Urban Risk and Well-being in Asian Megacities

Rapid urbanisation presents challenges such as inequality, informalisation and diversified, social needs for emerging cities. Informal and formal institutions and their impact on urban development and well-being vary across social classes and cities.

Endo, Shibuya, and their contributors provide a systematic and multifaceted overview of urban well-being. It explores the characteristics and complexities of urban well-being of lower and middle classes in Asian megacities. The book explains that social setting and socioeconomic condition of individuals and households play a critical role in urban well-being. It offers insights on the vulnerabilities and resilience of urban populations and the intertwined dynamics of social networks and what they mean for individual well-being.

This book will be a useful reference for students, researchers and academics in urban studies, Asian studies or development studies.

Tamaki Endo is Professor at the Graduate School of Humanities and Social Sciences at Saitama University. Her research interests include informal economy, urban development, inequality and global value chain. She received her PhD in Economics (2007) from Kyoto University. Main publications are *Living with Risks: Precarity & Bangkok's Urban Poor* (NUS Press association with Kyoto University Press, 2014), Goto, Endo and Ito [eds], *The Asian Economy: Contemporary Issues and Challenges* (Routledge, 2020).

Momoyo Shibuya is an Associate Professor at the Graduate School of Humanities and Social Sciences, Saitama University. She received her PhD from Macquarie University on ethnic relations of the Japanese transnational community in a social contextual shift. After completing her degree, she worked as a researcher in the media industry and at think tanks before joining Saitama University. Her research interests include ethnic networks and soft power contributing one chapter to *the Routledge Handbook of Soft Power* (2nd ed., forthcoming).

Urban Risk and Well-being in Asian Megacities

Urban Lower and Middle Classes in Bangkok, Shanghai, and Tokyo

Edited by
Tamaki Endo and Momoyo Shibuya

Routledge
Taylor & Francis Group
LONDON AND NEW YORK

First published 2023
by Routledge
4 Park Square, Milton Park, Abingdon, Oxon OX14 4RN

and by Routledge
605 Third Avenue, New York, NY 10158

Routledge is an imprint of the Taylor & Francis Group, an informa business

British Library Cataloguing-in-Publication Data
A catalogue record for this book is available from the British Library

ISBN: 9781032357133 (hbk)
ISBN: 9781032357140 (pbk)
ISBN: 9781003328155 (ebk)

DOI: 10.4324/9781003328155

Typeset in Galliard
by codeMantra

Contents

Figures

Photo

Tables

Boxes

Authors/Contributors

Tamaki Endo is Professor at the Graduate School of Humanities and Social Sciences at Saitama University. Her research interests include informal economy, urban development, inequality and global value chain. She received her PhD in Economics (2007) from Kyoto University. Main publications are *Living with Risks: Precarity & Bangkok's Urban Poor* (NUS Press association with Kyoto University Press, 2014), Goto, Endo and Ito [eds], *The Asian Economy: Contemporary Issues and Challenges* (Routledge, 2020).

Momoyo Shibuya is an Associate Professor at the Graduate School of Humanities and Social Sciences, Saitama University. She received her PhD from Macquarie University on ethnic relations of the Japanese transnational community in a social contextual shift. After completing her degree, she worked as a researcher in the media industry and at think tanks before joining Saitama University. Her research interests include ethnic networks and soft power contributing one chapter to *the Routledge Handbook of Soft Power* (2nd ed, forthcoming).

Asuka Imaizumi is an Associate Professor at the Graduate School of Humanities and Social Sciences, Saitama University, Japan. She specialises in Japanese economic history and received her PhD in Economics from the University of Tokyo. Her research interests include relationship between industrial development, technological progress and transformation of regional society, especially focusing on the case of Tokyo. Her recent publications include "Widespread Enthusiasm: Grassroots Participation and Regional Variation in Early Japanese Patenting, 1885-99" (*Technology and Culture*, vol. 63, no. 2).

Kaoru Kanai is a Professor at the Graduate School of Humanities and Social Sciences, Saitama University. She received her PhD from the University of Tokyo on Japanese employment system and part-time workers. Her research interests include gender and power relations, atypical employment in Japan.

Masato Miyazaki is a Professor at the Graduate School of Humanities and Social Sciences, Saitama University, and an Adjunct Associate Professor in the Institute for Public Policy and Governance at the University of Technology Sydney. He received his PhD in Economics from Keio University. His research interests focus on local public finance, expenditure and intergovernmental grants. His book *The Political Economy of Behaviours of Local Governments* (in Japanese) was published by Keio University Press in 2018.

Naoki Oishi is an Associate Professor at the Graduate School of Humanities and Social Sciences, Saitama University. He received his PhD in Economics from the University of Tokyo in family business history. His research interests include Japanese style management and organisation, and his current project is on trading companies' business models in Japan.

Preface and Acknowledgement

The initial idea for our research project, 'Urban well-being in Asian megacities', was realised in 2011 from discussions with faculty colleagues in different fields of economics and sociology. It focuses on risks and social networks. Prior to receiving official research funding, we had already planned a preliminary research trip to Taipei as our first destination in mid-March 2011. However, this trip never happened—on March 11, 2011, a major earthquake hit Eastern Japan. The Tokyo metropolitan area where we lived was also severely affected by the tremors.

In fact, on that day, Tamaki Endo was in Bangkok. A Thai fellow researcher shouted over the phone, 'Switch on the TV now! Earthquake hit Japan!'. The TV screen showed unrealistic scenes of the earthquake and tsunami. After rushing to call family and friends in eastern Japan, with no success, Endo returned to Tokyo on the morning of March 14. The usual two-hour bus ride from the airport to home took more than five hours on that day.

At the time, Momoyo Shibuya was in Phnom Penh on a study tour. News of the earthquake came through the coordinator, but the tour continued as scheduled. On the night of March 11, Shibuya received an international call from a family member living in Tokyo confirming that they were safe. Interestingly, local calls between family members living in the same district in Tokyo did not go through; however, international calls did. Eventually, Phnom Penh became the point of contact for the families in Tokyo.

After these experiences, both of us and other project members in Japan were still trying to fly over to Taiwan. Fortunately, all members of our project were safe, and flights on March 15, the day of our departure, were on schedule. However, we found that all airport buses and major trains around Tokyo megaregions ceased and we were unable to get to the airport—we were stuck in Japan.

Over the next few months, we anxiously endured the continuing aftershocks, while only fragmented and limited information about the nuclear accident was released. Meanwhile, we experienced scheduled power outages for two hours a day to save electricity since the Tokyo area was dependent on Fukushima and other Tohoku regions for its electricity supply. We learned that urban life can be vulnerable without basic social infrastructures.

Our discussion on risks and crisis as well as survival strategies in megacities was put forward in this unexpected and unusual circumstance. We managed to get a large research fund, the development fund from Saitama University between June 2011 and March 2014 for the project. Spending one year with preliminary research and planning, we chose three cities, Tokyo, Shanghai, and Bangkok, for our research fields. Despite the development stage of the countries, our interests were on commonalities shown under globalisation. At the same time, we were also interested in how the uniqueness of each city survives or is strengthened by interacting global socioeconomic change and dynamics. Both quantitative and qualitative research had taken place during 2012–2014, including some additional follow-up and data analysis after our research fund period ended.

However, the book took longer than we expected, and manuscripts were written through the COVID-19 pandemic which started from 2020—the systematic and worldwide crisis of the century. The pandemic taught us again that the topics we were addressing, risk and crisis responses in megacities, formal and informal institutions and subjective well-being, are of increasing importance even more. Megacities in Asia and other parts of the world are now facing new challenges derived from rapid and compressed development, continuous extraordinary events and shocks that have path dependency from the past, as well as influence prospects for better urban future. We hope that our book can be one of the sources to trigger future discussions involving researchers and practitioners in Asia and beyond.

The research project and the book could never have been completed without all the guidance and support obtained. Above all, we would like to first express our gratitude to people in all cities who took time to share their stories with us. We met some people face to face, and some were anonymous, but their testimonies—some actually did write really long stories in free columns of questionnaires—always made us think about their struggles, ambitions and hopes in urban life.

We would like to thank those for their academic stimulation, guidance and advice during the research and writing period: Professors Kunio Urakawa, Keiichiro Oizumi, Patricio Abinales, Gerard Finin, Chen Yun, Sandra Kurfurst, Tomohiro Machikita, Wataru Kusaka, Motoko Kawano, Ichiei Jo and Professor Emeritus Akira Suehiro—thank you. Deans and colleagues in the Faculty of Economics, Saitama University also encouraged us throughout the project period; special thanks to Professor Emirate Osamu Ito, Kazuo Usui and Yoshihiko Kamii for their support through the initial stage of projects, and to Professors Jongwon Woo and Hiroyuki Taguchi. The project became possible because of the research grant Development Fund of Saitama University. We also thank the Research Center for Sustainable Development in East Asia for their financial support.

We would like to express our gratitude for all works done by Ms. Chizuko Fujii, our project secretary; logistics of the project never went smoothly without her help. We also thank our assistant Chadatan Osatis who worked on data cleaning and translation. Shanti Volunteer association helped us with the Bangkok research and Ms. Sachiko Otani with the Shanghai research.

We would like to sincerely thank all comments from anonymous referees. We still have some homework left which we will keep working on in the future. We are highly indebted to Professor Timothy Bolt for his tremendous assistance and comments in editing and finalising the manuscripts. The chapters are now in much better shape because of this as well as his valuable advice. Finally, we would like to thank Yongling Lam and Payal Bharti at Routledge for their support and advice extended to us during the production process. However, the errors in this book are the sole responsibility of authors.

Tamaki Endo
Momoyo Shibuya
September 2022

1 Urban Risk and Well-Being in Asian Megacities

Tamaki Endo and Momoyo Shibuya

Introduction

The globalising world is facing increasing uncertainty. Our economic and social activities have become more interconnected than ever, accelerating the cross-border movement of goods, people, money, and information. This enhanced connectivity and mobility is the source of the rapid and compressed development of Asia. However, these very channels can suffer significant shocks from negative events such as crime, economic crisis, and pandemic diseases. In the era of economic interdependency, the factors influencing the regional economy of a country are not limited to just domestic factors and policies. Rather, external factors too have a significant impact on economic activities and social change (Endo and Oizumi 2020, 163). Such circumstances add dynamic complexity to our society, resulting in our lives being constantly exposed to risk and fraught with uncertainty.

These complex dynamics are largely driven by megacities and their global networks. Urban areas are more directly connected with global economic and social activities. In particular, emerging cities have been experiencing rapid and 'compressed' development, where phenomena and problems of both developed and developing countries occur simultaneously (Goto, Endo and Ito 2020; Whittaker et al. 2020), and policy agendas to improve one's well-being are more complex and challenging. We are now in the 'Urban Century', where urban populations have come to outnumber rural populations. In 2008, they exceeded 50% of the world population (United Nations 2019), with further growth expected in Asian and African cities (UNFPA 2014). What can make our urban life better—this simple yet complex question has been asked repeatedly, and in this increasingly urbanised setting, answering it is now more vital for our well-being.

The most basic definition of 'urban well-being' is being physically and mentally well, or at least improving, in one's life in an urban environment. Well-being, hence, has both material and subjective dimensions (Mahali et al. 2018), whereby the former includes socioeconomic aspects exemplified by health, economic conditions, and social relationships,[1] and the latter refers to how we perceive our own lives. The criteria of 'being well', however, may vary from person to person. In the era of uncertainty, the risks and actual shocks encountered, either at the individual or societal level, are among the key determinants of one's well-being.

DOI: 10.4324/9781003328155-1

The impact of urban risks and shocks in a city manifests itself unevenly across different social strata, reflecting differences in the level of vulnerability and ability of risk responses (Endo and Shibuya 2017, 2). Furthermore, community configurations and societal settings may lead to differences in survival strategies across cities, even when their urbaneness are similar. Indeed, Mahali et al. (2018), for example, argue that we should not simply apply the Global North's concept of well-being to the Global South, as structural factors differentiate the formation of both material and subjective well-being. We should rather look carefully at social and cultural settings and contextual differences. Analysing Asian urban life to define how we live and understanding what factors contribute to better urban well-being are crucial for our future well-being. Understanding commonalities and differences between middle- and lower-class well-being in/across megacities (Tokyo, Shanghai, and Bangkok in our book) will help illuminate how these individual and structural factors have intertwined with each other in the Asian context.

1.1 The Dynamics of Asian Megacities in the Era of Globalisation and Uncertainty

Asian megacities are now leading centres of economic development in the world, serving as centres for production and finance as well as consumption. Nevertheless, urban inequalities are widening and forming multi-layered stratification within the city (Endo and Oizumi 2020).

Bangkok and Shanghai are prime examples of such cities. They serve as multi-functional global hubs and lead their countries' economic development, as does Tokyo a long-standing Asian megacity. A person who visits these three cities will find similar landscapes such as high-rise office buildings, luxury department stores, mega shopping malls, and cosmopolitan consumers. At the same time, the rapid and compressed economic development and social transition of Thailand and China create a variety of policy dilemmas for these cities. For example, ageing had already started before the social security system was fully developed, and before they had made a successful transition from middle-income to high-income countries (Oizumi and Ito 2020). Despite the increase of white-collar workers in global business sectors, informal economy workers are still widely observed in Bangkok and Shanghai, which traditional development economics used to assume to be a phenomenon of 'developing' countries. The institutional response is not catching up due to financial burdens of dealing with 'new' and 'old' phenomena simultaneously, leaving spaces for informal mechanisms of risk responses to exert themselves.

However, it should be noted that Tokyo is not necessarily an 'advanced model' for these cities. Its population had reached 10 million as early as the 1960s (United Nations 2019) and is known as the first and largest megacity in Asia. The poor living conditions in the early post-war period have rapidly improved, showing a relatively equal distribution of living standards among Tokyo (23 wards) by the 1970s (Bansal 2018). Despite this spatial 'egalitarianism' in the past, both spatial and socioeconomic urban inequality increased in the 1990s (Hashimoto and Asakawa 2020; Hashimoto 2021). Since then, the 'informalisation' of the labour market and illegal shared houses or rooms have rapidly increased in Tokyo. Tokyo is now becoming similar to Bangkok and Shanghai in terms of the necessity of dealing with complex and multi-layered stratification. These substantial changes in the economic and social structures of the cities mentioned above were accelerated by globalisation, rapid urbanisation, and neoliberalisation. Now, megacities are not only a space of opportunity but also a space of risks.

1.2 Urban Risk Matters

The risk production mechanism is embedded in urban settings in global cities (Buscher and Mascareno 2012). Cities pose fundamentally different types of risks than rural areas in terms of characteristics of commodification, environmental hazards, and social relationships that are unique to urban living (Moser 1998; Fujita 2003; Endo 2014). Dense populations and high-rises increase the vulnerability to environmental and natural hazards, including the spread of infectious diseases. The market economy requires urban residents to engage in some sort of income-generating activities in order to meet basic needs and sustain the economic foundation of urban life, but the ties between urban residents tend to be tenuous. The more a society develops successfully with globalisation and shifts to a phase of late modernity, which weakens intermediate communities such as the family, local community, and enterprise (community at workplace), the greater the individualisation we experience, and as a result, we must be able to manage risks and survive on our own (Giddens 1991; Bauman 2000; Beck and Beck-Gernsheim 2002).

Urban residents face various types of urban risks in the course of their daily lives, and therefore their life is a continuous process of risk responses. It is impossible to avoid risks and shocks fully in urban life. Thus, the level of individual and household well-being in urban life is defined by the vulnerability and capability to deal with risks.

Urban risk is the possibility of loss caused in urban contexts that involve multi-dimensional factors. It can be both systematic and idiosyncratic (World Bank 2001). Nevertheless, the local context matters significantly, as place-specific risk accumulation processes, as well as people's perceptions and responses, would uniquely differentiate the same events (Endo and Shibuya 2019). The World Bank classifies risks according to their nature and level of occurrence along six dimensions: natural, health, social, economic, political, and environmental risks, and at three levels: the individual/household, household/community, and region/nation (World Bank 2001; see Table 1.1).

The impact of urban risks manifests unevenly among different social classes due to differences in their level of vulnerability and capability for risk response. The idiosyncratic risks individuals and households face daily are mainly in three areas—economic, social, and health. As one does not obtain food directly from

Table 1.1 Main sources of risk

Type of risk	*Idiosyncratic*	*Covariant*	
	Risks affecting an individual or household (micro)	*Risks affecting groups of households or communities (meso)*	*Risks affecting regions or nations (macro)*
Natural		Rainfall Landslide Volcanic eruption	Earthquake Flood Drought High winds
Health	Illness Injury Disability Old age Death	Epidemic	
Social	Crime Domestic violence	Terrorism Gang activity	Civil strife War
Economic	Unemployment Resettlement Harvest failure	Changes in food prices	Growth collapse Hyperinflation Balance of payments, financial or currency crisis Technology shock Terms of trade shock Transition costs of economic reforms
Political		Riots	Political default on social programs Coup d'etat
Environmental		Pollution Deforestation Nuclear disaster	

Source: World Bank (2001), p. 136.

nature and the land in an urban setting, earning money is essential to survive in the city. Unemployment or extreme poverty, therefore, might threaten the very foundations of life itself. Being healthy does have a positive effect on subjective well-being and quality of life. More importantly, it is basic capital for oneself in urban life (Moser 1998), as illness often leads to the loss of income. Moreover, new social transformations, such as the 'informalisation' of formal employment and ageing (for example, see Oshio and Urakawa 2008; Hashimoto and Asakawa 2020; Urakawa and Endo 2020, for the case of Tokyo), are creating new social vulnerabilities that increase the socioeconomic risks for certain age groups and social classes.

It is important to note that the causes of some of these risks are not always idiosyncratic, but rather systemic. For example, unemployment of an individual or household members might be the outcome of systemic shocks such as economic crises or other macro events. In that case, we have to be aware that, first, these shocks at the individual or household level need multi-layered responses (Endo 2014). Second, the impacts of macro shocks manifest unevenly. For example, in the discussion of natural disaster risks, IPCC (2019) conceptualised the damage one might suffer as being determined by how the three dimensions of hazard, vulnerability, and exposure interact (Figure 1.1). With certain societal events, for example, an earthquake or other natural disaster, it does not mean that one is exposed to that 'hazard' automatically; rather, one's 'exposure' to the hazard is dependent on one's physical distance from the hazard and degree of isolation from the impacts of the hazard. Once an individual or household is exposed, the depth and degree of damage that might be suffered from the event are also determined by their socioeconomic vulnerability. The 'capacity' of society to prepare for, mitigate, and absorb shocks after events and 'resilience' in the recovery process also affects the response process after shock, both in the short and long term. The World Bank defines 'vulnerability' as 'a high susceptibility to loss

Figure 1.1 Conceptualising risk.
Source: IPCC (2019, 46), Modified by author.

from negative shocks resulting from a system's exposure, internal conditions and risk management', and 'resilience' as 'the ability of person or system to recover from negative shocks while retaining or improving their functioning' (World Bank 2014, 61). This conceptual framework can be applied to other types of socioeconomic risks, such as economic crisis, depression, and pandemic.

To understand the risk response processes of urban residents, we need to understand the stratification that might form different levels of vulnerability among social classes. Moreover, when we compare different cities, we must look at the differences in social settings that shape the capacity and resilience of the society.

1.3 Survival Strategies and Social Networks

Both informal and formal mechanisms operate and interact in all risk response processes (Table 1.2), from risk preparation and mitigation to coping process after shock. As mentioned earlier, survival strategies might vary among cities or social classes and would take place at the individual, household, community, or societal levels, depending on the magnitude of the impact from urban risks, shock/crisis, and condition of resilience we have seen in the last section.

It is important to note that the level of risk occurrence is not always the same as the level of risk response. As mentioned earlier, 'unemployment', which manifests as risk at the individual level, may result from economic crisis or recession at the macro level (Endo 2014, 19). In this light, a formal mechanism at the societal level should be part of the important support channels in the individual risk response process. The state may play various roles in reducing and mitigating risks as well as providing safety nets after actual shocks happen to ease recovery process. In the case of a natural disaster, physical distance is a key determinant of exposure to the disaster, whereas in the case of an economic crisis, 'institutional' distance may determine the degree of shock one may suffer. Primarily, the societal setting of each city varies. As mentioned above, due to the financial constraints, as the provision of social security in middle-income countries is still limited, informal mechanisms might play a key role for certain groups in cities such as Bangkok and Shanghai. The interactive mechanism of the specific urban

Table 1.2 Stakeholders and Units for Risk/Shock Responses

	Stakeholders	*Units*
Informal Mechanisms	Individual and household	Individual Household
	Group based	Community (Association)
Formal Mechanisms	Market based	Enterprise NPO
	Publicly provided	State

Source: Made by author partly referred World Bank (2001), p. 141.

societal setting and the individual/household's conditions defines vulnerability and capacity in a specific response process.

Our analysis of survival strategies will focus on the 'coping with shocks' or post-shock phases. 'Reducing' and 'mitigating' risk phases also matter for managing and responding to risks, as they form precondition for the degree of impact. However, the interaction of different stakeholders and units in each phase is complex. To start our investigations from what actually happened to our respondents using quantitative analysis on the data from our survey affords us a better understanding of the commonalities and differences among different social classes in the three cities. In terms of social settings, the precondition of institutions in formal mechanisms and informal mechanisms are not always exclusive but sometimes complementary to each other.

Among formal mechanisms, the provision of social security by the 'state' is one of the most important preconditions of the societal setting. As we will explain in Chapter 2, class divisions in social security provision for Bangkok residents and Shanghai residents are wide, because there is no universal social security system in Thailand and China yet. However, all Tokyo residents, in theory, should be included in medical, employment, and pension welfare of some kinds. Among emerging cities like Bangkok and Shanghai where state provision is limited, NPO and other institutions might play a bigger role compared to Tokyo. We also have to pay attention to the unique characteristics of Shanghai (or China), with migrants controlled by the policy and house registration systems. Rural registration holders in Shanghai and urban registration holders cannot enjoy the same package of social security even though they may be working in the same sector in the city.

With or without sufficient formal mechanisms to respond to risks, however, informal mechanisms are also necessary to sustain urban lives. Informal mechanisms may include any kind of resources available for utilisation when people face risks and actual negative events, both monetary resources like property and assets and non-monetary ones, like, cultural capital and/or social capital through personal networks. This is not limited to the middle-income countries. Once a developed society advances and transitions to late modernity, people experience an individualisation that leaves them disembedded from their own social existence by dismantling intermediate communities such as classes, families, and occupational groups 'without reembedding' (Beck and Beck-Gernsheim 2002, xxii). As individuals are connected to society without buffers of communities, risks fall directly on them, and they are expected to respond to such risks on their own. In such a developed society, often with adequate formal resources, such as social security system, the diversity of employment forms increases and those who work in atypical or non-regular career patterns tend to be easily excluded from security coverage (Fujimura 2016); informal mechanisms are important for survival in such cases.

Moreover, due to the diversity in cities, a common coping strategy for everyone seems to be ineffective and, naturally, formal mechanisms may not work as designed. In emerging cities, the risk response strategies must be more complexly combined due to the diversity of people, in addition to the limitations of formal mechanism. Some people are embedded in traditional informal networks as a result of compressed development, while others are already facing 'individualisation' and the new social transition that developed countries are undergoing.

Our analysis primarily focuses at the level of the individual. The household is often treated as the core unit of analysis in surveys on living conditions. However, resource entitlement and degree of household cooperation create differences in the degree of one's well-being as well (Kabeer 2000; Endo 2014). Considering family as one of the informal institutions and surviving units, we start our investigation from the individual level. It should also be noted that the scale and timing of events determine the availability of response units and resources. The economic and social risks and shocks individuals and households face in their daily urban life in the life course, for example, lay-offs or illness, and unexpected events on a bigger scale, such as earthquakes, which affect the whole of society, may not have the same burden of response. The individual approach has the limitation of clarifying structural constraints to particular societal-level crises that respondents might experience over time. Despite these limitations, looking at their past experiences and perceived networks helps us to better understand how informal and formal mechanisms interact (or do not interact), what is available to people, and how they trust or do not trust these networks in urban life.

1.4 Outline of the Chapters and Data Set for Analysis

To discuss the individual well-being of the middle and lower classes of Asian cities, a series of quantitative and qualitative studies in Bangkok, Shanghai, and Tokyo were designed and conducted from 2011 to 2014. The quantitative data sets were collected through questionnaire surveys by face-to-face interview (Bangkok and lower class of Shanghai) and online (Tokyo and middle class of Shanghai) during 2012 and 2013. A common questionnaire with some additional localised options was designed and translated into the local languages. Qualitative research included in-depth interviews and participatory observation. Additional interviews were also conducted from 2014 onwards during the data cleaning and analysis periods. To depict the complex features of commonalities and differences among cities and social classes, the data were divided into six groups (middle and lower classes for each city) that were used as basic analytical units.

Chapter 2, 'Megacities matter', reviews the dynamics and dilemmas faced by three Asian megacities and clarifies their common background as urban settings and unique arrangements in social settings. Despite differences in development stages, there are many similarities in the macro features of the three cities, providing the rational for comparing them in the analysis. In the era of widespread globalisation, it is reasonable to expect more similarities among cross-regional megacities than among cities within a country (Endo and Oizumi 2020). In other words, a comparison of Bangkok with Shanghai and Tokyo might reveal more similarities than a comparison of Bangkok with secondary cities such as Korat and Chang Mai in Thailand. Simultaneously, despite commonalities in urbanisation dynamics, survival strategies and risk responses are embedded in the social context of each city. The comparison of these three cities will clarify how formal and informal mechanisms interact with and mutually impact each other. Then, Chapter 3, 'Asian megacity survey on well-being', introduces our survey methodology and the socioeconomic characteristics as well as subjective well-being of the research respondents in our data sets (approximately 2,740 respondents). Regarding subjective well-being (life satisfaction) indicators in our survey, one of the most interesting paradoxes is the extremely low score for life satisfaction of the Tokyo lower class. Despite being once the richest city in Asia with well-established formal social security system, why is Tokyo's lower class the most dissatisfied group of all covered across the three megacities? We will assess this subtopic in later chapters.

Chapter 4, 'Understanding urban well-being from a historical perspective', examines the historical context of material needs and life satisfaction in Asian megacity. Using Tokyo as a case study, the analysis shows that the economic development phase does not explain the lower level of life satisfaction in Tokyo than in other cities. The economic conditions of individuals and households differentiate the life satisfaction levels of the lower and middle classes within a given country. However, a time series survey on life satisfaction since the 1970s by the Tokyo municipality office suggests that the subjective well-being of the Tokyo lower class has deteriorated since the late 1990s. Historical changes in Tokyo's case suggest the importance of the social setting in shaping one's well-being.

Chapter 5, 'Perceived and experienced urban risks and life difficulties', deals with the potential risks and actual difficulties the middle and lower classes of these three cities experience. The analysis of the sequential stages of the past, present, and future perceptions of urban risks clarifies the nature of risks faced in urban life, what their priorities are, and how their actual needs and experiences form their future perceptions. It will show that one's past experiences and recent circumstances influence their subjective well-being and future perception, and thus, there is a path dependency for the prospects of life. It is, however, not a matter of fully eliminating risk and negative shock from one's life, but rather of the conditions for resilience and vulnerability.

Chapters 6 and 7 delve deeper into the post-shock phase, the roles of formal and informal institutions, and subjective well-being. Chapter 6, 'The networks of received and anticipated supports as a risk response to urban life in Asia', explores the social networks people can expect, access, and utilise to deal with risks and difficulties in their urban lives, considering how social networks can function as informal capital for an individual's subjective well-being. The data includes both kinds of social networks in effect and examine their perception as dependable, degree of intimacy, and capacity for helping, to draw out the structures of networks people have. Analysing such network structures with individual subjective life satisfaction would then help identify the types of social capital that the networks may be concerned with.

Chapter 7, 'Life satisfaction and social security in three megacities', looks at differences in formal institutions and mechanisms among the six groups. It also explains how these differences influence subjective well-being. There has been debate as to whether the availability of social security and formal support influences individuals 'subjective well-being'. The analysis of the different social classes in the three cities indicates that there are different expectations for not only the quantity but also the quality of social security services.

The concluding chapter (Chapter 8), 'Towards better urban well-being in Asian megacities', draws theoretical and policy implications from our survey. The chapter attempts to conceptualise urban well-being in Asia by focusing on the similarities and differences among six groups (middle and lower class in three megacities) in risk responses, survival strategies, and subjective well-being, as well as how they interact with social settings and historical contexts.

Note

1 Mahali et al. (2018) reviewed different scholars on well-being and examine whether it can be applied to the analysis of Global South. Individuals tend to intermingle the objective and subjective (or psychological) dimensions when asked about own lives and well-being (p. 381). Economic condition of individual is often focused for objective or material dimension of well-being. However, Mahali et al. (2018) point out that many studies clarify that 'relational well-being', including social capital, network, and relationships, are also key for one's well-being. The relational well-being can be associated with both objective and subjective dimension because resource entitlement is often physical, while the trust in it is subjective. In this book, therefore, we use the term 'socioeconomic' well-being in a wider sense, not limited to the individual material conditions but also including the relational/collective dimensions that respondents have and exercise in their urban life.

References

Bansal, B. 2018. 'Urban space in economic history: Tokyo as Asia's first megacity 1945–1970', PhD dissertation, GRIPS.

Bauman, Z. 2000. *Liquid modernity.* Cambridge: Polity Press.

Beck, U. and E. Beck-Gernsheim. 2002. *Individualization: institutionalized individualism and its social and political consequences.* London: SAGE Publication.

Buscher, C. and A. Mascareno. 2012. 'Mechanisms of systematic risk production.' In *Risk habitat megacity*, edited by D Heinrich, K Krellenberg, B Hansjürgens and F Martínez, 39–63. Berlin: Springer.

Endo, T. 2014. *Living with risks: precarity and Bangkok's urban poor.* Singapore: NUS Press in association with Kyoto University Press.

Endo, T. and K. Oizumi. 2020. 'Urbanizing Asia: cities transforming into mega-regions.' In *The Asian economy: contemporary issues and challenges*, edited by K Goto, T Endo and A Ito, 145–168. London: Routledge.

Endo, T. and M.K. Shibuya. 2017. 'Urban risk, risk response and well-being in Asian cities: the case of Tokyo, Shanghai and Bangkok', *Procedia Engineering*, 198: 976–984. https://doi.org/10.1016/j.proeng.2017.07.143

Endo, T. and M.K. Shibuya. 2019. 'Urban risk and surviving strategies: a case study of urban middle class and lower class in Asian megacities', paper presented at EURA-UAA Conference City Futures, University College Dublin, Ireland, June 20–22.

Fujimura, M. 2016. 'Trust and life in risk society' [Risuku shakai ni okeru shinrai to seikatsu], *Studies in Contemporary Sociological Theory*, 10: 31–43.

Fujita, H. 2003. *Toshi to bunmei no hikaku shakaigaku* [The comparative sociology of city and civilization]. Tokyo: University of Tokyo Press.

Giddens, A. 1991. *Modernity and self-identity*. Cambridge: Polity Press.

Goto, K., T. Endo and A. Ito, eds. 2020. *The Asian economy: contemporary issues and challenges*. London: Routledge.

Hashimoto, K. 2021. 'Time difference gentrification as a bloodless revolution: class structure and spatial polarization in the Tokyo metropolitan area after the 1980s.' *International Journal of Japanese Sociology*, 30: 23–63.

Hashimoto, K. and T. Asakawa, eds. 2020. *Kakusa shakai to toshi kuukan: Tokyo ken no shakai chizu 1990–2010* [Stratified society and urban space: social map of Tokyo mega region 1990–2010]. Tokyo: Kajima shuppankai.

IPCC. 2019. *IPCC Special Report on the Ocean and Cryosphere in a Changing Climate* [H.O. Pörtner, D.C. Roberts, V. Masson-Delmotte, P. Zhai, M. Tignor, E. Poloczanska, K. Mintenbeck, A. Alegría, M. Nicolai, A. Okem, J. Petzold, B. Rama and N.M. Weyer (eds.)], accessed 10 January 2021, <https://www.ipcc.ch/srocc/>.

Kabeer, N. 2000. *Power to choose: Bangladeshi women and labour market decisions in London and Dhaka*. London: Verso Books.

Mahali, A., I. Lynch, A. Fadiji. T. Tolla, S. Khumalo and S. Naicker. 2018. 'Networks of well-being in the Global South: a critical review of current scholarship.' *Journal of Developing Societies*, 34 (4): 373–400.

Moser, C. 1998. 'The asset vulnerability framework: reassessing urban poverty reduction strategies', *World Development*, 26 (1): 1–19.

Oizumi, K. and A. Ito. 2020. 'Ageing Asia: from demographic dividend to demographic tax.' In *The Asian economy: contemporary issues and challenges*, edited by K. Goto, T Endo and A. Ito, 191–208. London: Routledge.

Oshio, T. and K. Urakawa. 2008. 'The trend of poverty and redistribution policies in the first half of the 2000s' [Nisen nendai zenhan no hinkonka no keikou to saibunpai seisaku], *The Quarterly of Social Security Research*, 44 (3): 278–290.

United Nations Department of Economic and Social Affairs. 2019. *The world urbanization prospects: the 2018 revision*. New York: United Nations.

United Nation Population Fund (UNFPA). 2014. *State of world population*. New York: UNFPA.

Urakawa, K. and T. Endo. 2020. 'Uneqalizing Asia.' In *The Asian economy: contemporary issues and challenges*, edited by K Goto, T Endo and A Ito, 207–232. London: Routledge.

Whittaker, D., T. Sturgeon, T. Okita and T. Zhu. 2020. *Compressed development: time and timing in economic and social development*. Oxford: Oxford University Press.

World Bank. 2001. *The world development report 2000/2001: attacking poverty*. Washington, DC: World Bank.

World Bank. 2014. *The world development report 2014: risk and opportunity*. Washington, DC: World Bank.

2 Megacities Matter

Socioeconomic Dynamics and Subjective Well-Being in Three Megacities

Tamaki Endo and Momoyo Shibuya

Introduction

Megacities in Asia, especially in the emerging countries, have grown rapidly. Their 'compressed development' has resulted in a multi-layered stratification in the city. With increased globalisation, these megacities have become hubs of global networks for goods production and circulation of international finance, people, and information. Irrespective of the stage of the country's development, the Asian megacities exhibit cross-regional dynamics of growth and socioeconomic restructuring. Megacities attract not only domestic elites but also rich investors from across the globe. At the same time, the job opportunities available in the megacities attract the urban poor, including domestic and international migrant workers. In the last two decades, urban inequality has increased in megacities. In recent years, urban renewal projects resulted in gentrification in many megacities, threatening the residential and occupational spaces available for the urban lower class (for cases of Asian cities, see Lee, Shin, and Lopez-Morales 2016; Ortega 2016; Shatkin 2017; Chen and Shin 2019; Endo 2022).

The urban risks and response processes of shocks impact the urban well-being. The increase in uncertainty at the societal level in the 21st century not only threatens the life foundation of the most vulnerable groups in the urban areas but also causes damage to the middle class. The impacts of systematic risks and shocks, such as economic crises, and increased natural disasters and pandemics, manifest across regions and social classes. In terms of severity, some crises, such as the global pandemic, also lead to urban crises as cities are the most affected (for urban debate regarding the COVID-19 case, see Florida, Rodriguez-Pose, and Storper 2021; Glaeser 2021; McFarlane 2021).

However, despite the commonalities in the forces governing urban dynamics and driving socioeconomic changes in the megacities, response and survival strategies are adopted within the local context. The shock response processes differ based on individual and/or household conditions and social settings in the cities. Social settings include differences in labour market structures, social security systems, and social networks.

Considering the differences among cities, traditional development economics, which employs more linear development perspectives, used to assume that economic development would improve well-being of the residents, which lead

DOI: 10.4324/9781003328155-2

to expectation that Tokyo residents would enjoy better life than residents of developing cities. The basic economic foundation of life, including economic resources and stability, surely matters in an urban context. However, as many previous studies have already shown, economic well-being does not simply explain subjective well-being level. The Asia Barometer, a comparative survey across nations, has shown that subjective well-being, such as life satisfaction, is not related to the stage of economic development. This is because Japan as one of the most economically developed countries, reports relatively lower levels of satisfaction on an average (Inoguchi et al. 2006, 311; Suehiro 2009).[1] OECD and European Commission also have been working on measuring multi-dimension of well-being for decades (for example, see Stiglitz, Sen, and Fitoussi 2009; OECD 2011). Examining other aspects of urban well-being is equally important to understand both material and subjective urban well-being. In addition, even if people face the same type of risk or event, their subjective well-being might differ depending on their perception of risks, social networks, and the urban settings (Endo and Shibuya 2019). An understanding of these characteristics brings forth the implications for better well-being of individuals and introduction or adoption of urban risk management policies in the Asian context.

In this chapter, we will conduct an overview of the macro socioeconomic dynamics in the three cities, namely Tokyo, Shanghai, and Bangkok, and compare their social settings. We also aim to review previous studies on social networks and subjective well-being, including life satisfaction in the Asian context.

2.1 Megacities and Regions as Centres of Economic Development

2.1.1 Rapid Urbanisation and Formation of Megacities

The urbanisation process in Asia has some specific features. The rate of urbanisation in Asia has been less than the global average for many years. Except for Japan, most of the countries were rural-based. For example, the urbanisation rate of Japan was 54.4% in 1950, whereas for Thailand and China, it was 16.5% and 11.8%, respectively (United Nations Department of Economic and Social Affairs [UN DESA] 2014). As Figure 2.1 demonstrates, East and Southeast Asia, however, started to show rapid growth in their urbanisation rates from the 1990s (Endo and Oizumi 2020, 149). According to the United Nation's data, Asia's total urban population, including South Asia, which was about 35% in 1960, exceeded 50% of the world's urban population by 2005. In addition, the average urbanisation rate exceeded the world average by 2010 (UN DESA 2014).

Tokyo is one of the oldest and largest megacities in Asia. According to the population estimates of Statistics Bureau under Ministry of Internal Affairs and Communications (2022), its population reached 10 million in as early as 1962; and presently, it is inhabited by more than 13.5 million people. In 2015, 28.4% of Japan's total population (36.1 million people) was concentrated in the Tokyo mega region, which includes the surrounding three prefectures (i.e., Kanagawa, Chiba, and Saitama). These three prefectures serve as residential areas for those

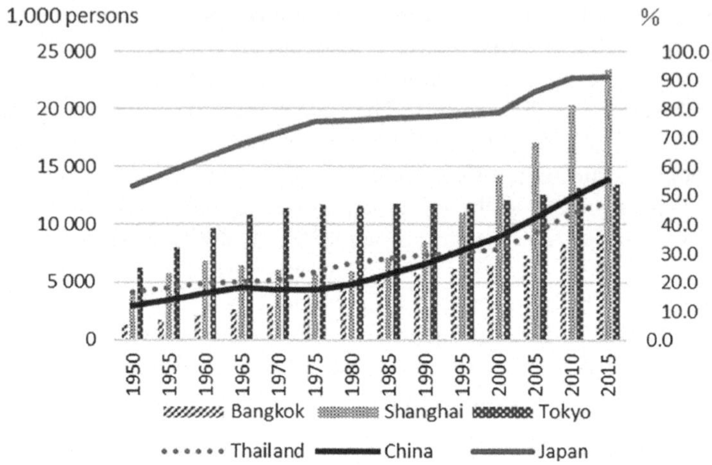

Figure 2.1 Urban population and urbanisation rate (1950–2015, every five years).

Source: World Urbanization Prospects: The 2018 Revision, except population for Tokyo. Tokyo population is from 'Population estimates', Statistics Bureau, Ministry of Internal Affairs and Communications (each year).

Note: 'World Urbanization Prospects' use Population of Kanto (Tokyo mega region, Tokyo metropolitan and surrounding provinces) for the data of Tokyo population. Therefore, we use data of Statistics Bureau of Japan for Tokyo.

who work or study in Tokyo. According to the 2015 census, the share of people who commute daily to other prefectures for school and for work from among the active population (comprising of people who are working or studying) accounts for 22.5% in Saitama, 20.4% in Chiba, and 18.5% in Kanagawa. The majority of these commute to Tokyo, which increases the city's daytime population to approximately 15.9 million people.

In contrast, Shanghai and Bangkok have undergone rapid urbanisation in terms of an increase in population. The population of Shanghai reached 10 million in the early 1990s, and that of Bangkok reached 10 million in the late 2010s (Figure 2.1). However, due to the high mobility of the residents, especially those who keep their resident registrations in their hometown, the population of these megacities reached 10 million much earlier. For example, it is often said that Bangkok's population reached 10 million in the early 2000s (Endo 2014).

The rate and extent of Shanghai's urbanisation are the most striking. The total population of Shanghai was only half of that of Tokyo in the 1970s and the early 1980s, but quickly caught up and exceeded Tokyo by 2000. In 2015, its population reached 23.5 million as per the official statistics. Despite the gradual increase in the Tokyo population in the recent years, the UN estimates that Shanghai's population will continue to increase and reach 30 million during the 2020s (UN DESA 2014).

Two features should be considered regarding the demographic and the social characteristics of these three cities. First, Tokyo has already started to face the problem of ageing, whereas Shanghai and Bangkok still have relatively young populations. According to the Bureau of Industrial and Labour Affairs of Tokyo

Metropolitan Government (2015, 27), the number of older people in Tokyo has trebled between 1980 and 2010. The ageing population (people aged over 65 years) reached 20.4% of the total population by 2010 and is expected to rise to 22.5% by 2040. Keeping with the trend, the proportion of the elderly in the working population increased to 10.2% in 2014. In contrast, the ageing population of Shanghai was 10.1% (as per the 2010 census, Shanghai Municipal Statistics Bureau 2019) and just 6.2% in Bangkok in 2010 (the National Statistical Office of Thailand [NSO] 2012).

Second, inward migrants exhibit different features in each city. The population of Tokyo continued to increase gradually with the social increase caused by those moving in due to work and to seek higher education until 2019 before the COVID-19 outbreak.[2] However, seasonal migration is rare. Instead, as we mentioned before, there is active inward mobility on a daily basis as people commute from the neighbouring prefectures. International migrants accounted only for 1.9% of the labour force in Japan in 2013; however, among total international migrants, 20.3% are living in Tokyo and 14.2% are living in the surrounding provinces of Toko megaregion including Saitama and Kanagawa prefectures (Bureau of Industrial and Labour Affairs of Tokyo Metropolitan Government 2015, 27).

In contrast, emerging cities such as Shanghai and Bangkok exhibit active dynamics of inflow of both (those wishing to be) permanent and temporary migrants. Both cities are attracting not only low-end but also high-end workers, including local and foreign workers, because of which a multi-layered and stratified labour market is created in these cities. In Shanghai, domestic migrants were found to be situated at the low end. Part of the dynamic is that China is known for its unique 'household registration system' (or *Hukou*) which started in 1958 to control inward urban migration, distinguishing between rural and urban registrations (Marukawa 2013). Those who were registered as rural residents, were either low-end workers or students, and had limited access to social security and other public services in the city. According to the Shanghai Municipal Statistics Bureau (2018), at the end of 2017, the population of long-term residents reached 24 million, which included 14 million permanent residents and an external population of 9.8 million. Until 2011, the statistics revealed the 'floating population' and it was estimated to be 2.2 million people who stayed less than six months and 9 million people who stayed more than six months in 2010 (Shanghai Municipal Statistics Bureau 2011). Most workers registered as rural residents are labourers employed in low-paid occupations. Shanghai does not accept foreign workers as low-end workers but is a destination for high-end workers. Shanghai municipality (2019) showed that 215,000 foreigners worked in Shanghai, which accounted for 23.7% of the nation's total, and the highest in the country (Shanghai Municipal Statistics Bureau 2019, 15). These figures show the multi-layered stratification of the cities.

In Bangkok, many domestic migrants who are low-end workers are already settled as permanent residents in the city and reside in 'slum' communities, including the second and the third generation (Endo 2014). Seasonal migrants can still be observed, but the seasonal gap of Bangkok residents in the statistics is no longer large.[3] For example, according to the Labour Force Survey of 2015, the population of Bangkok in Quarters 1 and 3 only differed by around 20,000 (NSO 2015). On the contrary, legal foreign migrants from the neighbouring countries such as Myanmar, Laos, and Cambodia account for more than three million people, and more than half of them are estimated to inhabit the Bangkok megaregions (BMR).[4] After the government eased the regulations prohibiting the migrants from travelling across provinces in 2015, the inflow of migrants to Bangkok and the BMR rapidly increased.[5] These migrants work in the so-called '3D works',[6] low-paid manufacturing, and service sectors. In other words, Bangkok's labour market employs a large number of foreign workers at both the low and high ends; high-end workers are mainly the expats working in multinational companies.

2.1.2 Megacities as Economic Centres

These megacities are the driving force for economic development and enjoy the economic benefits of being the hubs of global connectivity. Figure 2.2 shows the gross regional product (GRP) per capita in Bangkok and Shanghai. Both cities experienced soaring GRP per capita in the 2000s, which in 2015 reached to US$14,991 and $16,753, respectively. In the same year, the GDP per capita for Thailand and China were US$5,799 and $8,167, respectively. While Thailand and China are still in the 'middle-income' group according to the World Bank classification, both Bangkok and Shanghai are reported to have achieved the income levels of countries in the 'high-income' category (Endo and Oizumi 2020, 156). Bangkok and Shanghai went through rapid and compressed development, which was also observed in other emerging cities in Asia (Goto, Endo, and Ito 2020; Shin, Zhao, and Koh 2020; Whittaker et al. 2020; for the case of Seoul: Shin 2020).

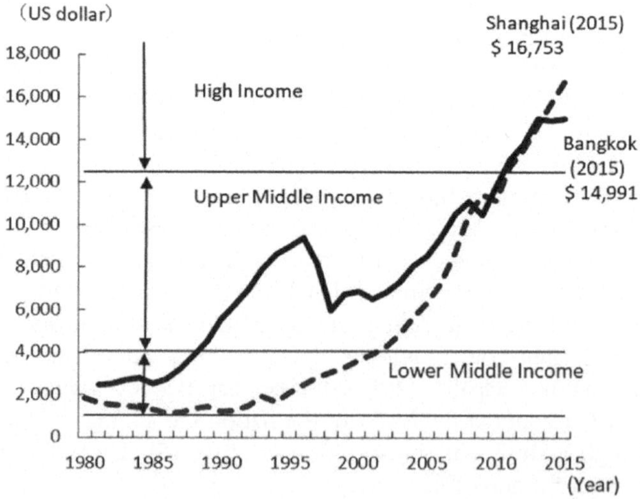

Figure 2.2 Per capita GRP in Bangkok and Shanghai (nominal exchange rate).

Source: Endo and Oizumi (2020, 155).

Original source: Made by author from Shanghai Statistical Yearbook for Shanghai, and NESDB, Gross Regional and Provincial Products for Bangkok.

Note: The definition of 2015 is as follows: High income country is 12,476 dollar and above, Upper-middle-income country is between 4,036-12,475 dollars, Lower-middle-income country is 1,026-4,035 dollars (World Development Indicators 2016).

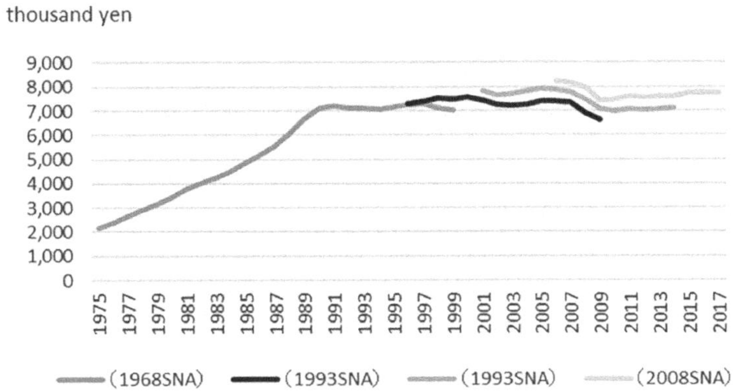

Figure 2.3 Per capita GRP in Tokyo (nominal).

Source: Annual Report on Prefectural Account (each year), Cabinet Office.

Note: The GDP and GRP are regularly revised with new criteria. There is no consistent time series data between 1970s to recent. The data is only available in yen.

In contrast, Tokyo reached its peak in 1990, and only gradual changes have been observed since then (Figure 2.3). However, GRP is much higher than the national average. For example, the GRP per capita of Tokyo was 7.7 million yen (US$63,425) in 2015 but the GDP per capita of Japan was 4.2 million yen (US$34,398)[7] (Tokyo Metropolitan Accounts 2017).

The economic concentration in megacities and regions has been outstanding. For example, Bangkok and its megaregions accounted for 29.1% and 66.2% of Thailand's GDP, whereas the Yangtze River Delta megaregion (Shanghai, Jiangsu Province, and Zhejiang province) accounted for 21.5% of the GDP in 2010, respectively.[8] Tokyo and its metropolitan areas (Tokyo, Kanagawa, Chiba, and Saitama) contributed to 18.4% and 32.4% of the country's GDP, respectively, in 2010 (IDE-JETRO 2015).

If we pay close attention to the internal work processes in the cities, the compressed development of emerging cities, like Bangkok and Shanghai, as well as the restructuring of the developed cities, such as Tokyo, created some similarities in the multi-layered and stratified urban structure. The next section will look at the internal work processes and the societal or urban settings that help understand the background of urban life for the lower and middle classes.

2.2 Socioeconomic Condition of the Urban Lower and Middle Classes in Bangkok, Shanghai, and Tokyo

How do lower and middle classes experience these rapid changes in cities? Are they able to reap the benefits of the rapid and compressed economic development? These are the basic questions that are likely to arise in our mind while looking at the economic figures of the cities. Many studies have shown that economic development contributes to decreasing absolute poverty (Rigg 2015; Urakawa and Endo 2020). Yet, the benefits of economic development do not trickle down automatically, but rising uncertainty makes the socioeconomic foundation of urban life vulnerable and fragile. This section views the socioeconomic conditions of the people living in the three cities at the macro level, which pertains to two fundamental aspects of the urban life of the people (i.e., occupation and residence). Then, the following section explores social networks and subjective well-being in the Asian cities.

2.2.1 Rise of Urban Inequality

Urban inequality has increased over the past two decades in all the cities. Figure 2.4a–4c shows the Gini coefficients of three cities. This clearly shows that the urban inequality started to increase since the 2010s in Bangkok and the early 2000s in Tokyo.[9] The Gini coefficients of both cities started to exceed the national average during the same period. The Gini coefficient in Japan, including Tokyo, declined in the late 2000s during the post-shock period of financial crisis of 2008 but started to increase again in the late 2010s. Bangkok's Gini coefficient has been rising to reach 0.51 in 2011; however, the Gini coefficient at the national level started to decrease slightly (national 0.48) (Office of the National Economic and Social Development Board [NESDB] 2015). Bangkok's Gini coefficient dropped in 2015 and has been fluctuating ever since. For China, the Gini coefficient specific to Shanghai in the time series was not available. Figure 2.4c shows the Gini coefficients of urban-rural areas. This suggests that inequality in the urban areas has been increasing and has recently exceeded the existing inequality in the rural areas.

Several studies have already revealed the common phenomena of increased intra-regional disparities in megacities and a decrease in inter-regional disparities. For example, Yusef, Sumner, and Rum (2014) analysed inequality in expenditures in Indonesia in 2013 and showed that the contribution of intra-regional inequality was greater than that of inter-regional inequality. Galbraith's (2012) study on inequality in China showed that the rise in inter-regional disparities began to slow down in the 2000s, while intra-provincial disparities and inequality within provinces continued to expand in the 2000s. He reported that inequality was particularly apparent in the urban areas of the coastal regions, including Shanghai. His study analysed the cause of this change and clarified that the increased disparity was associated with the restructuring of the industrial and labour market, such as growth of the service sector in megacities. Banks and other financial institutions continued to grow primarily in the urban areas such as Beijing, Shanghai, and Guangdong, resulting in employment generation and an increase in wages in these cities (Galbraith 2012, 240; Urakawa and Endo 2020).

Compared with the available studies on inter-regional disparities and national-level analysis of inequality, limited in-depth studies explore the reasons for increase in urban inequality. At the national level, researchers in Japan, which used to be known as a relatively equal country, have launched many studies on inequality since the 1990s. The debate over causes of inequality has now settled, and the major contributing factors outlined are as follows: (1) restructuring of the labour market and increase in the number of irregular workers; (2) ageing;

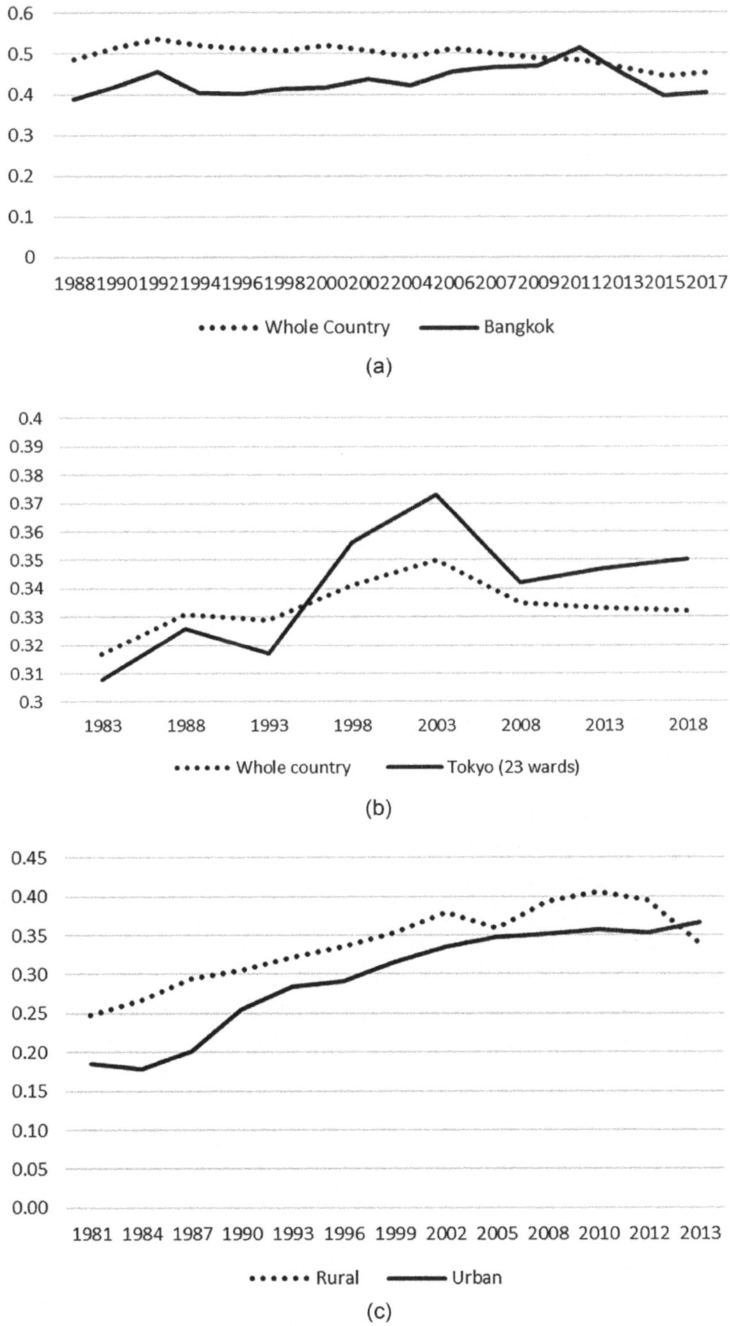

Figure 2.4 Gini coefficient: (a) Thailand and Bangkok, (b) Japan and Tokyo, and (c) rural and urban area in China.

Source: (a) NESDB (2017), (b) Hashimoto (2021), and (c) The World Bank, PovcalNet (Access date: Aug 25th, 2017).

and (3) limited redistribution compared with other developed countries (Ohtake 2005; Tachibanaki and Urakawa 2006; Urakawa and Endo 2020). With respect to Tokyo, Hashimoto (2021) reported that these factors, especially restructuring of the labour market, are major reasons for the growing inequality. More empirical research is needed to understand the causes of the increasing inequality in the urban areas (e.g., megacities), especially in the Global South, to provide significant insights for the future of the urbanising world.

2.2.2 Restructuring and Multi-layered Stratification of the Urban Labour Market

Let us now look at the characteristics of the urban labour market. This will help us understand the background of the rising urban inequality, the actual situation faced by people, and the cities' policy-related dilemmas. The compressed development brought multi-layered stratification in Bangkok and Shanghai, which Tokyo did not experience during the process of past development. However, the labour market in Japan has undergone 'informalisation' since the 1990s (Urakawa and Endo 2020; Hashimoto 2021), which has created a similar phenomenon in Tokyo's labour market to that observed in the emerging cities.

The unique aspect of emerging cities and countries are the high ratio of agricultural workers (in rural areas in the hinterland) and the self-employed. Figure 2.5 shows the ratio of the working population to workers and also the share of the agricultural workers of the country. By the time the working population reached its peak and started to decrease in Japan and Korea, the share of agricultural workers was already less than 10%. However, in Thailand, when the working age population peaked in 2010, and while ageing of society has already started, the proportion of agricultural workers remained high despite agriculture's share of GDP already falling to about 10%. The working age population ratio at peak was similar in Japan (69.9% in 1992) and Thailand (71.8% in 2010), though agricultural workers accounted for 6.3% and 38.2% of the population, respectively. The situation is the same with China too. It should be noted that Japan was already a high-income country and the second largest economy in the world in 1992, whereas Thailand and China are still middle-income countries in terms of per capita income. Some of these agricultural workers are also a source of seasonal or temporary migrants to cities. However, urban labour market cannot absorb all of these workers, either due to lack of qualifications and skill requisite for entry into the urban labour market, or due to lack of job opportunities. These structural characteristics of the labour market are likely to persist. Emerging countries must deal with the social issues confronted by the globalised urban areas and rural areas simultaneously.

Another important characteristic is the widely observed existence of an informal economy in emerging cities. Contrary to the prediction of traditional development economics, that the informal economy will shrink or disappear once the economy developed, this tends not to have occurred. Rather, globalisation, urbanisation, and the risk responses of people have encouraged the reproduction, and sometimes expansion, of informal economic activities (Jütting and

Figure 2.5 Ratio of agricultural workers and working age population (1980–2015).
Source: Oizumi and Ito (2020), p.198, tabulated from World Development Indicators.

Laiglesia 2009; Endo 2014; Chen and Carre 2020). The NSO of Thailand publishes annual statistics that provide details of the informal employment. According to their report, informal employment was 55.2% in 2016 for the whole country and 28.2% for Bangkok (NSO 2017). In China, while official statistics are not available, the International Labour Organization has estimated that the informal employment in China accounted for about 54% in 2016 (ILO 2018). A case study on six Chinese cities in 2010, which received support from the World Bank, considered three criteria and showed different estimations in the scale according to the definition (cf., Park, Wu, and Du 2012; Endo and Goto 2020).[10] An important finding of this study was that the number of informal workers doubled among the domestic migrant workers compared with the resident workers with urban registration. In addition, a large proportion of workers aged between 16 and 34 years belonged to the informal employment category (Park, Wu, and Du 2012). The large scale of the informal economy reflects the high ratio of self-employed workers in the urban labour market of emerging cities. Table 2.1a–c shows the labour market structures of the city compared to the whole country. The ratio of self-employed workers (or own account workers) in Tokyo has been declining in parallel with the decline in Japan, which had already reached 10% by the time the ageing of society become a significant policy agenda in the 1990s. In contrast, self-employed workers in both Bangkok and Shanghai accounted for approximately 20%. These cities have already become the hub of the global value chain and are regional centres of many multinational companies as well as headquarters of domestic conglomerates and enterprises that employ a large number of highly educated workers in the country in white collar jobs. In other words, both old and new kinds of work cohabit in the same cities.

Table 2.1a Labour market structure (occupational status, Thailand/Bangkok) (unit: %)

	Thailand						*Bangkok*					
	1970	*1980*	*1990*	*2000*	*2010*	*2017*	*1970*	*1980*	*1990*	*2000*	*2010*	*2017*
Employer	0.4	0.2	0.8	1.3	2.0	2.7	1.8	0.8	2.9	4.4	4.2	4.8
Own account worker	29.9	30.0	28.8	30.8	33.2	31.6	20.3	20.8	15.7	17.9	19.9	20.1
Employee	15.7	20.2	26.7	35.9	42.3	47.7	63.6	67.0	73.6	70.3	70.0	68.0
Unpaid family worker	54.1	49.7	43.8	31.9	22.2	17.8	12.4	11.3	7.7	7.2	5.3	6.9
Members of producers' cooperatives	–	–	–	0.1	0.3	0.2	–	–	–	0.2	0.7	0.0
Total	100.0	100.0	100.0	100	100.0	100.0	100.0	100.0	100	100.0	100.0	100.0
Labour participation rate			79.0	73.3	73.5	68.2			63.8	61.5	69.8	69.9
Agricultural workers			66.8	56.2	43.6	33.4			2.5	1.5	0.7	0.2

Source: NSO, Population and Housing Census 1970, 1980, 1990, 2000, 2010 (Whole Kingdom, Bangkok). Data of 2017 is from NSO (2017), The Labour Force Survey (Q3) Whole Kingdom 2017.

Note: Data of Bangkok for 1970 is total of Phra Nakhon and Thon Buri. "Unknown" is not included (except Bangkok data for 1970, which was 1.9%). Labour participation rate is for those above 15 years old (for 1970–1990, it is above 13 years old).

Table 2.1b Labour market structure (occupational status, China/Shanghai) (unit: %)

	China				*Shanghai*			
	1990	*2000*	*2010*	*2019*	*1990*	*2000*	*2010*	*2019*
Employer			2.3	2.7			3.9	3.8
Own account worker			64.2	36.6			38.1	20.3
Employee			31.7	57.9			55.0	73.3
Unpaid family worker			1.8	2.8			2.9	2.7
Total			100.0	100.0			100.0	100.0
Labour participation rate	85.6	84.1	78.4	78.2	77.5	54.9	56.5	
Agricultural workers	60.1	50.0	36.7	25.1	11.5	11.6	3.4	

Source: China Population statistics yearbook 2000, China Population & Employment statistical yearbook 2020, Shanghai Statistical yearbook 2002 and 2011.

Table 2.1c Labour market structure (occupational status, Japan/Tokyo) (unit: %)

	Japan					*Tokyo*				
	1977	*1987*	*1997*	*2007*	*2017*	*1977*	*1987*	*1997*	*2007*	*2017*
Employee	70.5	76.3	82.1	86.8	89.4	78.1	82.2	85.7	88.3	90.7
Self-employed workers	18.1	15.0	11.8	10.1	8.5	14.8	12.2	10.5	9.4	7.9
Family workers	11.4	8.7	6.0	2.8	1.8	7.0	5.5	3.7	2.0	1.1
Total	100.0	100.0	100.0	100.0	100.0	100.0	100.0	100.0	100.0	100.0
Labour participation rate	63.2	62.6	63.7	60.4	60.5	63.4	64.3	64.5	63.3	65.0
Agricultural workers	12.2	8.2	5.4	4.1	3.2	0.5	0.6	0.6	0.5	0.4

Source: Statistic Bureau of Japan, Labour Force Survey (each year).
Note: The survey is done by every five years (sample survey). Because of data limitation, Population census (1975, 1985) is used for labour participation rate for Tokyo (1977, 1987).

These phenomena associated with emerging cities are the consequences of the compressed development, in which transformation is rapid and socioeconomic changes occur simultaneously. As the ageing population started to increase before the country attained the status of a high-income country with a fully developed universal social security system, main policy concerns in the 2010s in both Thailand and China have included how to expand social security coverage. Most informal economy workers were not included in the social security provisions. Often middle-income countries start to provide social security first to the public workers and gradually extend the benefits to the private employees. However, the inclusion of agricultural workers and self-employed workers is a major challenge for middle-income countries due to the lack of sufficient budget as well as the weak capacity of workers to pay taxes (Oizumi and Ito 2020). In the case of Tokyo, the informal economy jobs seen in the Global South are not much recognised in the city. However, Tokyo currently faces the issue of 'informalisation' of employment, which will be discussed in later chapters.

With regard to the structure of the labour market, it is important to note that social security coverage has different characteristics among the studied cities. As discussed, Bangkok and Shanghai are at the similar stage concerning to expand social security coverage to 60%–70% of population who are not covered yet. The health insurance, social security, and worker compensation coverage in Thailand are shown in Table 2.2. Except for health insurance, which is a new health insurance scheme for the poor started in the early 2000s, coverage is very limited. The Ministry of Labour has also introduced a voluntary scheme for social security for self-employed workers which is designed closely mimic that for private employees (contributions from three stakeholders: state, employer, and employee), namely the two-stakeholder system with contributions from state and self-employed workers. Registration of workers is gradually increasing. However, only 10% of the self-employed workers had registered by the late 2010s.[11]

On the contrary, irrespective of the occupational status, some social security and welfare schemes are available in Tokyo, which extend from health to pension and employment, and some are voluntary depending on the employment contract (also see Chapter 7). However, informalisation of employment and increase of irregular workers or 'working poor' has been a social agenda since the late 1990s. Along with the decline in the international competitiveness of the Japanese enterprises and deregulation of labour markets, companies have rapidly replaced formal workers with irregular workers, who now account for approximately 40% of the national labour market and 20% of the labour market in Tokyo (Figure 2.6). These irregular workers are not entitled to the same benefits as formal workers, and the contribution of employers is also limited. Ironically, this deterioration of the employment system brings forth within Tokyo similar issues and policy challenges of the emerging cities such as Bangkok and Shanghai.

Yet, the result of redistribution is evident in Japan, but not in the two middle-income countries. Among many Organisation for Economic Co-operation

Table 2.2 Population who received health insurance by type of health insurance: 2009–2015 in Thailand

Health welfare	*Year*			
	2009	*2011*	*2013*	*2015*
Population receiving health welfare (%)	97.4	98.0	98.3	98.5
Type of health welfare (Universal Coverage: UC)	78.6	79.2	74.4	75.3
Social security system (SSS)/worker compensation fund	12.9	11.6	15.4	16.4
Civil servant medical benefits scheme (CSMBS)	8.2	8.8	8.6	7.5
Private health insurance	3.7	4.1	5.3	6.7
Health insurance covered by employer	0.4	0.5	0.7	1.0
Others	0.6	0.5	0.5	0.9

Source: NSO, Social Indicators 2017.

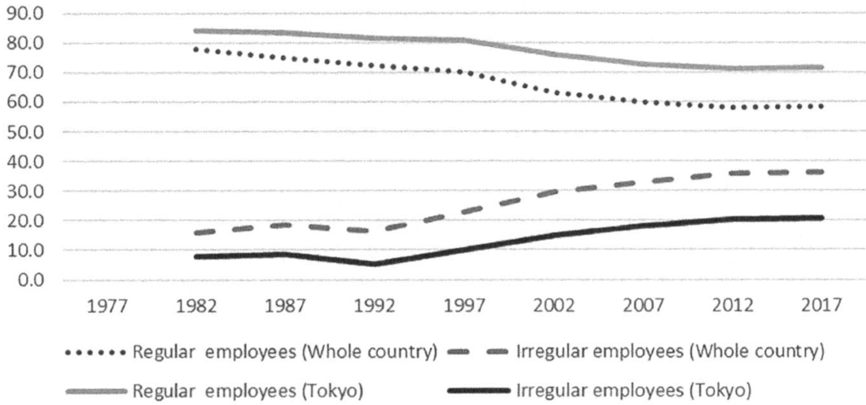

Figure 2.6 Irregular workers in Japan/Tokyo.
Source: Statistic Bureau of Japan, Labour Force Survey (each year).

and Development (OECD) countries, Japan has relatively weak but various redistribution policies that aim to reduce inequalities. According to the United Nations Development Programme, in the latter half of the 2000s, the redistribution efforts have led to a Gini coefficient of 0.370 before redistribution and 0.305 after, which they calculated as reflecting an 18% redistribution effect (UNDP 2013). However, the difference in Gini coefficients between the initial and redistributed incomes of middle-income countries is reflective of minimal change. The UNDP estimates that in China the Gini coefficient before and after redistribution was altered only by 6% from 0.42 to 0.40 in the latter half of the 2000s. In Thailand, the Gini coefficient remains unchanged (UNDP 2013; Urakawa and Endo 2020). It is worth noting that we should carefully examine whether the similarities, if any, between the three cities are due to the progress made by the emerging cities to extend social security benefits or due to deterioration of the welfare systems in developed cities like Tokyo.

2.2.3 The Residential Areas for the Urban Lower Class

Finally, let us briefly look at residential arrangement for the urban lower class. This is one of the significant indicators of urban equity because adequate housing is a fundamental human right. The living conditions of the poor are reflective of the city's management and their priorities in development and service provision and for whom these are intended.

UN Habitat (2016) revealed that despite the rapid development and economic prosperity of the Asian megacities, slum communities are still widespread. In 2014, 26.2% of the population of East Asian cities and 28.4% of Southeast Asian cities were slum dwellers. It was reported that in Bangkok, there were 2,057 communities in 2015 (BMA 2015) and 60%–80% of these communities were estimated to be the residential areas of urban lower class as per a wider definition

(Endo 2014, 2021; Yap and Leeruttanawisut 2016). Among them, the so-called 'congested community', or slum community according to a narrow definition, account for 644 communities. Notably, these communities from the perspective of residents provide multiple functions for people to survive in the city (cf., Endo 2014). Urban redevelopment projects, however, have accelerated the displacement of these communities in recent years, and the lower class has been increasingly pushed out from the inner city to the outskirts of Bangkok (Askew 2002; Endo 2022).

In the case of Shanghai, self-built communities in the inner city are rare because the government and private landlords do not allow people to build communities on empty lands. Urban villages' also exist at the periphery of the city and provide residence to rural migrants who work in the city (Wu 2016). Although the official statistics are limited, making it difficult to estimate the number of residents in the area, the increase in the land prices and the expansion of urban areas have made these suburbs targets of potential investment for developers. With the increasing pressure to relocate urban villages, new forms of informal settlements have emerged. For example, brokers rent a unit in a condominium apartment for middle- and upper-class residents, partition it into several smaller rooms—sometimes as many as 20 we heard during our field research in September 2012—with concrete walls to sublet (see Photos 2.1 and 2.2). Each unit is rented to low-income people. Against the backdrop of a shortage of vacant land and an increased threat of eviction in Shanghai (see Shao 2013 for Shanghai's transformation and demolition), this type of informal group-rented apartment is considered to be a 'contemporary slum' and is known as *qunzu* (Poon 2019; Endo 2020; Harten 2021; Harten, Kim, and Brazier 2021).

Photo 2.1 Brokers divide a unit in a condominium apartment for middle- and upper-class residents into smaller 'rooms' for the lower classes.

Photo 2.2 Inside a small partitioned room.

Interestingly, we can find similar informal residential arrangement appeared in recent Tokyo. In 2013, the Mainichi Newspaper reported that many illegally shared rooms with residential arrangements were found in Tokyo. A typical example is that a room in an apartment was divided into 12 small units, and each unit was rented out for approximately 1,200 yen (about US$11) per day.[12] The Ministry of Land, Infrastructure, Transport, and Tourism (MLIT) started a survey on illegal housing with shared rental rooms and their location (*Dappou house*) from September 2013 and began to pose regulations. The survey conducted in August 2016 found that there were 1,421 houses with illegal rental rooms in Japan. Among them, 79.6% of illegal housing facilities were found in Tokyo (MLIT 2016). In addition, a survey of the Tokyo Metropolitan Government in 2018 found that about 4,000 people can be estimated to be permanently living in Internet cafés in Tokyo (Tokyo Metropolitan Government 2018). Among them, 75.8% (approximately 3,000 people) were irregular workers without permanent residence. They are referred to as 'Net cafe refugees'.

Governments' responses vary depending on their rigidity and flexibility with respect to policy practice. In Japan, Net cafe refugees are mostly ignored. At the same time, regulations for illegal housing were enforced within a month after these illegal houses are reported in public news. In contrast, informal settlements in Bangkok and Shanghai are often tolerated until occupied land or buildings are to be used for the new development plans. There have been 'slum upgrading projects' in some sites in Bangkok or, at least, there has been implicit co-existence in these cities. However, since 2015, new issues are giving rise to tensions in Bangkok and Shanghai. These issues are accelerated by urban redevelopment projects (Wu 2016; Poon 2019; Endo 2022). These emerging cities are at turning points with rapid gentrification that is likely to take over the already limited residential options for the lower class.

2.3 Personal Networks and Quality of Life

Let us now focus on the personal networks as part of social relationships among Tokyo, Shanghai, and Bangkok in association with the subjective well-being of the people. Subjective well-being is a broad concept that includes both cognitive and affective evaluation of an individual's own life, often measured in the form of life satisfaction, fulfilment, or happiness (Diener, Oishi, and Lucas 2003). Here, we mainly consider the cognitive dimensions, or life satisfaction, which has often been measured and discussed through social surveys.

Personal networks of social relationships are often seen as a resource to enrich our lives and are referred to as social capital. As seen within the sustainable livelihoods' framework (Department for International Development [DFID] 1999), social capital is included as one of the five livelihood assets available to individuals to survive, along with human, natural, financial, and physical capitals. Recognising the specific importance of social capital, DFID describes it as a 'resource of last resort' for those in difficulty, as it may serve as a shock buffer, an informal safety net, or to compensate for a lack of other capital comprising livelihood assets (DFID 1999, 19).

2.3.1 Social Relationships in the City

The debate regarding personal networks as part of social relationships within cities vis-à-vis urbanisation has evolved around three arguments (Wellman 1979). The first is that the traditional kin and community-based relationships would be weakened ('Community Lost'); the second is that those relationships would persist ('Community Saved'); and the last is that those would be transformed (namely fragmentation and subculturation, 'Community Liberated').

The classical understanding of Wirth (1938) and the early Chicago School is that urbanisation weakens the close relationships between the family members, kin, and neighbours (i.e., primary relations) due to the mass influx of diverse kinds of people into the city and the increased social division of labour. Cities are considered as spaces with faceless anonymity, in which superficial, rational, and calculating relationships are formed, and people are required to live within such instrumental secondary ties. Although this 'community lost' perspective has impacted the society ever since, some studies have pointed out that the retention of primary relations can be observed even in urban settings, due to the existence of relatively homogenous living and/or working spaces. Evidence pertaining to the existence of urban communal solidarity networks, which have become a resource of support with respect to needs, have been found, described, and emphasised in fieldwork (e.g., Guns 1962; Keller 1968). Developed on the basis of the previous two arguments, the third perspective claims that the nature of the community undergoes transformation, which is exemplified in the discussions by Wellman (1979) and Fischer (1975). According to these, the development of transportation and communication within a city liberates human relationships from geographical constraints, and that people are likely to be a part of widely dispersed networks. Such networks enable people to create sub-communities and sub-cultures with a different kind of traditional kinship and local ties, according to their own interests. In addition, developments in communication technologies have led to further increase in virtual communities, which have been found in abundance in recent years. Social relationships within urban spaces should also be redefined to include virtual communities as an extension of the real world (Castells 2001). This complementary blending of virtual and real spaces is likely to change the way people connect, as well as the role that social relationships play in responding to risks or in other aspects.

2.3.2 Social Relationships in China, Japan, and Thailand

These urbanism debates above have been led by Western societies, and how the Asian societies are/have been experiencing the impact of urbanisation on their social relationship structure has not yet been fully revealed. In order to clarify this, reference made to social relations in the Asian region in general, or in each of three countries, to date has to be reviewed to start.

Asian societies have traditionally been characterised by familism, a family-centred patriarchal or collectivistic relationship for social interaction and trust. Familism can lead to nepotism or relational favouritism, which is contrary to the concept of social trust; thus, it is likely to have a negative impact on the social capital. In other words, dependence on the family prevents people from building trusting relationships with others, thus making them disinterested in society and making it difficult for them to pursue public interests (Fukuyama 1995). In a modern urban space having diverse population, the public sphere becomes more meaningful due to existence of trusting relationships. However, despite the transition to compressed modernisation, urbanisation, and globalisation, this traditional familism seems to perpetuate and is still influential in Asia. Lee (2013) used the data from the Asia Barometer, a public opinion survey for Asia, to show that although urbanisation has led to the nuclearisation of the family, familism is still prevalent in Asian cultures, particularly in Confucian cultures, in which economic development is evident.

These characteristics of Asian social relationships are also confirmed in the Hofstede, Hofstede, and Minkov's (2010) study of the six-dimension model of national culture.[13] Of the six dimensions, the dimensions most directly related to social relationships—power distance (PDI: strength of social hierarchy) and individualism (IDV: individualism vs. collectivism)—are reviewed. In these, many East Asian countries are found to be more accepting of hierarchical relations and appear to be more collectivistic. Among the three study countries, China and Thailand tend to reflect the more typically Asian characteristics: in contrast Japan, despite its Confucian influences, scores more moderately closer to the middle on both of these dimensions.[14]

Looking into further details, the Chinese social relationships, often referred to as *guanxi*, are like the web of social favour exchange networks. They are built with 'acquaintance (*shu*), intimacy (*qin*) and trustworthiness (*xin*)' (Bian and Wang 2016, 23), centring on family and kinship, but also extending to the surrounding pseudo-familial relationships, such as local communities or schools. This is also evident in the results of Asian value surveys, such as the Asia Barometer Survey (2004) and World Values Survey (WVS Wave 6, 2010–2014). Most surveys indicate that people's hometown and school, in addition to family, were important to them, and that their neighbours were trustworthy.

In contrast, in Japan, social relationships are expressed more in terms of *uchi* (in-group), *soto* and *yoso* (out-group and strangers), reflecting closeness and whether the individuals are reserved with one another (Nakane 1967; Doi 1971) with *uchi* mainly including one's own immediate family members. A distant and reserved relationship with people in the categories of *soto* or *yoso* is not given sufficient attention and trust building is not focused. *Uchi*'s unreserved intimate relationship, on the contrary, varies in scope depending on the context, and the fact that a person is included in *uchi* at a certain occasion does not necessarily mean that they are always trusting. In Asian value surveys, Japanese people are more likely to value their families, compared with the Chinese, but are less likely to value or trust other community members. Therefore, trustworthy relationships tend to be limited to a narrow range, such as immediate family.

Thailand also exhibits a tendency towards familism in the value surveys, but the family in the Thai context is unlike that in the two aforementioned countries. It is fundamentally a nuclear family, but as called *la famille anomique* (in English, anomie family; Todd 2008), it seems difficult to find clear and rigid family rules of inheritance, cohabitation, and so on, rather there is a lot of flexibility in practice. According to Hayami's (2019) study of care relationships in Thailand, family can be like a 'family circle' characterised by a flexibly structured relationship that is widely linked by lineage but beyond the household, extending outwards into a network.

2.3.3 Social Networks for Subjective Well-Being in Asia

Even though downsides of personal networks, such as pressure for in-group conformity and exclusion of outsiders, has been pointed out, or despite no clear causal links identified, many studies have reported a positive correlation between social capital and happiness, whereas there is a negative relationship between isolation and physical and mental health (e.g., Halliwell and Putnam 2004).

This issue has led to a discussion over subjective well-being and social capital, which originated in the individualistic societies of the West. However, with economic development, it has also attracted attention in Asia. In particular, in East Asia, an individual is considered a part of the community to which they belong. Hence, they have certain expectations from life based on the cultural values and consider social relationships important. Indeed, the findings of the Asia Barometer Survey show that life satisfaction in Asian societies is positively correlated with family and community relationships, and that social capital is essential for well-being in Asia rather than economic or human capital (Shin and Inoguchi 2010; Inoguchi 2014).

To the best of our knowledge, it is yet to be examined whether individuals derive satisfaction from the quantity of their social relationships or from the quality of their social interactions. Sun, Harris, and Vazire (2020) suggest the influence of personality and claim that the quality of relationships is important for introverted individuals. A closer look at the situation in Asian societies also reveals that the size of the network is not necessarily important; however, the people with whom one is connected and the nature of the connections have a significant impact on subjective well-being (Endo and Shibuya 2017).

Furusato and Sato (2014) compared the two types of networks, that is family and social communities, in Japan, and found that these networks contribute differently to subjective well-being in a social context. When income inequality in society is high, a large number of social community networks enhance subjective well-being, especially of individuals from low-income groups. Conversely, when inequalities are small, well-developed community networks are found to have a positive impact on subjective well-being. In other words, personal character, cultural values, and perception of one's own situation are involved in the personal networks of social relationships that lead to satisfaction with one's life.

It should be noted that similar kind of debates abounds, but most of them are being carried out at a national level, rather than at the city level. As mentioned above, human relationships in urban settings are different from those in rural areas. Therefore, the findings of national-level studies are not directly applicable at the city level in those countries. Of course, cities are not an entity separate from the country, but are spaces where people from diverse geographical backgrounds congregate; thus, the kinds of relationships established there are likely to be distinct from those in other regions where the population is relatively fixed. In addition, cities are full of risks, which make it difficult for individuals to survive without resources. In such an environment, the importance of social capital is likely to become even more apparent and significant.

In Asian cities, where family relationships are considered strong, it is yet to be uncovered whether the community has been lost, saved, or transformed, or in another different situation. Hence, it is important to analyse the human relations in a city by examining the nature of personal networks of social relationships that may help in dealing with risks in the Asian cities.

Conclusion

Asia has rapidly transformed into an urban society characterised by multi-layered stratification. As shown from the compressed development of the emerging cities such as Bangkok and Shanghai as well as the informalisation of certain social settings in developed cities, such as Tokyo, the three cities are facing similar challenges. With the increasing uncertainty and inequality, the lower- and middle-class urban residents are exposed to traditional and new risks simultaneously in their urban lives.

Megacities are a strategic analytical target to understand how individuals' objective and subjective well-being are defined and evolve over time and how individual conditions as well as social settings interact. This is because megacities are a conjuncture of complex dynamics of societal changes in a globalised and an urbanised world. Risks and shock/crises change social settings and vice versa; social settings are also a precondition of the risk/shock response process because formal institutions define the resilience and capacity of the society. Weak formal institutions can limit one's resilience at times of risks and crises, but it is not a one-to-one correspondence as informal institutions also matter.

Despite the rise of emerging cities as economic centres, social security, which is one of the important components in formal institutions, is not fully developed in emerging cities. The unique characteristics of the combination of formal and informal institutions in risk responses and survival strategies in the post-shock phases of emerging cities are different from those of the developed cities. However, as mentioned earlier, we can find commonalities prominently in the three cities (i.e., Tokyo, Shanghai, and Bangkok) as well. Social networks and subjective well-being are partly cultural, but at the same time, changeable over time in unique conditions of urbanity and social setting. After we present an overview of our dataset in the next chapter, the following chapters will discuss commonalities and differences among cities and classes with respect to each of the dimensions.

Notes

1 The Asia Barometer Survey was started in 2003 and responses from 800 people (between 20 and 60 years old) were collected for each country. In 2004, the survey was conducted in 13 countries which included questions about life satisfaction. Life satisfaction includes the following dimensions: economic (i.e., living standard, household income, housing, education, occupation) and non-economic dimensions (i.e., marriage, family life, relationships with friends and neighbours, environment, safety, and leisure).

2 According to the Ministry of Internal Affairs and Communications' survey (2022), outflow of population of Tokyo City (23 wards) exceeded inflow in 2021. The last time Tokyo experienced excess moving out of population was in 1996 in official record.

3 In the past, large gap in a number of active working populations used to observed between Quarter 1 and Quarter 3 of the year. For example, Quarter 1 and Quarter 3 of Labour Force Survey during 1980s show a few million person differences for whole country according to the harvest schedule. Many agricultural workers worked as seasonal migrants in the cities during off-season.

4 Bangkok megaregions include Bangkok and 11 surrounding provinces where most of the industrial estates are located. Thailand has 77 provinces altogether.
5 From the interview conducted on 1 November 2019, and internal document of Department of Employment, Ministry of Labour, Thailand.
6 '3D works' is often used to describe works with unfavourable conditions such as dirty, dangerous, and demanding.
7 The data in dollars could not be procured from the national statistics and the municipality. The dollar is calculated by using currency rate archives of International Monetary Fund. 1US dollar is 121.94 yen (average of December 2015).
8 In Southeast Asia, the size of the primary cities, which are often the capital and secondary cities, differ widely with respect to the populations. For example, secondary cities in Thailand such as Nakon Rachashima and Changmai only have about 400,000 people, whereas Bangkok has more than 10 million people. However, China has several urban centres with a population of more than 10 million such as in Shanghai, Beijing, Shenzen, and others.
9 Hashimoto (2021) calculated Gini coefficient of Tokyo from 'Housing and Land Statistical Survey'. Usually, the Gini coefficient published by Ministry of Health, Labour and Welfare is used for analysing the inequality in Japan. However, data for the cities is not available in the data set. The Gini coefficient of former survey tended to be lower than latter.
10 Informal employment is defined as: (1) workers who do not receive social security benefit; (2) workers without employment contract under law of 2009; and (3) those who fall into either of categories 1 and 2.
11 From reports and an interview with the Social Security Office, Ministry of Labour on 12 September 2018. The data has been procured from the internal documents. However, during the COVID-19 pandemic, the registration for voluntary social security scheme jumped up from less than 3 million to 10 million. However, benefits can be received after three months of contributions, and after this, some stopped paying contributions. It is challenge for Social Security Office how to involve these new registered people sustainably in post-shock period (from interview on 15 August 2022).
12 Mainichi newspaper first reported about illegal housing with shared rental rooms on 23 May 2013 and published a series of articles. About 40 articles on illegal housing appeared in the Mainichi newspaper between May and September 2013. MLIT launched the first survey in September 2013 and started to regulate the housing by adhering to the safety rules.
13 According to their study, six dimensions of culture are: individualism, power distance, masculinity, uncertainty avoidance, long-term orientation, and indulgence.
14 China scores 80 for PDI and 20 for IDV; Thailand scores 64 and 20; Japan scores 54 and 46, respectively.

Bibliography

Askew, M. 2002. *Bangkok: Place, Practice and Representation.* London: Routledge.

Bangkok Metropolitan Administration (BMA). 2015. *Satit krungthep* [Statistic of Bangkok]. Bangkok: BMA.

Bian, Y., and W. Wang. 2016. 'The social capital for self-employment in transitional China.' In *Rethinking social capital and entrepreneurship in greater China: Is guanxi still important?*, edited by J.H. Wang, and R.M. Hsung, 21–35. London: Routledge.

Bureau of Industrial and Labour Affairs of Tokyo Metropolitan Government. 2015. *Tokyo no sangyou to koyou shugyo 2015* [Industry and employment in Tokyo 2015]. Tokyo: Tokyo Metropolitan Government.

Castells, M. 2001. *The internet galaxy: reflection on the internet, business and society.* Oxford: Oxford University Press.

Chen, M., and F. Carre. 2020. *The informal economy revisited: examining the past, envisioning the future.* London: Routledge.

Chen, Y.L., and H.B. Shin, eds. 2019. *Neoliberal urbanism, contested cities and housing in Asia (The contemporary city)*. New York: Palgrave Macmillan.

Department for International Development (DFID). 1999. *Sustainable livelihoods guidance sheets.* London: DFID, accessed 30 July 2021, <livelihoodscentre.org>.

Diener, E., S. Oishi, and R.E. Lucas. 2003. 'Personality, culture, and subjective well-being: emotional and cognitive evaluations of life.' *Annual Review of Psychology*, 54: 403–425. doi:10.1146/annurev.psych.54.101601.145056

Doi, T. 1971. *Amae no kozo* [The anatomy of dependence]. Tokyo: Kobundo.

Endo, T. 2014. *Living with risks: precarity and Bangkok's urban poor.* Singapore: NUS Press association with Kyoto University Press.

Endo, T. 2020. 'Informal residential areas: the functions of "slum" communities from the urban lower-class perspective.' In *The Asian economy: contemporary issues and challenges*, edited by Goto, K., T. Endo, and A. Ito, 184–185. London: Routledge.

Endo, T. 2022. 'Urban redevelopment, spatial restructuring and displacement of communities in Bangkok.' *LSE working paper.*

Endo, T. and K. Goto. 2020. 'Informalizing Asia: The other dynamics of the Asian economy', In *The Asian Economy: Contemporary Issues and Challenges*, edited by Goto, K., T. Endo, and A. Ito, 169–187. London: Routledge.

Endo, T. and K. Oizumi. 2020. 'Urbanizing Asia: cities transforming into mega-regions.' In *The Asian economy: contemporary issues and challenges*, edited by Goto, K., T. Endo, and A. Ito, 145–168. London: Routledge.

Endo, T and M.K. Shibuya. 2017. 'Urban risk, risk response and well-being in Asian cities: the case of Tokyo, Shanghai and Bangkok', *Procedia Engineering*, 198: 976–984. doi: 10.1016/j.proeng.2017.07.143

Endo, T. and M.K. Shibuya. 2019. 'Urban risk and surviving strategies: a case study of urban middle class and lower class in Asian megacities', *Paper presented at EURA-UAA conference city futures IV*, University College Dublin, Ireland, 20–22 June.

Fischer, CS. 1975. 'Toward a subcultural theory of urbanism', *American Journal of Sociology* 80 (6): 1319–1341.

Florida, R., A. Rodriguez-Pose, and M. Storper. 2021. 'Cities in a post-COVID world.' *Urban Studies,* first published online 27 June 2021, doi: 10.1177/00420980211018072

Fukuyama, F. 1995. 'Social capital and the global economy.' *Foreign Affairs* 74 (5): 89–103.

Furusato, Y., and Y. Sato. 2014. 'Social capital and subjective happiness [Shukanteki kofukukan to sosharu kyapitaru]' In *Sosharu kyapitaru to kakusa shakai: kofuku no keiryo shakaigaku* [Social capital in an unequal society: the quantitative sociology of happiness], edited by R. Tsuji and Y. Sato, 189–208. Tokyo: University of Tokyo Press.

Galbraith, J.K. 2012. *Inequality and instability: a study of the world economy just before the Great Crisis*, Oxford: Oxford University Press.

Glaeser, E. 2021. 'Urban resilience.' *Urban Studies* 59 (1): 3–35.

Goto, K., T. Endo and A. Ito, eds. 2020. *The Asian economy: contemporary issues and challenges*, London: Routledge.

Guns, H.J. 1962. *The urban villagers: groups and class in the life of Italian-Americans*, New York: Free Press.

Halliwell, J.F., and R. Putnam. 2004. 'The social context of well-being', *Philosophical transactions of the Royal Society of London, Series B, Biological sciences*, 359 (1449): 1435–1446. doi: 10.1098/rstb.2004.1522

Harten, J.G. 2021. 'Housing single women: gender in China's shared rental housing market.' *Journal of the American Planning Association* 87 (1): 85–100.

Harten, J.G., A.M. Kim, and J.C. Brazier. 2021. 'Real and fake data in Shanghai's informal rental housing market: groundtruthing data scraped from the internet.' *Urban Studies* 58 (9): 1831–1845.

Hashimoto, K. 2021. 'Time difference gentrification as a bloodless revolution: class structure and spatial polarization in the Tokyo metropolitan area after the 1980s.' *International Journal of Japanese Sociology* 30: 23–64.

Hayami, Y. 2019. 'Potentialities of care in Southeast Asia.' In *Tonan Ajia ni okeru kea no senzairyoku* [Potentialities of care in Southeast Asia: Practice of life's connectivities], edited by Y. Hayami, 1–27. Kyoto: Kyoto University Press.

Hofstede, G., G.J. Hofstede, and M. Minkov. 2010. *Cultures and organizations: software of the mind*, rev. 3rd ed. New York: McGraw-Hill.

IDE-JETRO. 2015. *IDE world trend: social transformation of Asia from population census* [Ajiken warudo torendo: Tokushu jinkou sensasu kara miru Higashi Ajia no shakai daihendou], No.238 (August). Tokyo: IDE-JETRO.

Inoguchi, T. 2014. *Deta kara yomu Ajia no kofukudo* [Asian happiness degree read from data: international comparisons of quality of life]. Tokyo: Iwanami Shoten.

Inoguchi, T., A. Tanaka, S. Sonoda, and T. Dadabaev. 2006. *Human benefits and values in striding Asia: East Asia in focus country profiles, thematic analyses and sourcebook based on the Asia Barometer survey of 2004.* Tokyo: Akashi Shoten.

International Labour Office (ILO). 2018. *Women and men in the informal economy: a statistical picture,* 3rd ed. Geneva: International Labour Office.

Jütting, J.P., and J.R. Laiglesia. 2009. *Is informal normal?: toward more and better jobs in developing countries.* Paris: OECD.

Keller, S.I. 1968. *The urban neighborhood: a sociological perspective* (No. 33). New York: Random House.

Lee, L., H.B. Shin, and E. López-Morales. 2016. *Planetary gentrification.* Cambridge: Polity Press.

Lee, Z. 2013. 'Familism in Asia [Ajia ni okeru kazokushugi].' In *Risuku no naka no Higashi Ajia* [Risk in East Asia], edited by S. Sonoda, 191–217. Tokyo: Keiso shobo.

Marukawa, T. 2013. *Gendai Chugoku keizai* [Contemporary Chinese economy]. Tokyo: Yuhikaku.

McFarlane, C. 2021. 'Repopulating density: COVID-19 and the politics of urban value.' *Urban Studies* published online 9 June, 2021. doi: 10.1177/00420980211014810

Ministry of Internal Affairs and Communications. 2022. *Report on internal migration in Japan derived from the resident registers.* Ministry of Internal Affairs and Communications, accessed 1 September, 2022, <https://www.stat.go.jp/english/data/idou/index.html>.

Ministry of Land, Infrastructure, Transport and Tourism (MLIT). 2016. *Progress about regulation and guidance of illegal rental rooms* [Ihou kashirūmu no zesei shidounado no joukyo ni tsuite], Press release on 17th October, Tokyo: MLIT Department of Housing.

Nakane, C. 1967. *Tate-shakai no ningen kankei* [Japanese Society]. Tokyo: Kodansha.

NESDB (Office of the National Economic and Social Development Board). 2017. *The report on poverty and inequality in Thailand* [Rai-ngan kan Wikhro Sathanakan kwaam Yaak jon lae kwaam Leuam lam nai Prathet Thai 2017]. Bangkok: Office of the National Economic and Social Development Council.

NSO (National Statistical Office). 2012. *The 2010 population and housing census: Bangkok.* Bangkok: National Statistical Office.
NSO. 2015. *Labour force survey: Bangkok (Quarter 1 and 3).* Bangkok: National Statistical Office.
NSO. 2017. *The informal employment survey 2017.* Bangkok: National Statistical Office.
OECD. 2011. *How's life? 2011: measuring well-being.* Paris: OECD Publishing.
Ohtake, F. 2005. *Nihon no fubyoudo* [Inequality in Japan]. Tokyo: Nippon Keizai Shimbun Press.
Oizumi, K., and A. Ito. 2020. 'Ageing Asia: from demographic dividend to demographic tax.' In *The Asian economy: contemporary issues and challenges*, edited by K. Goto, T. Endo, and A. Ito, 191–208. London: Routledge.
Ortega, AA. 2016. *Neoliberalizing spaces in the Philippines: suburbanization transnational migration, and dispossession.* Lanham: Lexington Books.
Park, A., Y. Wu, and Y. Du. 2012. 'Informal employment in urban China: measurement and implications.' *Working Paper (No.77737)*, World Bank.
Poon, L. 2019. 'When affordable housing in Shanghai is a bed in the kitchen', Bloomberg CityLab, <https://www.bloomberg.com/news/articles/2019-07-15/shanghai-s-illegal-and-crammed-affordable-homes>.
Rigg, J. 2015. *Challenging Southeast Asian development: the shadows of success.* London: Routledge.
Shanghai Municipal Statistics Bureau. 2011. *Shanghai statistical yearbook 2011.* Shanghai: Shanghai Municipality.
Shanghai Municipal Statistics Bureau. 2018. *Shanghai basic facts 2018.* Shanghai: Shanghai Municipality.
Shanghai Municipal Statistics Bureau. 2019. *Shanghai basic facts 2019.* Shanghai: Shanghai Municipality.
Shao, Q. 2013. *Shanghai GONE: domicide and defiance in a Chinese megacity.* Maryland: Rowman & Littlefield.
Shatkin, G. 2017. *Cities for profit: the real estate turn in Asia's urban politics.* Ithaca, NY: Cornell University Press.
Shin, H.B. 2020. 'Urban transformation "Korean Style": lessons from property-based urban development.' In *Exporting Urban Korea? Reconsidering the Korean Urban Development Experience,* edited by S.H. Park, H.B. Shin, and H.S. Kang, 58–80. London: Routledge.
Shin, D.C., and T. Inoguchi. 2010. 'Avowed happiness in Confucian Asia: Ascertaining its distribution, patterns, and sources.' In *The quality of life in Confucian Asia*, edited by D.C. Shin and T. Inoguchi, 223–245. Dordrecht: Springer.
Shin, H.B., Y. Zhao, and S.Y. Koh. 2020. 'Whither progressive urban futures? Critical reflections on the politics of temporality in Asia.' *City* 24 (1-2): 244–254.
Statistics Bureau, Ministry of Internal Affairs and Communications. (each year). 'Jinko suikei [Population Estimates]', accessed 12 September, 2022, <https://www.stat.go.jp/data/jinsui/index.html>.
Stiglitz, J.E., A. Sen, and J.P. Fitoussi. 2009. *Report by the commission on the measurement of economic performance and social progress.* Paris: Commission on the Measurement of Economic Performance and Social Progress.
Suehiro, A. 2009. 'Happiness and hope in Asia [Ajia no koufuku to kibou].' In *Kibougaku 1 Kibou wo kataru* [Social Science of Hope 1: Talking about hope], edited by Institute of Social Science, Y. Genda, and S. Uno, 81–123. Tokyo: University of Tokyo Press.

Sun, J., K. Harris, and S. Vazire. 2020. 'Is well-being associated with the quantity and quality of social interactions?' *Journal of Personality and Social Psychology* 119 (6): 1478–1496.

Tachibanaki, T., and K. Urakawa. 2006. *Nihon no hinkon kenkyu* [A study of poverty in Japan]. Tokyo: University of Tokyo Press.

Todd, E. 2008. *The diversity of the world: family and* modernity [La diversité du monde: famille et modernité]. Translated by F Ogino. Tokyo: Fujiwara shobo.

Tokyo Metropolitan Accounts. 2017. *Annual report on Tokyo metropolitan accounts for 2017* [Tomin keizai keisan heisei 29 nendo nempo]. Tokyo: Tokyo Metropolitan Accounts.

Tokyo Metropolitan Government. 2018. *Research report on irregular workers who lost housing* [Jukyo soshitsu huanteishuroushanado no jittai ni kansuru chousa houkokusho]. Department of Welfare and Social Security, Tokyo: Tokyo Metropolitan Government.

UNDP (United Nations Development Programme). 2013. *Humanity divided: confronting inequality in developing countries.* New York: UNDP.

UN Habitat. 2016. *World Cities Report 2016: Urbanization and Development: Emerging Futures.* Nairobi: UN Habitat.

United Nations Department of Economic and Social Affairs (UN DESA). 2018. *The world urbanization prospects: the 2018 Revision.* New York: UN DESA Population Division.

Urakawa, K., and T. Endo. 2020. 'Unequalizing Asia: from poverty to inequality.' In *The Asian economy: contemporary issues and challenges*, edited by K. Goto, T. Endo, and A. Ito, 209–232. London: Routledge.

Yap, K.S., and K. Leeruttanawisut. 2016. 'Informal settlements in Bangkok: origins, features, growth and prospects.' *Public goods versus economic interests: global perspectives on the history of squatting*, edited by Anders, F., and A. Sedlmaier, eds. London: Routledge.

Yusef, A., A. Sumner, and I. Rum. 2014. 'Twenty years of expenditure inequality in Indonesia, 1993–2013.' *Bulletin of Indonesian Economic Studies* 50 (2): 243–254.

Wellman, B. 1979. 'The community question: the intimate networks of East Yorkers.' *American Journal of Sociology* 84: 1201–1231.

Whittaker, H., T. Sturgeon, T. Okita, and T. Zhu. 2020. *Compressed development: time and timing in economic and social development.* Oxford: Oxford University Press.

Wirth, L. 1938. 'Urbanism as a way of life.' *American Journal of Sociology* 44 (1): 1–24.

Wu, F. 2016. 'Housing in Chinese urban villages: the dwellers, conditions and tenancy informality.' *Housing Studies* 31 (7): 852–870.

3 Asian Megacity Survey on Well-Being

Momoyo Shibuya

Introduction

In the previous chapter, we discussed the macro-socioeconomic dynamics of Asian megacities. Apparently, Asian megacities may look similar to other global cities, but hiding inside them are living spaces weaved from their own peculiar historical and social contexts. While the lives of the people living in these megacities appear to be globalised, a local flavour can also be detected upon deeper examination.

This chapter will draw a picture for readers of three Asian megacities before we delve deeper into the dimensions of their urban lifestyles. To this end, this chapter first briefly outlines the survey design and then further data on the urban characteristics of Tokyo, Shanghai, and Bangkok, obtained from the responses to the questionnaires. The data in this chapter will serve as a reference for the following chapters.

3.1 Survey Details

3.1.1 Procedure and Scope

We conducted the Asia megacity survey in three cities, namely Tokyo, Shanghai, and Bangkok, from 2012 to 2014. The timing coincided with a period of events that foreshadowed the shape of the present-day global society. During this specific time, financial crisis, conflicts, terrorism, natural disasters, and epidemics occurred, making many aware that we were in an 'age of risks' on a global scale.

The survey targeted middle- and lower-class residents who were the main earners for their households in each city based on the research intention to reflect and portray people's urban lives according to the economic situation. The thresholds for classifying respondents into the middle or lower class were determined with reference to: the advice of local researchers and research agencies, the data from the respective statistical office in each city, and the considerations of economic indicators in each city (e.g. personal income and consumer prices in the survey year). In Bangkok, the middle class was defined as those having a monthly income between Thai baht (THB) 15,001–50,000, and the lower class

DOI: 10.4324/9781003328155-3

with THB 15,000 or less. In Shanghai, the middle-class threshold was set at a monthly income between renminbi (RMB) 4,001–15,000, while the lower class with RMB 4,000 or less. In Tokyo, the middle class was those having a yearly income between Japanese yen (JPY) 3,000,001–8,000,000, and the lower class was less than JPY 3,000,000.

The questionnaire combined two types of questions: some questions appeared in all questionnaires, whereas others were city-specific. The questionnaire part common to all cities included questions on individual attributes (i.e. age, sex, and family composition), history of city residence, working conditions, perceived risks of living in an urban area, available public and private support, life satisfaction, and sense of fulfilment. Questions on urban residence history included the place of origin, total years of residence in the city, number of moves in and out of the city, current residence, and length of residence. Working conditions were asked regarding job type, employment status, length of employment, number of job changes, working hours per week, and most recent income. Regarding the perceived urban risks, respondents were provided with options for what they considered the risk of urban living and asked to select the relevant ones from the list. The options included economic (finance, work, and housing), social/personal (personal relations, family issues, and health issues), or environmental (living environment and natural disasters) (see Chapter 5 in detail). For the public and private support resources available, respondents were asked to name up to three specific people or institutions they had sought and would seek help from when problems arose. Then, life satisfaction was measured as self-reported on a 10-point scale. Furthermore, respondents were asked whether they felt satisfied with some presented activities to identify what makes life fulfilling for them.

Regarding city-specific questions, we incorporated different versions of questions due to the specific national circumstances in social security schemes and household registration systems into the questions and response options. For instance, the options of social security schemes were prepared in the context of the systems of that specific country, such as employment insurance, pensions, and health insurance. In addition, as the public services available differ according to household status (urban or rural registration) in China, a question asking about registration status was added to the Shanghai version of the questionnaire.

Each questionnaire was drafted initially in Japanese, translated into English, Chinese, and Thai, and subsequently back-translated to ensure content equivalence. The questionnaires were distributed online or face-to-face in each city; responses were collected online for both classes of Tokyo and middle class of Shanghai and through face-to-face interviews for lower class of Shanghai and both classes of Bangkok. All respondents were randomly selected, except for the lower class of Bangkok, in which the survey was conducted within accessible selected communities. Ultimately, the sample sizes were 766 in Bangkok, 700 in Shanghai, and 1,261 in Tokyo.

3.1.2 Demographic Profile of Respondents

Table 3.1 provides an overview of respondents' characteristics by city. In the results discussed later in this chapter, six groups (two classes in each of the three cities) were used as the basic analysis unit; however, numbers on the whole city population were also used where appropriate. Respondents in the three cities differed slightly in their numbers and demographic composition. Still, all data were carefully analysed, and we compared the questionnaire results with existing data for each city.

The median age of survey participants in Bangkok, Shanghai, and Tokyo stood at 43.0, 35.8, and 43.9, respectively. In Tokyo, the higher median age was the same in both classes, and the age profile for survey participants was similar to the whole city population (i.e., 44.0 years) based on results of a national survey for the same period (Statistic Bureau of Japan, 2016). Contrariwise, Shanghai respondents had the lowest median age among the three surveyed cities, which reflects the relative youthfulness of the city's middle class. Upon comparing the numbers for Shanghai in our survey with the estimated median age (i.e., 39.5 years) for the whole population in the city (Shanghai Municipal Bureau of Statistics, 2015), we believe that to be a little skewed towards younger respondents in our survey. Similar to Shanghai, Bangkok also showed a trend towards the younger respondents for the sample from the middle class and older from the lower class; meanwhile, the estimated median age for the whole population in Bangkok was 36.9 years (National Statistical Office Thailand, 2016), the lowest of the three cities based on official reports. In our survey, the results for Bangkok were skewed towards higher ages, particularly for the lower class.

Regarding the proportion of locals and internal migrants (who are originally from other regions), most Shanghai respondents were locals, with internal migrants accounting for only 19.7% of the middle class and 28.5% of the lower

Table 3.1 Summary of respondents' sex, age, and internal migrant rate

City	*Bangkok*	*Shanghai*	*Tokyo*
Middle class	412	300	631
Age (Median)	39.3	32.6	43.7
Male:Female	48.5:51.5	50:50	51.5:48.5
Internal migrant rate	66.0	19.7	53.4
Lower class	354	400	630
Age (Median)	46.8	39.0	44.1
Male:Female	46.5:53.5	50:50	53.3:46.7
Internal migrant rate	63.3	28.5	52.1
Total	766	700	1,261
Age (Median)	43.0	35.8	43.9
Male:Female	47.6:52.4	50:50	52.4: 47.6
Internal migrant rate	64.8	24.7	52.7

Source: by author.

class. According to municipal statistics of Shanghai, the registered population share among residents is about 60% (Shanghai Municipal Bureau of Statistics, 2015). Although this 'registered population' variable may include internal migrants, which hinders our ability to make simple conclusions, the comparison of the survey results with official information about the city suggests that the proportion of local respondents in this survey was higher than that of locals in the city, in general at the time. Incidentally, the most common reason for internal migration was to get an employment.

In our survey, internal migrants in Tokyo accounted for more than half of the middle and lower classes (53.4% and 52.1%, respectively). A national survey reported that 45% of the residents were born outside Tokyo (National Institute of Population and Social Security Research, 2019); therefore, our Tokyo sample comprised a slightly higher proportion of migrants. Like Shanghai, the most common reason for moving to Tokyo was work, whereas other common reasons were to pursue higher education and job transfer.

The Bangkok sample included an even higher proportion of migrants compared with the two other cities, for 66.0% of the middle-class respondents and 63.3% of the lower-class respondents. In its general population, the estimation was that internal migrants accounted for just over 40% of the population at the time (National Statistical Office Thailand 2010). This figure is not significantly different from that of the other two cities, indicating that our survey respondents are more likely to be internal migrants than in the real Bangkok, or the other cities. The main reason for their migration was work, followed by pursuing higher education and marriage for the middle class. For the lower class, it is followed by accompanying their parents' relocation to their new job.

3.2 Survey Results

3.2.1 Residential Status

One way to assess how urban residents lead their lives is by examining how frequently and to where they move (residential mobility). On average, largely similar patterns were recorded regardless of city and class with all six samples typically staying resident in the same area/district for about 30 years and reporting an average of three residence changes during this (Table 3.2).

Nevertheless, apart from that, pattern differences among the six groups can naturally be observed. In Shanghai, 87.3% of the middle and 65.0% of the lower-class respondents reported living in their own houses. This high rate of house ownership in Shanghai seems to resonate well with the result of the AsiaBarometer survey of 2004 (Inoguchi et al. 2006), which found that 65% of Chinese respondents answered positively about the importance of having a comfortable house in one's life. When asked if they would like to continue living in the city in the future, a high percentage of Shanghai respondents said yes (over 90% in both groups).

In Tokyo, only 45.6% of the middle class and 35.9% of the lower class lived in their own houses, with more respondents reporting living in rented houses

Table 3.2 Summary of residential status

		Bangkok		*Shanghai*		*Tokyo*	
		Middle	*Lower*	*Middle*	*Lower*	*Middle*	*Lower*
Years in the city (years)		22.8	32.6	27.9	32.1	30.0	30.9
Move (average times)		2.57	2.89	2.28	3.06	3.07	2.99
House/Unit	(%)						
[Owned]		34.30	82.90	87.30	65.00	45.60	35.90
[Rented]		49.90	14.00	11.30	32.80	53.70	62.40
[Lodgings]		10.50	2.80	1.30	2.00	0.60	1.70
Wish to stay in the future	(%)	54.40	69.50	94.00	91.50	75.90	67.10
[Local]		68.60	79.40	94.60	99.30	83.30	73.80
[Internal migrant]		47.10	63.70	91.50	71.90	69.40	61.00

Source: by author.

(50.1% and 57.8%, respectively). This relatively low percentage of ownership in Tokyo seems linked to the fact that only 43% of Japanese respondents in the AsiaBarometer agreed with the idea of owning a comfortable house. Contrarily, not a low percentage – 75.9% of the middle class and 67.1% of the lower class – said they would like to continue living in Tokyo.

In the Bangkok data, the lower class were more likely to live in their own houses (82.9%), while the middle class were more often in rented houses (49.9%) than in their own (34.3%). Interestingly, while the AsiaBarometer survey found that Thailand, rather than China, had a higher percentage of respondents stating that owning a comfortable house was more important to them, there are differences in orientation by class. The lower class in Bangkok lived in their own houses[1] like in Shanghai, while the middle class were inclined to live in rented houses, more similar to Tokyo. The intention to continue living in Bangkok in the future was only held by 54.4% and 69.5% of the middle and lower classes, respectively.

These results seem to be related to the values of urban dwellers and the proportion of internal migrants. Home ownership rates are often determined by economic conditions. But it is also influenced by whether people consider owning a house to be stable and preferable or ownership to be land bound (i.e. whether they consider renting to be more precarious or more flexible). Comparing the results for locals and those from other regions, a higher proportion of locals reported a desire to continue living in the city, irrespective of city or class. It is possible that factors such as whether there are other places to which they feel attached and whether they have values that match the urban lifestyle may have influenced the results.

3.2.2 *Family*

In this subsection, we will see the distribution of people's families in cities. To begin with, Tokyo respondents were found to live in relatively small families.

As shown in Table 3.3, there is a noticeably high proportion of singles (45.5% of the middle and 61.1% of the lower class) and divorced people (10.6% and 13.3%, respectively), whereas a low proportion of married people (40.6% and 23.5%, respectively). The average number of household members also reflected this, with a particularly high proportion of single-person households among the lower class (1.8 persons on average). Regarding children, the average number among middle class was 0.7 with this just 0.5 among lower class, suggesting many households without children. Furthermore, families typically had few relatives living in the same area as themselves (an average of 0.6 among the middle class and 0.5 among the lower class).

Contrastingly, many people in Shanghai lived with their families. Of the middle class, 79% were married, and in the lower class, 63.5% were married. Similar to Tokyo, the average number of children was low with an average of 0.6 in both the middle and lower classes, suggesting that many families do not have children. However, the Shanghai middle-class households did have an average of 3.5 members, the largest average households among the six groups surveyed. As for the number of relatives living in the same area/district, the middle class in Shanghai also has the highest of all six samples, at 2.27 persons. Conversely, the lower classes have an average of 2.2 people in their families, and the lowest number of relatives in the neighbourhood, at 0.29. Although there are not as many single-person households as in Tokyo, family size differs between the middle and lower classes, suggesting that different living environments and lifestyles have developed.

Bangkok also had a higher proportion of married people than Tokyo. In contrast with Shanghai, the lower class (68.3%) had a higher proportion of married people than the middle class (55.3%). For the lower class, as there was a relatively high rate of divorced and widowed, the proportion of singles was the lowest among the studied groups. The average number of family members living together was 2.5 for the middle class and 3 for the lower class, with at least one child (1.6 on average for both classes). As for the number of relatives living

Table 3.3 Family structure

	Bangkok		*Shanghai*		*Tokyo*	
	Middle	*Lower*	*Middle*	*Lower*	*Middle*	*Lower*
Married	55.3	68.3	79.0	63.5	40.6	23.5
Single	36.4	13.9	19.7	32.3	45.5	61.1
Divorced	4.1	8.5	1.3	3.3	10.6	13.3
Widowed	4.1	9.3	0.0	1.0	3.3	2.1
Family size	2.50	3.00	3.51	2.20	2.08	1.81
Child	1.57	1.67	0.64	0.64	0.71	0.50
Relatives	0.86	1.92	2.27	0.29	0.62	0.56

Source: by author.

Note: Figures of marital status are in percentage (%); average family size, child, and relatives are in persons.

in the same area, the middle and lower class had an average of 0.86 and 1.92, respectively. Contrary to Shanghai, in Bangkok, the lower classes lived in larger families than the middle classes.

These figures show that the middle class in Shanghai and the lower class in Bangkok were more likely to live with their families and have nearby relatives, whereas other groups lived alone or in relatively small family circles, particularly common for the lower class in Tokyo. However, even for the two groups that lived with their families, the number of family members is by no means large. Furthermore, the number of children is not high, given the estimated total fertility rate in the region (2.2 in 2015; for 1.65 for East Asia and 2.27 for South-East Asia. United Nations, 2022). Therefore, the family communities in which people in the three cities are embedded are all relatively small.

3.2.3 Education and Work

The data on educational attainment, which allows for inferences about cultural capital, as well as individual attitudes and values for social activities, indicated a significant disparity between the middle and lower classes in the proportion of respondents with higher education across all cities. The biggest gap between economic classes was observed in Shanghai, where 96.3% of middle-class and only 31.0% of lower-class respondents reportedly had a tertiary education background. All respondents had more than primary education, except 1.3% of the lower class. In Bangkok, this gap was small compared to Shanghai but still clearly showed the differences between the classes as well as within each class. In the middle class, 50.7% of the population had a higher education background, while 20.1% had only primary education. Conversely, in the lower class, 11.5% had higher education, though the majority (57.9%) had only up to primary education. Tokyo also had a large disparity between classes, with 82.1% of the middle class having tertiary education, while among the lower class, this was slightly more than half of that (44.0%). However, within the same class, the differences are not as clear-cut as in Bangkok, with only 2.4% of those in the lower class having only primary education.

No correlation between occupations and educational attainment was identified in the data. Occupational trends and preferences seemed to be according to the city rather than educational background.

In Shanghai, most respondents were full-time employees (89.7% of the middle class and 77.3% of the lower class). Of these, people in public sector employment characteristically accounted for 37% in the middle class and 30% in the lower class. In both classes, a few were self-employed, and less than 10% of those had a second job. This survey asked about people's work values, such as whether they preferred an unstable but discretionary job or a job with no discretion but stability, and about two-thirds of the Shanghai respondents chose a stable job. This result is consistent with the current situation. The average length of current employment was about seven years, irrespective of occupation. Despite an over threefold wage gap on average between the middle and lower classes (USD 1105.30 for the middle class compared to USD 355.38 for the lower class), working hours were slightly longer in the lower class, 46.4 hours per week, than in the middle class, 41.8 hours per week.

Meanwhile, Bangkok had a higher proportion of self-employed people (61% of the middle class and 44.1% of the lower class[2]) and fewer full-time employees (31.5% and 29.0%, respectively), showing a different pattern among the three cities. Our survey also asked respondents elsewhere to choose between unstable but discretionary work and stable work with little discretion, with three-quarters of the Bangkok respondents choosing unstable but discretionary work. This result seems to be linked to their actual work practices. Presumably, because many people were self-employed, both classes had many respondents who worked six days a week, and the average weekly working hours were longer than in other cities (53.3 hours per week on average for the middle class and 56.8 hours per week for the lower class). However, the average length of their current work was 8.5 years for the middle class and 11.9 years for the lower class, and only around 10% of the respondents had a second job, indicating that they were not necessarily moving from one job to another.

In Tokyo, self-employment also accounted for a modest proportion (12.8% of the middle class and 18.6% of the lower class), though the core of both the middle and lower classes were full-time employees (71.6% and 43.7%, respectively), most of whom worked for private companies. For the lower class, however, part-time employees also accounted for 29.7% of the sample. As a result, the average number of years in their current job varied between 7.55 years (lower class) and 11.28 years (middle class). Besides, on average, working hours were shorter in Tokyo than in the other cities, at 43.2 hours per week in the middle class and 42 hours per week in the lower class. However, more people have a second job than in the other two cities, and the figure was 17.9% in the lower class and 12.9% in the middle class. On the binary choice question asking about their work values, contrary to Bangkok, Tokyo respondents chose stable work with limited discretion at around 70%. From this, we can conclude that respondents in Tokyo, especially among the lower class, were seeking stability but, in reality, were unable to live in such a way (see Box 2a).

3.2.4 Household Finance and Social Security Schemes

This section moves on to examine the situation of household finances and social security. The first notable point is the number of workers in the household. In the household, the money available is not simply equal to the respondent's income, and the meaning of the security available can be very different. Breaking down single and married households, single-person households in all cities were likely to have one worker. Married households in Bangkok and the middle class of Shanghai had more than one worker, while in Tokyo and the lower class of Shanghai had often only one worker and were less likely to have a dual-earner lifestyle.

Regarding household income, the middle class in Bangkok earned almost twice as much as the lower class (Table 3.4). Over 60% of both the middle and lower classes responded that they had savings; only 37.1% of the middle class and roughly three-quarters of the lower class had debt. The debt amount of the lower classes is about six times greater than household income or roughly equal amount to that of the middle-class households. The balance between savings and debt as a proportion of household income was found to be −0.62 for the middle class, which is not very significant. In contrast, for the lower class, it was −4.93, indicating that debt is much greater than household income. The main reason for debt was house purchases. In Shanghai, the income gap between the middle and lower classes was large, with the middle-class average approximately three times higher. Concerning savings, all respondents in the middle class had savings, and the amount saved was about 17 times their income (62.5% of the lower class had savings with an amount of nine times their income). Relative to Bangkok, fewer respondents had debts, with only 19.8% of the middle class and 8.8% of the lower class. For both groups, the reason for debt was typically the purchase of a house. The ratio of net savings (reported savings minus debt) to household income indicated that the middle class had three times the higher savings ratio than the lower class (8.17 and 2.47 times, respectively). Finally, in Tokyo, like in Bangkok, the middle class earned about twice as much as the lower class. However, in Tokyo, savings and debt were characteristically large relative to household income. Among the middle class, 77% had savings, which on average were 11.7 times their income, and 30.7% had debts, which averaged almost 21.9 times their income. The situation was the same in the lower class, with 66% having savings averaging 12.2 times the household income. Debt was held by 26.2% and for these respondents averaged 8.5 times the household income. Where Tokyo differs from other cities is that the middle class had more debt than the lower class. Notably, the main reason for debt differed significantly: for the middle class was to buy a house, whereas, for the lower class, it was to cover daily living expenses.

Table 3.4 Household finance

	Bangkok		*Shanghai*		*Tokyo*	
	Middle	*Lower*	*Middle*	*Lower*	*Middle*	*Lower*
Wage	642.21	384.97	1,105.3	355.38	3,828.35	1,942.9
Household Income	1,112.27	646.94	1,961.83	576.01	4,609.55	2,368.94
Household saving	2,545.91	633.92	33,514.97	5,424.24	53,996.27	28,940.76
Household debt	3,237.88	3,821.71	17,487.94	4,000.1	100,814.01	20,251.35
(Saving–debt)	−691.97	−3,187.79	16,027.03	1,424.14	−46,817.74	8,689.41
/household income	−0.62	−4.93	8.17	2.47	−10.16	3.67

Source: by author.

Note: Figures of wage, household income, household saving, and household debt are median, in US dollars.

Table 3.5 Social security schemes

	Bangkok		Shanghai		Tokyo	
	Middle	*Lower*	*Middle*	*Lower*	*Middle*	*Lower*
Unemployment insurance	7.8	12.9	23.7	54.8	56.7	78.0
Health insurance	51.6	73.4	91.3	45.9	72.9	80.4
Pension	4.4	2.8	94.0	62.7	69.6	70.7
Retire allowance	4.4	3.4	0.0	14.0	44.5	21.1
Bonus	30.2	19.6	74.0	39.8	54.5	33.9

Source: by author.

Although a straightforward comparison of work-related social security schemes is not possible due to differences in the systems by country, the survey findings are compiled here. Our survey asked about respondents to indicate their coverage for each of the following: unemployment insurance, health insurance, pension, retirement benefits, bonuses, and others (Table 3.5).

Fewer people in Bangkok had access to unemployment insurance, pensions, and retirement benefits. Unemployment insurance was available to 7.8% of the middle class and 12.9% of the lower class, while pensions and retirement benefits were even less available to 4.4% of the middle class and 2.8% of the lower class. Compared to these, health insurance was much more common covering 51.6% of the middle class and 73.4% of the lower class. These results, including the limited number of people receiving bonuses (30.2% of the middle class and 19.6% of the lower class), may be because most Bangkok respondents were self-employed and included fewer company employees. Shanghai's middle class was covered by a high proportion of health insurance (91.3%), pensions (94.0%), and bonuses (74.0%). However, only 23.7% were covered by unemployment insurance, and no one was contracted to receive any retirement benefits. Contrarily, in the lower class, access to all schemes was generally low (45.9% for health insurance, 39.8% for bonuses, 54.8% for unemployment insurance, and 62.7% for pensions), although the coverage for retirement benefits was not common (14.0%). In Tokyo, all schemes had a reasonable level of coverage rates. The coverage was even higher in the lower class for health insurance (72.9% for the middle class and 80.4% for the lower class[3]), unemployment insurance (66.7% and 78.0%, respectively), and pensions (69.6% and 70.7%, respectively). However, the coverage rate was not so high for bonuses, 54.5% for the middle class, and 33.9% for the lower class, and for retirement benefits, 44.5% for the middle class and 21.1% for the lower class, which is often considered to be a Japanese-style company package.

3.2.5 Life Satisfaction

This section focuses on possible factors contributing to respondents' subjective well-being under the above-described conditions. First, let us start by looking at the life satisfaction scores across the study cities.

Of the three cities, Tokyo's average score was noticeably the lowest. In a scale of up to 10 for highest possible self-reported life satisfaction, the middle class scored 5.84, and the lower class 4.84. Furthermore, when taking a closer look at the response ratios (Figure 3.1), 25% of the middle class and 40% of the lower class reported a score of 4 or less. Shanghai scored slightly higher than Tokyo. The middle class scored 6.95 and the lower class 6.12, with the difference between the middle and lower classes being smaller than in Tokyo. Examining the response ratios, approximately 70% of the middle class responded with a score of 7 or above, and less than 10% scored 4 or below. Even in the lower class, the number scoring 4 or below was just under 20%. Bangkok scored even higher than the other two cities. Notably, there was no difference between the scores of the classes, with the middle class scoring 7.31 and the lower class 7.32. Furthermore, very few of both groups scored below 4. Instead, approximately 70% scored 7 or above, and around 10% (and about 20% in the lower class) scored a perfect score of 10.

Further, the survey contained a question on what made them experience a sense of fulfilment, which is also related to well-being, with a list of options. The options were: working, studying, playing sports, resting, spending time with family, spending time with friends, and doing volunteer work.

In Tokyo, the middle and lower classes reported feeling fulfilled when resting (64.3% of both classes) and playing sports (54.5% of the middle class and 57.1% of the lower class). For the middle class, this is followed by working (48.3%), spending time with friends (47.9%), and further behind by spending time with family (42.2%). In the lower class, spending time with friends (48.1%) and working (39.7%) came next, followed by spending time with family (31.0%). Whereas in Shanghai, the middle class showed high response rates for all options, though the most frequent responses were spending time with family (80.3%) and working (77.3%). In addition, this group featured a high number of responses for doing volunteer work (38.0%). Conversely, for the Shanghai lower class, responses

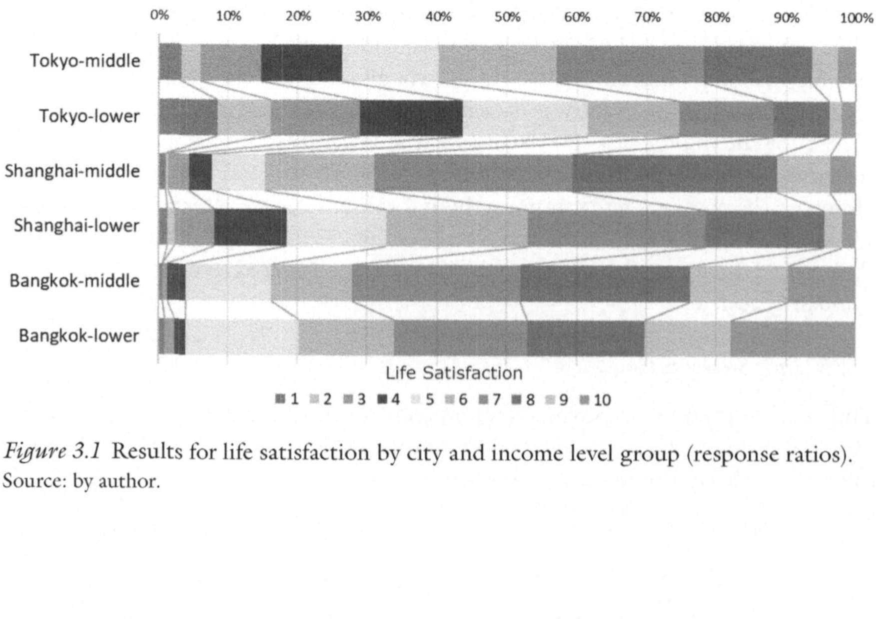

Figure 3.1 Results for life satisfaction by city and income level group (response ratios). Source: by author.

were concentrated on spending time with family (88.0%) as well as with friends (76%). Among the Bangkok middle class, most respondents chose to rest (78.2%) and spend time with family (69.4%), while the lower class concentrated only on spending time with family (77.8%).

From these results, it appears that in Tokyo, compared to the other two cities, people felt more fulfilled by personal activities, and family was not a source of fulfilment. Comparatively, in Shanghai and Bangkok, social connections with others were the source of a sense of fulfilment. The things that gave a sense of fulfilment were also slightly different between the middle and lower classes, indicating that the expansion of the subjective world and the nature of values may differ between them.

Other factors that may impact subjective well-being were also examined, such as whether people had problems in their urban lives and hoped to resolve these in the future. When examining whether there is a statistically significant correlation between the problems people have and their self-rated life satisfaction, the Tokyo data showed a correlation between life and work problems and satisfaction in the middle and lower classes (Table 3.6). The same was true for the Shanghai data. In Bangkok, for the middle class, life problems were related to satisfaction, but work problems were not; for the lower class, neither problems in life nor at work were related to satisfaction. Solving these problems also seemed to affect satisfaction in Tokyo and Shanghai but not Bangkok.

Contrastingly, having a life dream was found to have little correlation with life satisfaction. In Tokyo, more than 60% of both income groups answered that they have a dream. The common dreams mentioned by both income groups were related to work, such as 'to have an ideal job' and 'to start a business'. Notwithstanding, the responses were still heterogeneous, suggesting that residents of this city have individual and diverse dreams. Yet, life satisfaction scores did not change depending on whether people have a dream for their lives. The correlation between reasons for not having a life dream and life satisfaction was only significant in the case of satisfaction with current life and no possibility of fulfilling the dream, regardless of the classes they belong to. In Shanghai, 39.3% of the middle class and 63% of the lower class had life dreams. The most common dream mentioned in Shanghai was buying one's own house, reported by 26.3% of the middle class and 24.9% of the lower class. Contrarily, the most common reason given for not having a dream was no possibility of realising it (27.2%). Interestingly, those with dreams had lower average life satisfaction scores than those without. Only in the lower class was a correlation between having a dream and life satisfaction. Like in Shanghai, 43.3% of the middle class and 67.4% of the lower class in Bangkok also reported having a life dream, but no correlation exists between having a dream and life satisfaction. Only in the lower class did having a life dream increase life satisfaction scores. Starting a business (35.6%) was the most common dream for the middle class, while for the lower class, it was to buy their own house (23.5%). There was no correlation with life satisfaction, perhaps because the reason for not having a dream was being satisfied with one's current life.

Table 3.6 Correlation coefficients with life satisfaction

	Bangkok				*Shanghai*				*Tokyo*			
	Middle		*Lower*		*Middle*		*Lower*		*Middle*		*Lower*	
	ρ	*n*	ρ	*n*	ρ	*n*	ρ	*n*	ρ	*n*	ρ	*n*
Life problem	.319**	412	.099	357	.279**	300	.455**	400	.332**	631	.439**	630
Job problem	.092	408	.036	319	.351**	300	.365**	314	.305**	595	.378**	532
Problem solved	.015	320	–.114	279	–.406**	93	–.325**	380	–.238**	489	–.287**	494
Dream	–.026	412	–.029	356	.085	300	.143**	400	–.007	631	.045	630
No dream												
[satisfied]		127		58	.248**	300	.360**	148	.362**	200	.489**	209
[realised]		19		1	.041	300	.038	148	–.015	200	.051	209
[no hope]		38		22	–.152**	300	–.189*	148	–.321**	200	–.384**	209
[no idea]		48		29	–.012	300	–.064	148	–.084	200	–.124	209

Source: by author.
Note: **>.01, * >.05.

These results suggest that residents in each of the surveyed cities differ in their perceptions of what is an 'ideal' life and that their life satisfaction is somewhat influenced when: they have problems and are unable to live this 'ideal' life; these problems are not solved; they do not perceive that their hopes and dreams are attainable. Tokyo has exceptionally low life satisfaction compared to other cities, but this does not mean that more people have problems or that are difficult to solve. Rather more people have dreams compared to other cities. Upon closer look at the data, however, it came to light that Tokyo is a 'solitary' society with diverse problems and dreams, and that no simple comparisons with others can be made. Comparatively, Shanghai and Bangkok are spaces where people feel more comfortable living within the family and social relationships and where, for better or worse, the values of a desirable society may be understood comprehensively.

3.3 Summary: Tales of Three Cities, Two Classes

This chapter has provided an overview of the survey findings. More detailed analyses can be found in the subsequent individual chapters of this book, but this section will summarise the features of the survey results seen in this chapter as a story.

Bangkok middle class: *Life has been very satisfying. After living in this city for almost 27 years, we have a family with children (renting houses, though). Although working long hours and without unemployment insurance or pension, running our own business is going well. We prefer to work independently than to be used by other people in the first place. Now, we prefer to stay in this city for the future, but not quite sure.*

The surveyed middle class in Bangkok has many university graduates but is probably characterised by more independent self-employed than office workers. Their laid-back attitude towards money, and the fact that they neither save nor have much debt, may indicate their lifestyle based on living comfortably within their income, if at all.

Bangkok lower class: *Although categorised in the lower class, our life is not that bad. It is satisfying and fulfilling to live in our own house (though in informal settlement), surrounded by family and relatives, and that makes us willing to continue living in Bangkok in the future. Even though we couldn't go on to a school, there are jobs we can do on our own in the city, and thus we can manage to survive. Of course, there are problems as well as debt, but that is life.*

Interestingly, the lower classes in Bangkok do not feel so unhappy even though they are not so well-off in the measurable attributes of income, social security, education, and so on. Possibly, this is because the centre of their life consciousness is their family or perhaps because they accept their life as it is.

Shanghai middle class: *Born in Shanghai, and with family and relatives nearby, we don't have too much trouble. Furthermore, having gotten married and bought a house, we see no reason why we should not live in Shanghai in the future. After finishing postgraduate studies, with stable employment in the public sector, which we had hoped for, our income is not too bad. However, we have to save as there is almost no unemployment insurance or retirement benefits. Having said that, it is also pleasant to do volunteer work outside a regular job as it gives us a sense of fulfilment.*

Shanghai middle class live stable lives, surrounded by family and relatives, with secure jobs and places to live. Kinship is an important part of Chinese society, and precisely that has happened. Simultaneously, however, they are well educated and enjoy civic activities such as volunteer work, demonstrating an urban lifestyle similar to those in developed Western countries.

Shanghai lower class: *Unless you have moved here from somewhere else, leaving Shanghai may not be an option for you. Still, we have problems at work and in life, to be honest. As we are not well educated, our salaries are not high even if we work full-time in the public sector. We also have a fear of getting sick because we are not covered by social security like health insurance. Family and relatives don't live nearby, which means you have to manage on your own... But we have dreams to fulfil.*

People in the lower class of Shanghai live a solitary life, far from the image of Chinese society, where kinship is highly valued. Their financial situation is also not so good. However, the fact that people living in Shanghai who dream of their own 'Shanghai Dream' may be the source of this city's growth.

Tokyo middle class: *Despite living a middle-class lifestyle, we are unsatisfied with our lives. We are indeed full-time employees after university, working 9 am–6 pm, with two days off a week as well as decent salaries and benefits. But owning a house is not a must for us; buying a house would need massive debt. Many of us remain single, have no children, or have no relatives living nearby. Still, after having lived in Tokyo for 30 years now, we can't imagine living anywhere else. We will just keep living here.*

Apparently, for the Tokyo middle class, traditional family and kinship relationships seem to have dropped out of the centre of life. The environment for individual human development and social infrastructure is relatively well-developed, and people enjoy convenience and comfort. And yet, these factors do not necessarily translate into life satisfaction.

Tokyo lower class: *Life is very tough. We would prefer a stable job but have to work part-time and can't see a bright future ahead. Perhaps having not gone to college, we don't have much choice. We are trying our best to save money, but even so, we sometimes have trouble making ends meet daily. There are many problems concerning work and life, and having a family is also a big challenge. Even though Tokyo has been home to us for a long time, the thought of moving to another place sometimes crosses my mind.*

In the context of Tokyo, a city with a fairly well-developed environment for individual human development and social infrastructure, respondents from the lower class live in relatively precarious jobs and insecure economic situations, which significantly undermines their well-being. With many of them living alone, often making it difficult for them to rely on others in their families, they are precisely the ones facing the challenges of a risky society.

Note

1 The Bangkok lower class's 'own houses' often refer to either self-built housing in informal settlements or housing project sites supported by the government. Since the 1990s, under the 'slum' upgrading policy, provisional housing registration has been implemented regardless of former land conditions (including cases of illegal dwellings). The provisional housing registration has enabled the infrastructure development in the concerned area (e.g. electricity and water supply). It also functions as a personal asset and certificate, with the provisional housing registry providing the address required, for example, when applying for a new job (Endo 2014).

2 According to Table 2.1a (Chapter 2), self-employed workers occupy about 20% in Bangkok, but this higher proportion of them in the present survey may be due to the fact that survey targeted the main earner in the household and the process of conducting the survey.

3 Japanese health insurance is compulsory, but there are cases where people do not join due to changes in their employment situation or for other reasons. Or some may not even be aware that they are covered through their company. In this survey, the answers were given by the respondents themselves.

References

Endo, T. 2014. *Living with risks: precarity and Bangkok's urban poor.* Singapore: NUS Press in Association with Kyoto University Press.

Inoguchi, T., A. Tanaka, S. Sonoda, and T. Dadabaev, eds. 2006. *Human beliefs and values in striding Asia: East Asia in focus: country profiles, thematic analyses, and sourcebook based on the AsiaBarometer survey of 2004.* Tokyo: Akashi Shoten.

National Institute of Population and Social Security Research. 2019. *Eighth national survey on migration, 2016 Population and social security survey.* Tokyo: National Institute of Population and Social Security Research.

National Statistical Office Thailand. 2010. *Preliminary report the 2010 population and housing census.* Bangkok: National Statistical Office Thailand.

National Statistical Office Thailand. 2016. *Report on population characteristics: the 2015–2016 survey of population change.* Bangkok: National Statistical Office Thailand.

Shanghai Municipal Bureau of Statistics. 2015. *Shanghai statistical yearbook 2014.* Beijing: China Statistics Press.

Statistic Bureau of Japan. 2016. *The 2015 population census of Japan.* Tokyo: Statistic Bureau of Japan.

United Nations, Department of Economic and Social Affairs, Population Division. 2022. *World population prospects: the 2022 revision.* New York: United Nations.

4 Understanding Urban Well-Being from a Historical Perspective

Asuka Imaizumi

Introduction

As discussed in Chapter 3, the results of our questionnaire survey on urban well-being (hereafter, WB data) indicated that the life satisfaction of both middle- and lower-class Tokyo residents was the lowest among all the cities studied. National level surveys, such as AsiaBarometer Survey (Inoguchi et al. 2005, 310-325), also showed similar results. Based on these findings, some have attributed the lower satisfaction of Japanese respondents to their national characteristics (e.g., Dadabaev 2005). However, a population's level of subjective well-being can change over time. This chapter will describe the decline in life satisfaction of Tokyo residents during the first decade of the 2000s. Our WB data captures the period when urban dwellers' well-being was near its lowest point in nearly half a century.

This historical trend raises questions regarding why and how the level of life satisfaction fluctuates. Urban social structures can also undergo changes; subjective well-being in urban life in that time must be influenced by society's basic characteristics, diachronic changes, and regional variations. While economic downturns may impact, ignoring the possibility of social transformation or simply attributing everything to macroeconomic conditions may hinder our understanding of the various factors that have lowered satisfaction.

Analyses of social changes require long-term perspectives, and changes over time do not diminish the value of less recent surveys. It is possible to obtain insights into causal relationships and the broad effects of slow changes. In this sense, our WB survey data remain relevant despite having been collected almost a decade ago, before the COVID-19 pandemic.

This chapter focuses on understanding Tokyo residents' life satisfaction from a historical perspective, mainly through surveys conducted by the Tokyo Metropolitan Government (TMG, the administrative office of Tokyo Prefecture). With relatively strong provision of formal support channels, including government policies and stable company employment, Tokyo's experience can offer an opportunity to consider the effect and limitations of these in securing a population's livelihood and well-being. Section 4.1 provides background information, and Section 4.2 describes the long-term trends in life satisfaction as well as relevant changes in Tokyo residents' perceptions of economic conditions and their future anxieties. Section 4.3 offers our interpretation of the trend data. These analyses elucidate the structural

DOI: 10.4324/9781003328155-4

features and their changes over time, which affect the well-being of urban dwellers in Japan. This will provide helpful insights into their current and future well-being.

4.1 Historical Perspective for Interpreting Urban Dwellers' Well-Being

4.1.1 Japanese Economic History and Urban Society in Tokyo

The population of Tokyo, which was already the political centre of the Tokugawa shogunate established at the beginning of the 17th century, expanded further during Japan's modernisation and industrialisation following the Meiji Restoration in 1868. During the First World War, population growth in Tokyo Prefecture accelerated, and the trend in the subsequent period can be divided into roughly three stages. In the first, population grew rapidly from 4 million in the 1920s to 11 million in the 1960s, interrupted by a short but sharp drop during the Second World War. After reaching over 11% of the national population, in the second stage, the population of Tokyo levelled off temporarily and the share of the national population living in Tokyo declined for three decades from the 1970s to the 1990s. In the third, the population growth resumed with an inflow of people and economic concentration, under the shadow of the severe damage caused by the collapse of the bubble economy at the beginning of the 1990s. Tokyo is currently back at being home to approximately 11% of Japan's national population (Ito 1983; TMG, Tokyo Statistical Yearbook 2020).

Tokyo's periods of rapid population growth, briefly reviewed above, induced social transformations that included not only the shift from a rural to an urban society but also changes within the urban society. Among the three stages mentioned above, the first and third stages both saw significant population growth, but different mechanisms of population inflow as well as the social structures that were produced.

In the 1950s, during the middle of the first stage of population growth, R. P. Dore closely observed ordinary urban residents in a neighbourhood near the centre of Tokyo (Dore [1958] 2013). He revealed much about the foundations of urban society at that time as well as its possible direction of change. According to his observations, Tokyo's urban society in the 1950s was basically formed by small and settled communities that closely resembled village life, especially for housewives who were focused around the home and neighbourhood. This was despite 'the working of all those forces which tend to make city life anonymous and atomic', such as 'the rapidity of residential changes, the increase in secondary contacts, the tendency for the man's primary contacts to develop on occupational lines and to be independent of territorial propinquity' (267).

The number of big businesses and white-collar workers has increased since the 1920s, the beginning of the first rapid population growth, leading to the formation of a new middle class in urban society. However, from the pre-war period to the rapid-growth era, the core of urban society comprised the self-employed, owners of small shops and workshops, as well as their families and employees (Bestor 1989; Tamano 1993, 2005; Tanimoto 2002, 2005). The share of the self-employed and family workers in Tokyo was stable (around 20%) in the post-war period until the 1980s, but then declined. Small- and medium-sized enterprises (SMEs), here defined as those with 29 or fewer workers, offered approximately 30% of employment until the 1990s. Thus, the self-employed, family, and SME workers represented half of Tokyo's workers until the 1980s (MIC, 1957–2018). The core members of neighbourhood associations (e.g., *chōkai*, *chōnaikai*) were such small business owners and shopkeepers in each region, and they engaged at the grassroots level of local administrations, including organising cultural events such as festivals (Dore [1958] 2013, 269–287; Bestor 1989; Tamano 1993, 2005).[1]

However, the same statistics also indicate that around 80% of Tokyo workers were categorised as employees, with the proportion having further expanded since the 1990s (MIC, 1957–2018). The importance of 'occupational' affiliation (Dore [1958] 2013, 267) became fundamental to post-war Japanese society. The Japanese economy, politics, and other social settings comprised *kigyō shakai*, the 'company-oriented society' or 'corporate society', integrating people's lives and well-being with corporate growth in the post-war period (Watanabe 1990, 2004). This integration was based on the Japanese employment system, which was usually characterised by periodic recruiting of new graduates, lifetime employment, seniority-based wage system, and enterprise unions. Although it was known for putting pressure on people to prioritize their employment commitments, this integration secured people's welfare and livelihoods through corporate employment rather than the national redistribution system. Of course, not all enterprises have adopted this typical Japanese employment system, especially smaller firms. However, continuous economic growth, subsidies for the self-employed and SMEs, and relatively equal access to education – the main channel for obtaining stable employment – convinced people that they could also benefit from economic growth based on companies, whether currently for themselves or for their children (Watanabe 1990, 2004; Goto 2001; Miyamoto 2008; Takeda 2012; Honda 2014).

This scheme was also characterised by *familialism*, a concept in which primary importance is attached to interdependence within families (Esping-Andersen 1999, 45–67, 90–92; 2000, 5–8; 2001, ix–xii; Miyamoto 2008, 166). Dore asked Tokyo residents in the 1950s about 'who bears the responsibility for looking after the sick and unemployed', and received the answers of 'family' and 'state' in almost equal numbers, that is, 37 and 38 out of 102 respondents, respectively (Dore [1958] 2013, 75).[2] Although the preference for support from the 'state' was equally noticeable, the results represented the 'general preference for personal contacts over impersonalized procedures', to which Dore added a comment referring to this as 'the much-discussed "particularism" of Japanese society' (76). Tokyo residents, as with the general Japanese population, tended to rely on mutual aid within the family. However, the family's forms are not immutable. Enjoying increasing income during Japan's economic growth, the nuclear family model of a male breadwinner with stable employment and his housewife as well as family relying on his wages became the foundation of the company-oriented society (Kimoto 2004; Ochiai 2004; Honda 2014). Osawa (2011, 23–24) called this the 'male breadwinner model' of a 'livelihood security system'. Some criticised the system as being contrary to the values of gender equality and pluralism. Nevertheless, this model, as well as the company-oriented society, was not only sustained after the period of rapid growth ended but was actually strengthened as Japan experienced the economic slowdowns from the mid-1970s to the 1980s (Watanabe 1990, 2004; Goto 2001; Kimoto 2004, Osawa 2011; Tanaka 2017, 201–206).

The urban society demonstrated complex reactions to these socioeconomic changes. Tokyo recruited juvenile workers from Japan's rural regions during the rapid economic growth from the mid-1950s to the 1960s. In many cases, these juveniles secured live-in jobs in small shops and workshops before forming nuclear families in urban society (Kase 1997, 37–45, 169–175). The self-employed individuals and proprietors of SMEs were the main subjects of administration in local communities, but their socioeconomic standing gradually receded (Tamano 2005, 259–278). Aside from neighbourhood associations, the increasing number of housewives generated another form of solidarity by organising social movements, for example calling for educational facilities, mutually dependent on the reformist regional governments in the 1970s (Tamano 2005, 115–200). Some workers who moved to Tokyo alone found an alternative support community in the growing religious groups, such as Sōka Gakkai (Bestor 1989, 30; Kase 1997, 198–218; Tamano 2005, 203–255). Such phenomena reflected the formation of networks other than the traditional regional ties and some people certainly tried to utilise these. Some of these networks also gained political importance. However, these channels were gradually diluted in urban society as the 'new middle class' grew and a new generation took over (Tamano 2005, 119–278). The increasing population accelerated the development of suburban residential areas outside central Tokyo, leading to the formation of a new type of urban society with a 'new middle class', which was partly reflected in the above-mentioned pause in the population growth during the second stage (Tamano 2009).

Following the collapse of the bubble economy at the beginning of the 1990s, the Japanese economy struggled with the 'lost decades'. The company-oriented society faced explicit difficulties during this long-lasting and severe economic downturn. Companies were unable to maintain their previous costly employment practices. Exacerbating the situation was that there were fewer alternative channels for security and integration in individuals' lives. Watanabe (2004, 28–30) pointed out that this systemic crisis led to a rapid increase in unemployment, suicides, crimes, and homelessness in the late 1990s. Globalisation and neoliberalism further fuelled criticism, forcing people to free themselves from the previous socioeconomic structure. However, there were no clear alternatives (Miyamoto 2008; Honda 2014; Tanaka 2017, 207–219; 2020, 172–188).

Tokyo's population growth in the third stage began along with such socioeconomic difficulties. The deregulation of land use triggered by the economic downturn facilitated this trend (Minagawa 2020, 123–198). Under this dismantlement of the company-oriented society, an increasing number of people were unable to obtain decent stable employment, as seen in the decrease in regular employment mentioned in Chapter 2. Some people were sinking even below the 'labour class', described by Hashimoto (2020) as an 'underclass' lacking various reserves or social security generally designed for those in regular employment.

Their livelihood and life satisfaction were strongly affected. The damage from the lack of stable employment can also be seen in demographic behaviours, such as the higher unmarried ratio (Hashimoto 2020, 99, 175).

Among Tokyo residents, the ratio of single-person households rose by approximately 13 percentage points, to 47.3%, between 1985 and 2015. The percentage of households with one or two members reached 71.5% in 2015. The unmarried ratio[3] among people aged 25–39 years rose from 35.1% in 1985 to a peak of 51.2% in 2005 and then declined slightly to 42.3% in 2015.[4] This decreased the gender gap in the unmarried ratio mainly by increasing the non-marriage rate for women (TMG, Tokyo Statistical Yearbook 1986, 1990, 1995, 2000, 2005, 2010, 2015). Of course, this trend included not only the formation of the expanded 'underclass' but also family pluralism. Nonetheless, the long-term trend was for men and women to choose or be forced to choose small families.

Dore ([1958] 2013) wrote that the urban society tended to be 'anonymous and atomic' (267). However, the structure of urban societies and experiences of city life have changed over time. Tokyo was a society of small business owners and shopkeepers, followed by nuclear families based on male breadwinners with stable employment. This model has gradually been eroded, especially after the bubble economy, by social transformations in both employment and families. The following sections explore the interrelation between structural changes and Tokyo's urban well-being, especially considering the population growth under the socioeconomic difficulties of the 2000s.

4.1.2 Long-Term Observation of Urban Life

Our examination should begin with long-term data on the urban lives of the Tokyo residents. Since 1970, the Tokyo Metropolitan Government has conducted an annual 'Survey of Public Opinion on Urban Life', which was renamed 'Survey of Public Opinion on Citizens' Lives' in 1998 after being merged with another survey on citizens' demands (1970–2022, hereafter, SCL).[5] The SCL is best suited for our research purpose since its annual surveys focus on Tokyo (prefecture-wide) residents and their perceptions of urban life. Some of its perennial questions have provided invaluable insight into changes over the decades. For example, since 1977, the SCL has asked respondents to answer the question 'Are you satisfied with your current life?' with one of the five response options: 'very satisfied', 'moderately satisfied', 'rather dissatisfied', 'very dissatisfied', or 'no idea', without any rewording.[6] A similar question regarding life satisfaction has been included in the governmental 'Survey of Public Opinion on People's Lives' since 1964 (Cabinet Office 1964–2021, hereafter, SPL). We can derive detailed implications for subjective well-being by combining these data sources.

The following sections examine historical fluctuations in self-reported life satisfaction using SCL data. Combining the SCL's historical data with our WB survey's one-time cross-sectional data, we can analyse urban well-being within a wider context. Data from different surveys may not be directly comparable.[7] Furthermore, we did not use the SCL's micro row-level data but only the aggregated information reported by the TMG. Thus, the information we derived relied on whether the relevant data were reported. Bearing these limitations in mind, we could use the data to form a general interpretation of trends.

4.2 Historical Changes in Life Satisfaction

4.2.1 Long-Term Trends in Life Satisfaction

Our WB data showed that Tokyo respondents, especially those in the lower-income group, were less satisfied than respondents in the two other studied cities. However, our data represented a snapshot of a single point in time. The SCL longitudinal data showed that Tokyo residents' self-reported life satisfaction fluctuated over time. Figure 4.1 shows the share of respondents who answered that they were 'satisfied' (the sum of 'very' and 'moderately') versus 'dissatisfied' (the sum of 'rather' and 'very') with their lives in the SCL surveys from 1977 to 2021.[8] Added to this plot was also the one-time snapshot of the three cities from our WB survey, with self-reported life satisfaction (with responses 1–5 classified as 'dissatisfied' and 6–10 as 'satisfied').[9]

According to Figure 4.1, our survey data on WB appeared reasonable enough in the historical trend of life satisfaction among Tokyo residents. The SCL 2013 reported that 53.8% of the respondents were satisfied and 41.3% were dissatisfied, whereas our data reported that 49.2% were satisfied and 50.8% were dissatisfied.

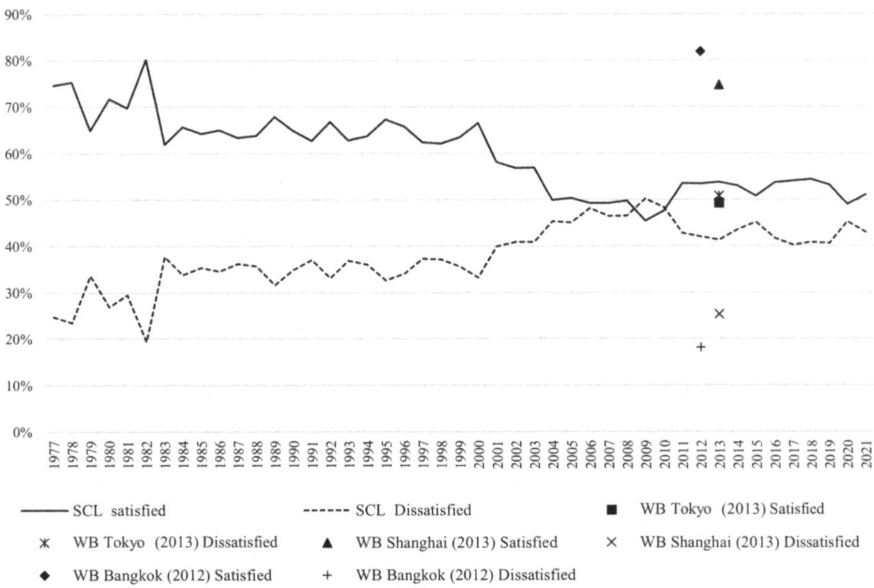

Figure 4.1 Life satisfaction in the SCL and WB data.

Source: Made by author based on SCL and WB data.

Note: The percentages indicate the share of respondents who reported being 'satisfied' or 'dissatisfied' with their lives. Totals do not sum to 100% as there are other possible responses: 'no idea' and 'no response'. In 2016, the minimum age for inclusion in the SCL survey was lowered from 20 to 18 years old. The SCL survey changed the data collection method and increased the number of targets for 2020 and 2021. The results of the WB survey for Shanghai, which was implemented in 2012 and 2014, are indicated in 2013.

While we only surveyed people those who earned individual annual incomes under eight million yen, the SCL had no income-level restrictions. Therefore, a lower life satisfaction score was expected from our sample. We considered the effect of income later on.

The share of respondents who reported being 'satisfied' tended to be low in Tokyo. However, the level varied significantly over time. From the mid-1980s to 2000, a fairly consistent 60%–70% of individuals reported being 'satisfied'. The 21st century ushered in a decline in satisfaction and rise in dissatisfaction, with the lowest satisfaction rate occurring in 2009. Although the satisfaction levels rose again after 2009, they did not return to their previous highs.[10] Figure 4.1 reminds us that the Tokyo residents' satisfaction shifted noticeably at the turn of the century.

To analyse the decline in life satisfaction, we must carefully examine the differences across age, gender, and income levels. The WB data indicated that people in the youngest and oldest age ranges were more satisfied than the middle generations in Tokyo. In addition, the proportion of satisfied women was higher than that of men in Tokyo, whereas the other two cities showed no explicit tendencies. Age and gender gaps can be important clues for interpreting trends in life satisfaction.

In Figures 4.2a and 4.2b, life satisfaction is shown for males and females according to age ranges based on the SCL data. Despite the higher levels of satisfaction among older people and women, life satisfaction for all age ranges and both sexes declined in the 2000s, just like they did in Figure 4.1. The variance among gender and age range groups narrowed in the long term. Although the gaps were also visible in the WB data in 2013, the attributional differences were in the long-term decline according to the SCL data.

Moreover, the WB data also reflected an obvious gap between the middle- and lower-class groups based on individual income. The SCL only offered life satisfaction based on household income level, so this chapter used household income levels: 'HHLower' indicated respondents whose household income was less than three million yen; 'HHMiddle' indicated those whose household income was from three million up to nine million yen; and 'HHUpper' indicated those whose household income was nine million yen or more.[11] (The upper limit of the 'HHMiddle' income was nine million yen instead of eight million yen used in the WB data, because the income groupings that the SCL used could not be divided at eight million yen.) In addition, for the pre-1990 data, 'HHLower' indicated those whose household income was under two million yen; 'HHMiddle' indicated those whose household income was from two million up to five million yen; and 'HHUpper' indicated those whose household income was five million yen or more.[12] Around 10%–30% of respondents, those who answered the question about household income level with 'no idea' or 'no response', are excluded from this calculation.

Figure 4.3a shows the trend in the life satisfaction for the three household income groups. Further, it shows the aggregation and WB data. All the income groups declined during the first decade of the 21st century. In addition, the gaps between 'HHLower', 'HHMiddle', and 'HHUpper' were obvious and widened. The ratios for the 'HHUpper' were relatively stable, whereas those for the 'HHLower' declined by more than 20 percentage points. Focusing on the latter, Figure 4.3b impresses on us that in the 2000s, the shares of those who reported being 'satisfied' and 'dissatisfied' with their lives were clearly reversed for this household income group.

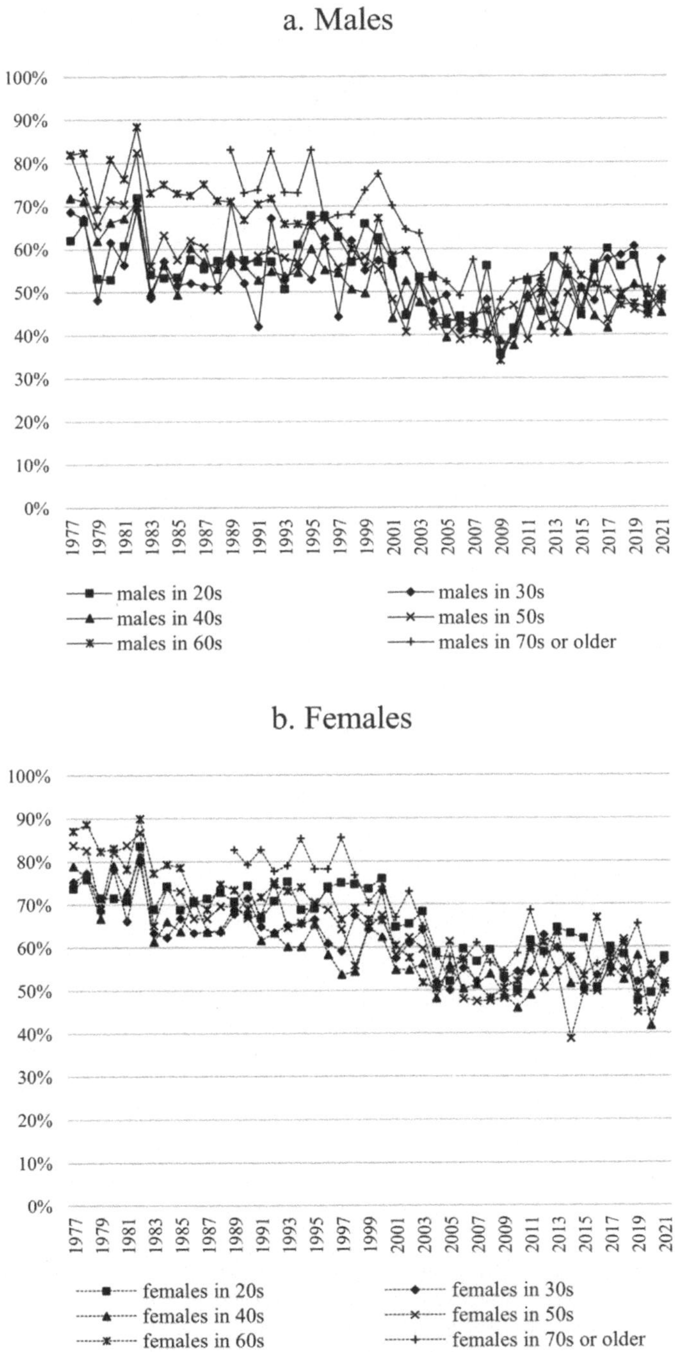

Figure 4.2 Trends in life satisfaction by age and gender: (a) males and (b) females.

Source: Made by author based on SCL data.

Note: The percentages indicate the share of respondents who reported being 'satisfied' with their lives. Prior to 1988, the data for males and females 'in 60s' included all respondents over 60 years old. The SCL survey changed the data collection method and increased the number of targets for 2020 and 2021.

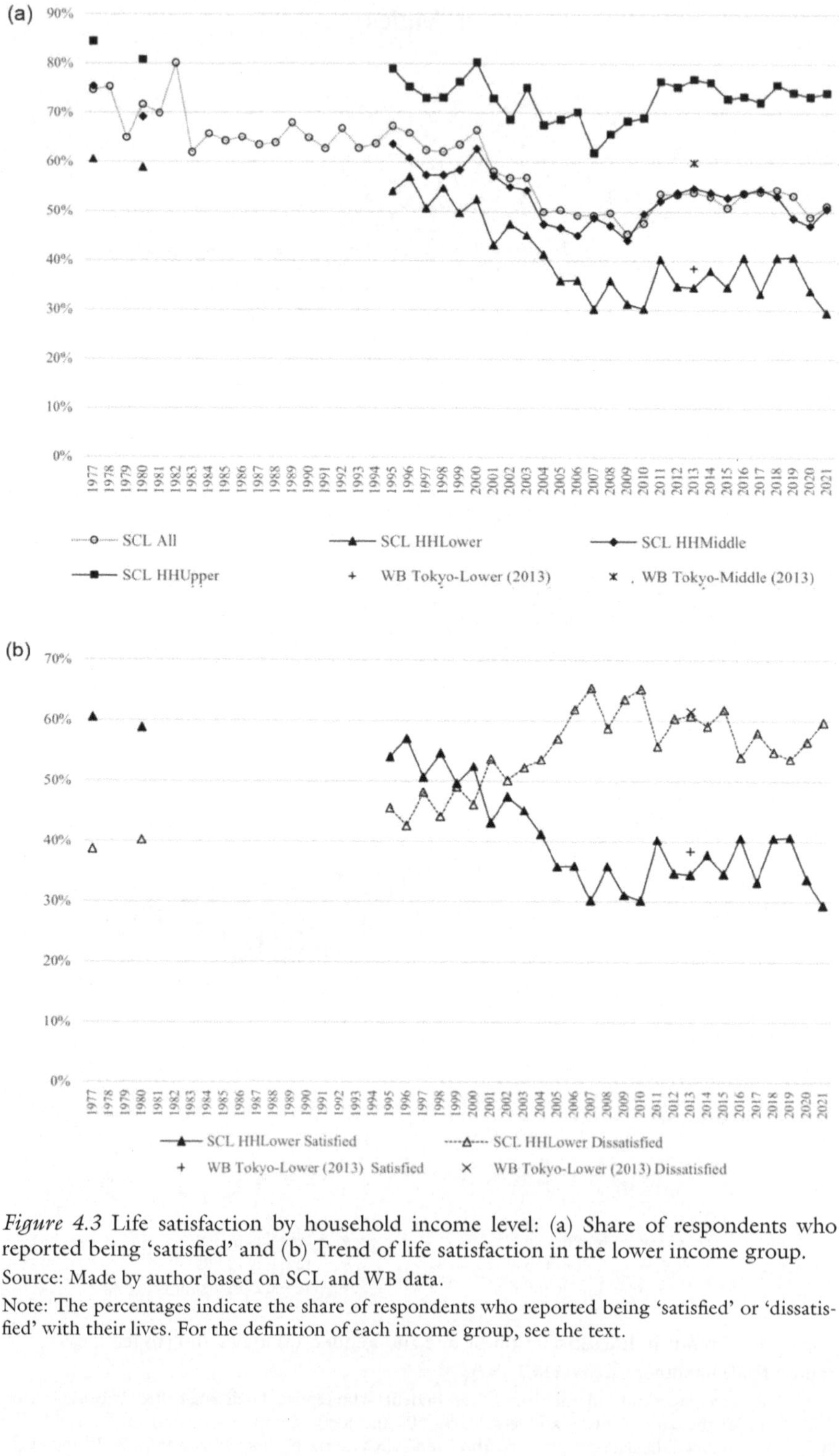

Figure 4.3 Life satisfaction by household income level: (a) Share of respondents who reported being 'satisfied' and (b) Trend of life satisfaction in the lower income group.

Source: Made by author based on SCL and WB data.

Note: The percentages indicate the share of respondents who reported being 'satisfied' or 'dissatisfied' with their lives. For the definition of each income group, see the text.

In summary, there was a general decline in self-reported life satisfaction in the first decade of the 21st century. In the 1990s, more Tokyo residents of both sexes, all generations, and all income groups reported being 'satisfied' with their lives. The situation began to change, as the turn of the century approached. Although the declining trend was common across all categories, the age and gender gaps shrank, whereas the gaps across household income groups widened. Our 2013 WB data depicted the exact point in time when the overall proportion of satisfaction dropped to nearly its lowest level, reshaping the gaps.

4.2.2 *Deteriorating Economic Conditions and Increasing Future Anxiety*

The previous section discussed the decline in life satisfaction in the first decade of the 21st century. The trend differed according to the categories of urban residents, and the changes might be related to structural factors. The mechanism underlying this decline is the next question to be addressed.

The downturn of the Japanese economy in the 1990s, discussed in Section 4.1.1, undoubtedly affected the life satisfaction of Tokyo residents. The SCL asked respondents whether they thought their households' economic circumstances[13] were worse (harder), better (easier), or had not changed compared with the previous year. The results indicated that most respondents felt that their circumstances generally worsened in the 2000s and stabilised at a worsened level through the 2010s, which seemed consistent with the reported fluctuations in life satisfaction.

The respondents' self-reported scores for their sense of economic sufficiency also fluctuated. The SCL asked respondents about their perceptions of the households' economic circumstances, offering five options: 'my present economic circumstances are sufficiently well-off', 'my present economic circumstances are not bad', 'my present economic circumstances are not sufficient', 'I cannot survive with present economic circumstances' and 'no idea'. As shown in Figure 4.4, the share of people who chose 'my present economic circumstances are not enough' or 'I cannot survive with present economic circumstances' – namely, those who denied having a surplus – peaked at over 60% in 1974 when the oil shock caused inflation, declined to 37% in 1992, then reversed to peak again at 57% in 2009. If the trend was broken down by household income group, the share of those who denied having a surplus rose overall, except for the 'HHUpper' group. The variance among the income levels widened; starting from smaller gaps in the 1990s, the income level of the 'HHUpper' showed almost no change in the 2000s, whereas the 'HHLower' showed an increase of around 20 percentage points. The deflation in the first decade of the 21st century (MIC 2022) seemed to have contributed to the maintained economic circumstances of middle- and upper-income residents but did not have the same benefit for lower-income groups; rather, it might have damaged their lives by reducing employment and producing insufficient income.

The concrete reasons for life dissatisfaction might offer further clues to understanding how economic conditions lowered the life satisfaction of Tokyo residents. The SCL assessed the reasons for dissatisfaction (multiple responses

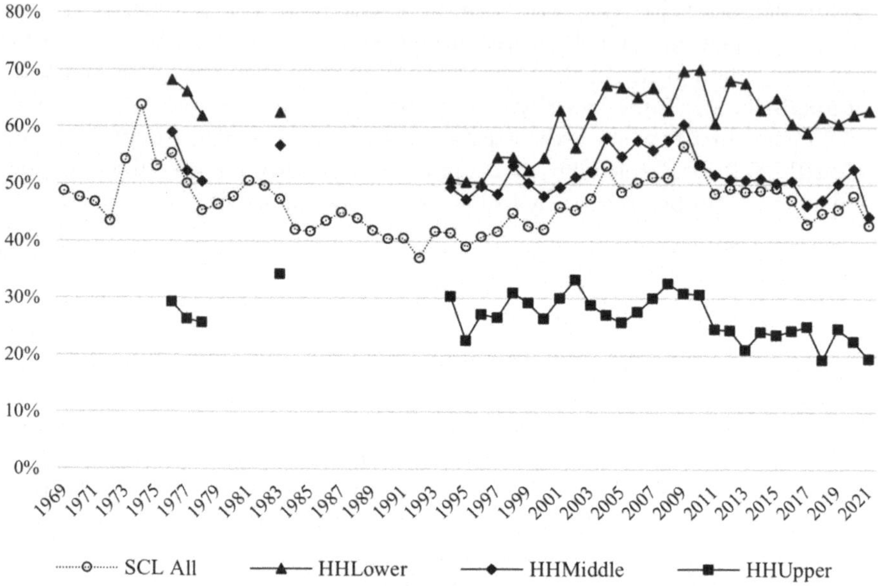

Figure 4.4 The proportion of 'no surplus for life'.

Source: Made by author based on SCL data.

Note: The percentages indicate the share of respondents who report not having surplus income. For the definition of each income group, see the text.

possible) regarding those who answered 'rather' or 'very' dissatisfied with their lives. The results are presented in Table 4.1. Note that this result was not screened by income level. The most common response (between 52% and 67%) was 'because of the insufficient amount of saving', with a response rate almost twice as large as the second reason, from 1998 to 2018.

Even though the majority expressed concern about their lack of savings, fewer individuals cited insufficiencies in basic needs (e.g., housing, food, and clothing) in comparison to insufficient time or money for enriching their lives (e.g., 'insufficient time for hobbies and education'). The answer of 'insufficient housing'[14] decreased in frequency after 2003. Thus, we can interpret the rising anxiety about savings as the enhanced anxiety that the respondents anticipated concerning future demands rather than current needs.

Table 4.1 also shows that the answers of 'having worries and anxieties' and 'not healthy' increased in frequency. The respondents' intensifying anxiety about health and illness was another clue. The SCL assessed in another question, 'What makes you anxious considering your future life?' (also with multiple responses possible). Since the survey started continuously asking this question in 2005, among the choices for this question, 'own health or illness' garnered the most responses. A similar question was also asked in 1998: 'What makes you feel anxious considering the present as well as future?' with multiple responses possible, including 'my own health'. If comparing these, the frequency of the

Table 4.1 Reasons for dissatisfaction

	1998	*2003*	*2008*	*2013*	*2018*
Insufficient saving	52.2%	62.1%	63.0%	66.9%	64.0%
Insufficient time for hobbies and education	26.3%	30.2%	28.7%	25.8%	27.8%
Cannot be involved in sports or leisure activities at will	15.9%	20.9%	19.7%	17.5%	18.9%
Cannot buy wants such as furniture and cars	18.6%	23.8%	22.4%	24.5%	21.6%
Insufficient housing	24.4%	28.2%	22.6%	19.5%	16.8%
Insufficient diet	11.8%	10.1%	12.8%	10.6%	9.9%
Insufficient clothing life	8.6%	10.4%	9.5%	7.3%	7.4%
Having worries and anxieties	15.3%	23.9%	25.6%	26.1%	26.1%
Not healthy	15.5%	22.7%	22.0%	22.0%	26.6%
Work or study going wrong	18.6%	18.4%	17.5%	16.9%	13.9%
Family life going wrong	2.5%	6.9%	4.7%	5.1%	7.3%
Human relation with friends and acquaintances going wrong	2.9%	2.6%	2.3%	2.3%	1.7%
Lack of fulfilment of social contribution	10.2%	10.8%	8.6%	9.3%	7.7%
Others	4.3%	5.1%	4.4%	6.4%	6.6%
No idea	3.0%	0.5%	2.2%	2.4%	0.9%

Source: Made by author based on SCL data.
Note: The percentages indicate the share of those who chose that item as a cause of their dissatisfaction (multiple answer). The author reorganised the item order.

answer concerning own health rose from 40% in 1998 to 64% in 2018. We could logically expect older people to be more anxious about their health than younger people. However, we found the same pattern of increase from younger respondents (from 17% to 44% for respondents in their 20s).

These facts suggest that general economic fluctuations enhanced anxiety and suppressed life satisfaction among Tokyo residents. With the shrinking household size (Section 4.1.1), more people of both sexes found it necessary to accept responsibility for their own lives and future risks, and deal with them on their own. Presumably because of this, they became more concerned about their savings as well as own health. Tokyo residents entered a new century, an era of enhanced self-help anxiety.

4.2.3 Uneven and Condensed Impact of Socioeconomic Transformation

Japan's economic challenges stoked future anxiety and suppressed overall life satisfaction. However, the economic fluctuations had complicated and uneven impacts on Tokyo residents based on the structural characteristics of Japanese society. There were three main impacts according to the SCL data: life satisfaction declined among older people, younger people had enhanced future anxieties, and women's overall life satisfaction fell.

Until the 1990s, older generations (people aged 60 years and over) reported high life satisfaction (Figure 4.2. See also Table 4.2 below). In the 2000s, life satisfaction declined to a level similar to that of the other generations. The number of older respondents was consistently large and increasing, reflecting Japan's ageing society and generational response bias. Therefore, a decline in their life satisfaction substantially affected the overall weighted average of life satisfaction. Yamada (2012) pointed out the problems of Japanese social security for elderly people in the 2000s, referring the increasing fragility of Japan's social security system, changing family configurations, and deteriorated working conditions before retirement. It is also generally believed that the decrease of family size has led to a rise in solitude of elderly people (Tachibanaki 2011, 14–69). The decline of life satisfaction might have reflected these factors.

In addition, significant cognitive changes were observed among the younger generation, as elucidated by a cohort analysis. Table 4.2 shows the life satisfaction ratios for 1979, 1989, 1999, 2009, and 2019 from the SCL data.[15] Every cohort showed a proportional decline in satisfaction ratios between 1999 and 2009. The gap was the largest for respondents born between 1970 and 1979, for the period between 1999 and 2009. For example, among the men in this cohort, approximately 30 percentage points fewer answered that they were satisfied with their lives in 2009 than did in the 1999 survey.

Returning to the SCL's question about anxiety, younger respondents, especially those born in the 1970s, reported increased anxiety for the future in the 2000s. As described in Table 4.3, the number of people born in the 1970s[16] who cited 'future income' as a source of their anxiety rose between 1998 and 2008. Of course, it was natural for people in their 30s to require more capital than those in their 20s. However, when compared with the following decade, the rising anxiety among people in their 30s in 2008 (i.e., the cohort born in 1969–1978 in Table 4.3) seemed unique. There was a similar effect for respondents answering 'nothing' to the question asking what they had future anxiety about. Between 1998 and 2008, more people reported experiencing anxiety regarding the future. Again, the rise was largest for men and women in the cohort born in 1969–1978 (around 20 and 10 percentage points, respectively) in 2008.

The cohort born in the 1970s is known as the 'Ice Age' or 'Lost' generation. It includes children of baby boomers,[17] who encountered the 'Ice Age' of job hunting from the late 1990s to the mid-2000s[18] as they entered their 20s and faced difficulties in finding decent jobs. Hashimoto (2020, 59–64) defined the 'Ice Age generation' as people born between 1973 and 1986. The documentary that coined the phrase 'Lost Generation' defined it as those born between 1972 and 1982 (Asahi Shimbun 'Lost Generation' Press Team 2007, 15–35). Although the definitions vary, they commonly indicate that the socioeconomic crises of the 1990s have coloured their job-hunting and marriage experiences. They faced an inevitable gap between expectations, of both their own and/or of their parents, and reality, whereas the following generations could anticipate the changes.[19]

Table 4.2 Cohort difference of life satisfaction

		1979	*1989*	*1999*	*2009*	*2019*	*Gap points*			
							1989–1979	*1999–1989*	*2009–1999*	*2019–2009*
Males	All	57.7%	64.6%	59.6%	39.3%	51.9%	6.9%	–5.0%	–20.3%	12.6%
	Born in 1990–1999					58.2%				
	Born in 1980–1989				35.8%	60.5%				24.7%
	Born in 1970–1979			65.8%	35.6%	51.7%			–30.2%	16.1%
	Born in 1960–1969		57.4%	55.0%	38.7%	45.8%		–2.4%	–16.3%	7.1%
	Born in 1950–1959	53.1%	56.4%	49.7%	45.3%	47.2%	3.3%	–6.7%	–4.4%	1.9%
	Born in 1940–1949	48.1%	58.7%	58.2%	34.0%	51.3%	10.6%	–0.5%	–24.2%	17.3%
	Born in 1930–1939	61.8%	71.0%	55.8%	48.0%		9.2%	–15.2%	–7.8%	
	Born in 1920–1929	65.4%	71.0%	73.6%			5.6%	2.6%		
	Born in –1919	69.3%	83.1%				13.8%			
Females	All	71.0%	70.8%	67.2%	51.0%	54.1%	–0.2%	–3.6%	–16.2%	3.1%
	Born in 1990–1999					47.4%				
	Born in 1980–1989				53.0%	51.9%				–1.1%
	Born in 1970–1979			73.6%	52.3%	58.0%			–21.3%	5.7%
	Born in 1960–1969		70.6%	64.3%	48.8%	44.9%		–6.3%	–15.5%	–3.9%
	Born in 1950–1959	71.5%	67.8%	64.7%	48.1%	49.2%	–3.7%	–3.1%	–16.6%	1.1%
	Born in 1940–1949	68.6%	69.3%	64.6%	50.5%	65.5%	0.7%	–4.7%	–14.1%	15.0%
	Born in 1930–1939	66.7%	69.5%	66.5%	54.5%		2.8%	–3.0%	–12.0%	
	Born in 1920–1929	69.0%	73.4%	70.4%			4.4%	–3.0%		
	Born in –1919	82.3%	82.7%				0.4%			

Source: Made by author based on SCL data.
Note: The percentages indicate the share of respondents who reported being 'satisfied' with their lives. Grey cells indicate a cohort whose year range has no upper age bound. For 2019, 'All' excludes those aged 18–19 years old.

Table 4.3 Cohort difference of future anxiety: future income

		1998	*2008*	*2018*	*Gap points*	
					2008–1998	*2018–2008*
Males	All	39.8%	48.1%	44.0%	8.3%	–4.1%
	Born in 1989–1998			46.5%		
	Born in 1979–1988		54.4%	54.9%		0.5%
	Born in 1969–1978	36.6%	58.7%	44.9%	22.1%	–13.8%
	Born in 1959–1968	51.3%	52.1%	46.2%	0.8%	–5.9%
	Born in 1949–1958	42.6%	49.7%	46.9%	7.1%	–2.8%
	Born in 1939–1948	48.5%	43.2%	31.4%	–5.3%	–11.8%
	Born in 1929–1938	34.5%	28.3%		–6.2%	
	Born in –1928	19.0%				
Females	All	36.0%	45.3%	43.2%	9.3%	–2.1%
	Born in 1989–1998			42.9%		
	Born in 1979–1988		54.5%	56.3%		1.8%
	Born in 1969–1978	39.4%	53.1%	49.7%	13.7%	–3.4%
	Born in 1959–1968	46.2%	53.3%	50.7%	7.1%	–2.6%
	Born in 1949–1958	50.7%	56.9%	52.9%	6.2%	–4.0%
	Born in 1939–1948	42.0%	38.6%	20.3%	–3.4%	–18.3%
	Born in 1929–1938	21.3%	19.8%		–1.5%	
	Born in –1928	13.5%				

Source: Made by author based on SCL data.
Note: The percentages indicate the share of respondents who cited 'future income' as a source of their future anxiety (multiple answers). Grey cells indicate a cohort whose year range has no upper age bound. For 2018, 'All' excludes those aged 18–19 years old.

Besides these changes, the attitudes of female residents showed a unique transformation. Table 4.2 also describes the cohort differences in life satisfaction among women. As previously mentioned, the level of life satisfaction for women in Tokyo has generally been higher than that for men. In addition, the female life satisfaction tended to show similar levels among age groups. However, the life satisfaction level of women fell significantly in the 21st century. The sex-based gap in life satisfaction shrank over time, especially in the 2010s. One reason for this seems to be the shifting gender roles and smaller families, as discussed in Section 4.1.1. Of course, gender roles did not disappear. Many scholars have documented that the increase in female workers without appropriate reorganization of gender roles has concentrated the burden on women (Esping-Andersen 1999, 45–72; 2009; Osawa and Namba 2011). As Esping-Andersen (1999, 47–72; 2000, 5–8; 2001, xi) pointed out, familialism itself could damage family formation. These factors might have contributed to the decline in women's life satisfaction.

Just to check, we also performed the same analysis of life satisfaction with the periodic SCL data from two years earlier each time (i.e., 1977, 1987, 1997, 2007, and 2017) to avoid the influence of the global economic downturn in 2008. Similarly, we examined the impact of taking the SCL of a year later (i.e., 1980,

1990, 2000, 2010, and 2020). In both cases, the basic patterns and descriptions were similar to the cohort analyses discussed above, indicating that the changes explained were not an accident of data bias but structural.[20]

The widened gaps in life satisfaction between household income levels discussed in the previous section should be interpreted by considering the influence of all three of these points. For the overall decline in life satisfaction, the gaps observed across age groups and between genders (basically unchangeable attributes) shrank, whereas the gap by household income widened. In other words, presumably because of the further atomization among Tokyo residents, economic conditions came to dominate over the base demographic factors in determining respondents' urban well-being. In addition, the compressed transformations severely affected the generation born in the 1970s, significantly lowering their well-being and trapping them as the 'Lost' generation.

4.3 Well-Being in the Transforming Urban Society

4.3.1 Urban Well-Being in the National Scope

The historical analyses in the previous sections discussed the intensified anxieties behind Tokyo residents' increasing dissatisfaction. Although its enhancement has been correlated with economic conditions, we should interpret the impact based on changing socioeconomic structures, such as family configurations, employment, and social security. For example, the problems of the 'Lost Generation' were not caused solely by economic fluctuations but also due to structural reasons. Under the characteristic employment practices described in Section 4.1.1, the overall economic conditions at the time of graduation could define employees' whole lives. The impact of the economic downturn was exacerbated by employment practices, and while the impact was felt by all, much of the pain was concentrated onto a single generation entering the workforce then (Machimura 2009; Tanaka 2017, 207–210; Hashimoto 2020).

These changes over time, however, are not limited to urban societies but have affected all of Japan. As Yasui, Debnar, and Tarohmaru (2013) emphasised, Tokyo's characteristics should be viewed through comparisons with other areas in Japan. Tanaka, Higashi, and Yugami (2020) evaluated the economic environment in the 23 wards within Tokyo as 'the sole winner' (14) from the 1990s onward. Their evaluation was based on its higher share of high-income employees (seven million yen or more), a lower share of low-income employees (three million yen or fewer) compared with other cities, towns, and villages and its income average with no significant decline even after the collapse of the bubble economy. Tokyo's high effective opening-to-application ratio, although also with high possibility of mismatch, suggests that the city has relatively more openings than qualified applicants; reflecting this, Tokyo's net population inflow has been positive in the 21st century (Tanaka, Higashi, and Yugami

2020), which can be seen in Figure 2.1 in Chapter 2 and is also mentioned in Section 4.1.1. Focusing on the situation in the 2000s, the period relevant to the discussions in the previous section, Yasui, Debnar, and Tarohmaru (2013) compared wage distribution among prefectures in Japan in 2005 and reported that the increase of inequality based on the growth of both upper- and lower-end service occupations in Tokyo, which was discussed in Sassen's (2001) 'global city' concept, has been mitigated by the growth of clerical work (see Box 1).

In addition, it should be noted that since the previous company-oriented society itself hindered economic opportunities for key groups, in particular women's, the dismantlement of this system was in a sense a 'door-opening' (Kimoto 2004, 328–332; Osawa 2011, 55–56). As Tanaka, Higashi, and Yugami (2020) emphasised, Tokyo has especially attracted women, as indicated by the higher share of high-income (seven million yen or more) female employees and a higher net population inflow of females. As advanced education for women has become the norm, more women seek the same professional opportunities as men (Osawa and Namba 2011, 187–193). In this sense, Tokyo represents a city with expanded opportunities, and it is unlikely that restoring its previous system would improve urban well-being.

To paraphrase, despite several decades of economic stagnation, Tokyo seems to remain a better destination for both men and women seeking jobs and motivated to succeed through a self-reliant mindset. Of course, the expansion of the 'underclass' menaces the stability, sustainability, and integration of society (Hashimoto 2020). The underclass includes irregular employees and gig workers,[21] the numbers of whom increased significantly in the 2010s. Their increase itself, however, indicates the existence of a strong labour demand in Tokyo and people applying for such roles.

Nonetheless, relatively higher social and economic opportunities in Tokyo along with the freedoms which accompany these do not necessarily lead to anxiety-free and higher life satisfaction. Figure 4.5 shows Tokyo's life satisfaction derived from the SCL data used to mirror the nationwide life satisfaction levels derived from the government's SPL (Cabinet Office 1964-2021). However, only the former declined in the 2000s, and the gap widened after 2004.[22] Of course, it is difficult to compare data derived from different sources; the SPL also offers the life satisfaction level for Tokyo residents (the 23 wards only), which is similar to the national level and does not show an obvious decline in the 2000s. The Tokyo trend in the SPL data seemed similar to the trend in the SCL data for higher middle-income or lower upper-income households (7–9 and 9–11 million yen). The discrepancies between SPL and SCL findings require further investigation in future studies. However, these at least indicate that Tokyo, 'the sole winner' (Tanaka, Higashi, and Yugami 2020, 14) in the nationwide economic downturn, did not necessarily outperform the rest of Japan in terms of life satisfaction.

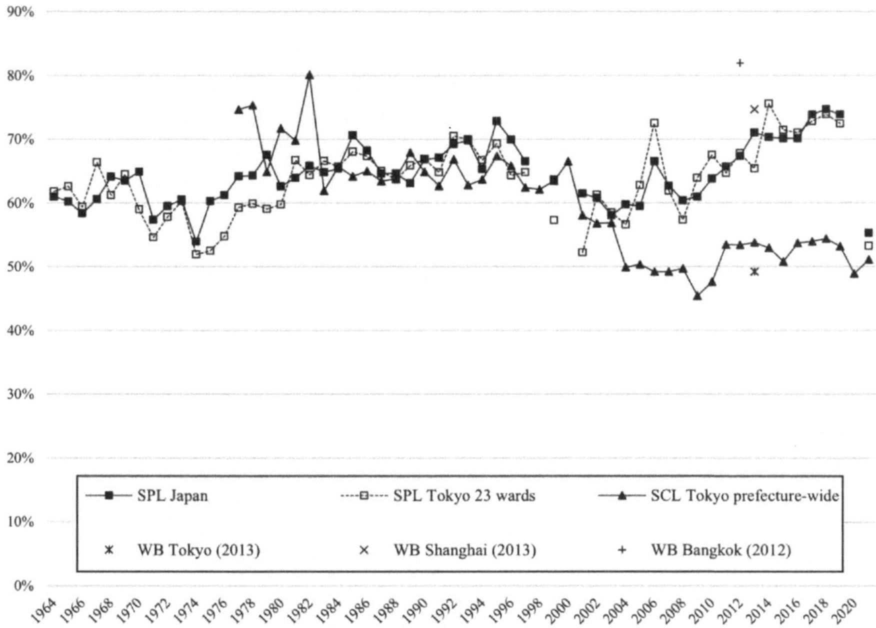

Figure 4.5 National and urban life satisfaction.

Source: Made by author based on SPL, SCL, and WB data.

Note: The percentages indicate the share of respondents who reported being 'satisfied' with their lives. For the years when the SPL survey was conducted twice, I adopted the figures from the first survey. The SPL survey was not conducted in 1998, 2000, and 2020. It changed the data collection method and decreased the number of targets in 2021 allegedly due to the COVID-19 pandemic. See also note on Figure 4.1.

4.3.2 Self-Reliance, Formality, and Urban Well-Being

Tokyo residents' life satisfaction has been modest despite the city's favourable economic opportunities compared with other regions. Relatively well-off livelihoods in Tokyo usually require longer working and commuting times (Tanaka, Higashi, and Yugami 2020, 14–15), which can certainly be part of the explanation. The SPL indicates that Tokyo residents often show lower satisfaction with housing conditions. Congestion negatively affects residents' quality of life.

However, ultimately, the suppression invites us to consider the possibility of 'the fragility of formality'. Under fluctuating economic conditions, even a formal job cannot permanently stabilise people's lives, and there are a greater number of irregular workers, as mentioned in Section 4.1.1. Without stable employment, the higher cost of living can shake people's fundamental living status, even though their lifestyles may currently be affordable. Favourable economic opportunities can rather enhance anxiety over future risks. After all, employment is a contractual, potentially temporary state, not an inviolable property of individuals.

Channels to support individuals' resilience to risks and shocks, on the contrary, have been threatened, as explained in Section 4.1.1. The company-oriented society offered life security through enterprise employment with family wages. People mould their lives to prioritize fulfilling their employment requirements (Watanabe 1990, 2004; Goto 2001; Kimoto 2004; Takeda 2012; Honda 2014). The male breadwinner model, with fewer productive activities based inside the home, resulted in shrinking neighbourhood networks (Dore [1958] 2013, 253–268; Tamano 2005). It is debatable whether and to what extent neighbourhoods once contributed to life security in urban areas like Tokyo (Dore [1958] 2013, 257–258; Ochiai 2004, 91–95). Nevertheless, when companies gave up their role in public integration, people often found themselves abandoned without other reliable networks (Tachibanaki 2011; Takeda 2012; Honda 2014).

Even with various critics, there is no room to doubt that relatively large contributions from 'formal' channels, namely corporate employment and the provision of government social security in the post-war period, have distinguished Japan from other developing countries. Livelihood protection systems and social insurance programs, such as unemployment insurance, were introduced in the late 1940s. In the late 1950s, the government established universal health insurance and national pension systems (Goto 2004; Kamimura 2004; Tanaka 2017, 85–89. See also Chapters 3 and 7).

However, under the company-oriented society structure, the employee-employer relations were primarily non-confrontational; rather, employees worked together with employers to expand corporate profits. The government's role was not perceived to be to supervise companies to secure workers' shares nor was it to redistribute companies' profits to ordinary people, but cooperating with companies to expand corporate profits. The expansion of corporate profits then supported employees and their families based on the Japanese employment system. People rarely fought for their rights to social security, partly because it was not necessary when the economy thrived under the company-oriented scheme. More essential is the concept of interdependence within the family and the basic tendency to disregard the focus on individuals' rights, making people hesitant to claim their rights to public support and even internalising the criticism of those, including themselves, who do (Watanabe 1990, 2004; Goto 2001, 2004; Tomie 2007; Miyamoto 2008; Tanaka 2017, 85–104; 2020, 157–176).

Tokyo offers evidence of the fragility of relying on formal channels: entrusting the source of people's livelihood and living to third parties, namely companies and/or the government, without solid recognition of rights to support to which everyone is legally entitled. After companies faced difficulties in the 1990s, there remained insufficient social security, less high-quality employment options, weakened communities, smaller families, and people firmly internalising the virtue of 'self-reliance' (Goto 2001; Tachibanaki 2011; Honda 2014; Hashimoto 2020).

Men and women came to be the core units of responsibility and decision-making in their own lives and thus were expected to deal with any risks by themselves. The differences among demographic groups receded, and one's economic status came to prevail as the determinants of livelihood. Beck (1992) described a similar situation as the 'individualisation' in 1980s Germany. This drift, as Beck described, resulted from the development of the welfare state. The liberation of people from traditional relations standardised individuals and forced them in turn to be dependent on and controlled by markets and institutions (87–102, 127–138).

Based on the concentration of relatively prosperous companies, Tokyo remains a better destination for men and women seeking job opportunities and the more favourable lifestyle options cities can offer. Nonetheless, or perhaps because of that, people cannot be free from anxiety, lowering their life satisfaction within this highly urban society.

Conclusion

Historical analysis can offer a sense of our position and how we arrived there. The current low level of life satisfaction in Tokyo reflects its decline during the first decade of the 21st century. Economic stagnation worsened people's expectations of future risks and, by extension, urban dwellers' sense of well-being. The impacts on each group were uneven because of the differences and changes in socioeconomic structures.

Urban society tends to be described as 'anonymous and atomic' (Dore [1958] 2013, 267), but its extent and form can change. For decades, after Dore's observations of Tokyo, companies came to take a central position along with other social security institutions to integrate people through economic growth. However, such formal channels could not guarantee people's well-being in an era of risks and uncertainty. With their preference for family-based personal resolutions and the expansion of formal channels, Tokyo residents now display their unique mechanism leading to some of their difficulties: self-reliance besieged by frigid formality, with shrinking families that lack a broad range of informal channels.

Although diminished and shaken, companies' contributions are still significant in Japan, and no stable alternative system has yet replaced these. With a shortage of other options and supporting channels, people rush to creaky boats and cannot be free from anxiety.

Acknowledgements

The author is grateful for helpful discussion with Isamu Mitsuzono for sharing his insights into the history of company-oriented society in Japan. The responsibility for any failures lies with the author.

Box 1 Employment and Life of Low-Income Single Women in Tokyo

Kaoru Kanai

While Japan is known as one of the most economically developed countries in Asia, it also has one of the largest gender gaps in East and Southeast Asia. According to the 2022 Global Gender Gap Report ranking for 146 countries, Thailand, China, and Japan have overall Global Gender Gap Index rankings of 79, 102, and 116, respectively. Japan scores particularly low in the areas of political and economic gender equality (World Economic Forum, 2022). Japan's gender gap has not narrowed for years. Even in Tokyo, where there are more working women than in other regions in Japan, the situation has not gone far enough to change.

Statistics show that in Tokyo, female migration from rural areas has indeed gradually increased since the 1980s and continues to increase. During the first two decades of the 2000s, the net inflow rate (incoming minus outgoing population) of women into the city centre (23 wards) was considerably higher than that of men (Tanaka, Higashi, and Yugami, 2020). Many of these women move to Tokyo for work, though the problems surrounding them indicate that the gender gap continues to exist.

First, women work but are paid less than men. According to the Employment Status Survey compiled by the Statistics Bureau of Japan, the proportion of high-income workers in Tokyo with annual incomes of over 7 million JPY has remained stable at approximately 27% for men from 1992 to 2017, while the proportion for women has only slightly increased from about 4% to 6% (Tanaka, Higashi, and Yugami, 2020). The results of the National Tax Administration Agency (2017) show that the average annual salary for all employees, including part-time workers, over the same period was about 4.32 million JPY, with men earning 5.32 million JPY and women 2.87 million JPY (1 USD = 113.19 JPY in 2017). Wages in Tokyo come at the cost of longer working hours and long daily commutes, yet around 60% of working women only earned less than 3 million yen as of 2017. Moreover, after they return to work after childbirth, their wages do not rise easily due to the excuse of 'inadequate' work experience, resulting in them failing to benefit from the seniority-based wage system. Their annual income hit a ceiling of around 3.8 million JPY even they are working as full-time workers.

Second, nearly half of all female workers are in non-regular employment. Until the early 1990s, young female regular employees were in charge of clerical work. However, due to labour market deregulation and cost-cutting during the recession, companies changed their recruitment strategies and replaced many of these posts with non-regular employment. Even if they are employed on a non-regular basis, women have to indulge to some extent because they themselves wish to work in clerical positions. Japanese women have reported a high preference for clerical jobs and the number of clerical jobs in Tokyo was on the rise until 2017 (which is latest data we can get) but was decreasing in rural areas (Employment Status Survey, 2017). This is one factor contributing to the influx of women to Tokyo.

Furthermore, it must also be pointed out that women often choose to move to Tokyo to liberate themselves from rural shackles and the pressure from their parents demanding their marriage. In other words, it is an escape from the traditional gender norm. They cannot be bothered to be constantly 'worried' by those around them asking if they have married or given birth yet. In Tokyo, there is no one around to put such pressure on them.

Working in such low-paid, precarious conditions, with no strong desire to marry, it is not uncommon for working women in Tokyo to remain single. The proportion of women living alone in Tokyo was between 40% and 50% for all age groups in 2018, which is higher than in rural areas (Statistics Bureau of Japan, 2018). For singles, the cost of living, including rent, is relatively high, making it difficult to secure a good living environment and making it financially unaffordable. In particular, lower-income women end up struggling to make ends meet. Although there are probably sufficient options of housing even for women with lower incomes, renting a room generally requires a guarantor who is a full-time employee and has a stable income, which limits women's options in the rental market. The deposit is also a burden. Deposit payment equivalent to two months' rent and 'key money', a non-refundable payment to the landlord, are required; in other words, renters need to prepare a total of four months' rent upfront. These high initial costs can pose a serious burden for low-income single women.

This can be illustrated by a specific narrative from an interview conducted by the author in 2022 on the life and work prospects of a single woman who is a low-income office worker in Tokyo. Ms. A, a clerical worker in her late 40s, graduated from a well-known private university and lives alone in Tokyo on an annual income of around 3 million JPY. Unable to find employment in her hometown, she came to Tokyo where clerical jobs were abundant. She arrived in the city in her 30s, eager to escape the pressure from her parents to marry. Having lived in the metropolis now for 13 years, she described the difficulty in finding a safe and secure place to live in Tokyo for the 80,000 JPY or so a month that she can afford to pay for rent. Inexpensive rentals within a 30-minute commute to her place of work in the city centre tend to be located in noisy areas, have poor neighbourhood security, and are typically old, mouldy wooden structures with rooms facing north that get little sunlight. Rents are cheaper in the suburbs of Tokyo's mega region, but the daily commute can be a long and crushing ordeal leading to accumulated fatigue. Ms. A has moved six times in constant search for a safe place to live with an easier commute.

Given the high initial costs of deposit and key money for each rental room, these frequent residential changes have been a huge financial strain for her. While she now has adapted to live alone in Tokyo, she sees no future in her career development. She is trying to save money and thus can barely afford to eat out. She worries about supporting herself after retirement. If she loses her job, life will get tougher even earlier, and she wonders how she will be able to continue paying rent. She believes her family will take care of her, if necessary, but she is the youngest child and will very likely outlive everyone else in her family. She has resigned herself to the possibility that she may eventually have to live on welfare.

Unsurprisingly, such a way of life results in low life satisfaction for women, especially single lower-income women, in Tokyo. The lack of a safe and secure home and living environment, as well as lack of career and financial prospects, contribute to lower life satisfaction and burden their lives. While gender norms are believed to be changing in Tokyo, data show no significant change in the gender gap in labour market structures, which leave women in the low-income group, who make up the majority, vulnerable in their survival. The results of our survey provide insight to the problems that arise when women congregate in cities in the face of lacking progress in narrowing the economic gender gap.

References

National Tax Administration Agency. 2017. *The Statistical Survey of Actual Statistics for Salary in the Private Sector*, accessed 30 August, 2022, <https://www.nta.go.jp/publication/statistics/kokuzeicho/minkan2017/minkan.htm>.

Statistics Bureau of Japan. 2017. *Employment Status Survey*, accessed 5 September, 2022, <https://www.e-stat.go.jp/en/>.

Statistics Bureau of Japan. 2018. *Housing and Land Survey*, accessed 30 August, 2022, <https://www.stat.go.jp/data/jyutaku/index.html>.

Tanaka, Y., Y. Higashi, and K. Yugami. 2020. 'The Characteristics of "Tokyo" as a Labour Market [Rodo shijō "Tokyo" no tokuchō]'. *Nihon Rodo Kenkyu Zasshi* 718.4-17.

World Economic Forum. 2022. *Global Gender Gap Report*, accessed 30 August, 2022, <https://www3.weforum.org/docs/WEF_GGGR_2022.pdf>.

Notes

1 Neighbourhood associations were once prohibited under the occupation authorities because of their contribution to the Second World War, but they later regained popularity (Bestor 1989, 66–77; Dore [1958] 2013, 269–275).

2 Men responded 'state' more frequently, while women more often responded 'family'.

3 'Unmarried' means people who were never married, excluding those who were divorced or widowed.

4 The reverse U shape of the unmarried ratio could be interpreted as a change in family-formation patterns around 2005. However, housing behaviours could also affect

this trend; if newlyweds moved to the suburban prefectures, Tokyo's unmarried ratio would increase; if they stayed in Tokyo after marriage, the ratio would decrease.

5 This chapter calls this survey the 'SCL', regardless of the period. The explanations and data on the SCL are based on issues of the SCL unless otherwise stated.

6 In 1983, the section in which this question was asked was moved to the first section assessing economic conditions, so it might now be more associated with economic conditions.

7 Our WB dataset for Tokyo adopted a quota method allocating almost the same number of respondents for each cell (gender × age range × income group) for the total samples (1,261 respondents). The SCL uses a stratified two-stage random sampling method that classifies Tokyo into several areal strata, in which 3,000 targets (4,000 targets after 2020) are proportionally allocated. The number of valid responses for the SCL is around 2,000, showing a gradual decrease. Both datasets cover the Tokyo Prefecture (23 central wards and other cities or towns). The WB data exclude the islands of Tokyo Prefecture, whereas the SCL started covering these since 1996, though even combined with several other included suburban areas still only make up around 3% of respondents. We surveyed only the primary earners; the SCL included all people aged 20 years or above (18 or above after 2016). We collected our Tokyo data through internet surveys, while the SCL surveys were conducted through individual interviews until 2020, when they switched to postal and internet collection. The SCL respondents tend to be those who are settled in and committed to the regional community. It includes more female than male respondents. Only around 50% of younger people respond to the SCL compared with around 70% of elderly people. The respondent shares of unmarried, single- or two-member households are lower than the prefectural average indicated in TMG (1986, 1990, 1995, 2000, 2005, 2010, 2015).

8 Totals do not sum to 100% as there are other possible responses which are not shown: 'no idea' and 'no response'.

9 Dividing the ten levels of satisfaction into two just categories risks losing nuances. Categorising level five is especially problematic as it can be chosen to avoid an obvious judge. However, since we mainly focus on the proportion of people being satisfied with their lives in the following analyses, few significant problems will be caused by considering 6–10 as 'satisfied'.

10 The results of the SCL after 2020 reflect the effects of the ongoing COVID-19 pandemic and a change in the data collection method.

11 Since the WB data only included the lower- and middle-income groups, 'HHUpper' was provided just for reference. Some respondents belonged to different income groupings depending on whether they were sorted by individual or household income. In the WB data, such cases accounted for around 35% of the respondents in 'Tokyo-Lower' and 20% in 'Tokyo-Middle'.

12 As mentioned earlier, we used only the aggregated information reported by the TMG and only had the continuous data reported after 1995.

13 The original questionnaire uses a vague Japanese word '*kurashi*', including the meaning of 'life', 'livelihood', and 'life circumstances'.

14 The original questionnaire uses a vague Japanese word '*jūseikatsu*', meaning life from the perspective of housing environment.

15 The way to interpret the differences and changes by cohort, this chapter learned from NHK Broadcasting Culture Research Institute (2020).

16 Because there was no comparable question in the 1999 SCL, we compared data in the years 1998, 2008, and 2018. Therefore, the cohorts were not in round years. We interpreted the cohort born in 1969–1978 as 1970s.

17 Japan's baby boomers are those born in the late 1940s and early 1950s. Their children, with most born between the late 1960s to the mid-1970s, were also numerous, slightly less than their parents. The latter half of this 'baby-boomer junior' generation overlapped with the 'Ice Age generation' (Hashimoto 2020, 64–68).

18 Hashimoto (2020, 58–64) defined this as 1994–2007 and said that job-hunters in the middle years of this period (around 2000) were most severely affected.

19 This chapter substituted those born in the 1970s for the 'Ice Age generation' because of the data availability. We could have undertaken the cohort analyses with the surveys from 1981, 1991, 2001, 2011, and 2021; or from 1982, 1992, 2002, and 2012, but with these sets, it was difficult to compare their perception within a decade around 2000. In addition, the 2011 data might have been influenced by the Great East Japan Earthquake.

20 The results of the SCL after 2020 included the influences of the COVID-19 pandemic. The SCL in 2008 was conducted from the end of August to the beginning of September, before the global financial crisis triggered by the collapse of Lehmann Brothers. When analysing the sets of SCL surveys from 1978, 1988, 1998, 2008, and 2018, the gap in life satisfaction ratio between 1998 and 2008 for males born in 1969–1978 showed a smaller decline compared to the other cohorts. This difference was partly because their satisfaction ratio in 1998 was lower than those for males in their twenties in 1997, 1999, or 2000.

21 Gig workers can formally be classified as self-employment, but a considerable share of these workers face a precariousness which can be recognised as more characteristic of the 'underclass' (see also Box 2a and b).

22 The data of SPL in 2021 showed a drastic drop, presumably reflecting the influence of COVID-19 pandemic and the change of data collection method (from individual interviews to postal collection).

References

Asahi Shimbun 'Lost Generation' Press Team 2007. *Rosuto Jenerēshon: samayou 2000 man nin* [Lost Generation: 20 Million People Adrift]. Tokyo: Asahi Shimbun sha.

Beck, U. 1992. *Risk Society: Towards a New Modernity.* Translated by Mark Ritter. London: Sage Publications.

Bestor, T.C. 1989. *Neighborhood Tokyo.* Stanford, CA: Stanford University Press.

Dadavaev, T. 2005. "Japan: Family, Values, and Interests of The Modernised Society." [Nippon: kindaikashakai no katei, kachikan, kanshin.] In *Ajia baromētā toshibu no kachikan to seikatsu sutairu: Ajia yoronchōsa (2003) no bunseki to shiryō* [Values and Life Styles in Urban Asia: A Cross-Cultural Analysis and Sourcebook Based on the AsiaBarometer Survey of 2003], edited by T. Inoguchi, M. Basáñez, A. Tanaka, and T. Dadabaev, 37-46. Tokyo: Akashi Shoten.

Dore, R.P. (1958) 2013. *City Life in Japan.* Paperback edition. Abingdon: Routledge.

Esping-Andersen, G. 1999. *Social Foundations of Postindustrial Economies.* New York: Oxford University Press.

Esping-Andersen, G. 2000. *Posuto kōgyōkeizai no shakaiteki kiso: shijō, fukushikokka, kazoku no seiji keizaigaku* [Social Foundations of Postindustrial Economies: Political Economy of Markets, Welfare States, and Families]. Translated by M. Watanabe and K. Watanabe. Tokyo: Sakurai Shoten.

Esping-Andersen, G. 2001. *Fukushi shihonshugi no mittsu no sekai: hikaku fukushi kokka no riron to dōtai* [The Three Worlds of Welfare Capitalism: Theory and Dynamism of Comparative Welfare States]. Translation supervised by N. Okazawa and T. Miyamoto. Kyoto: Minerva Shobo.

Esping-Andersen, G. 2009. *The Incomplete Revolution: Adapting to Women's New Roles.* Cambridge: Polity Press.

Goto, M. 2001. *Shūshuku suru Nihongata <taishūshakai>: keizai gurōbarizumu to kokumin no bunretsu* [Shrinking Japanese Type of <Mass Society>: Economic Globalism and Division of the Nation]. Tokyo: Junposha.

Goto, M. 2004. "The Structure of Japanese Type of Social Security: Its Formation and Conversion." [Nihongata shakaihoshō no kōzō: sono keisei to tenkan.] In *Kōdo seichō to kigyō shakai* [Rapid Economic Growth and Company-Oriented Society], edited by O. Watanabe, 190–221. Tokyo: Yoshikawa Kobunkan.

Hashimoto, K. 2020. *Andākurasu 2030: okizari ni sareru 'hyōgaki sedai'* [Underclass 2030: The Abandoned 'Ice Age Generation']. Tokyo: Mainichi Shimbun Shuppan.

Honda, Y. 2014. *Shakai o musubinaosu: kyōiku, shigoto, kazoku no renkei e* [Reorganising the Society: for the Cooperation of Education, Work, and Family]. Tokyo: Iwanami Shoten.

Inoguchi, T., M. Basáñez, A. Tanaka, and T. Dadabaev eds. 2005. *Ajia baromētā toshibu no kachikan to seikatsu sutairu: Ajia yoronchōsa (2003) no bunseki to shiryō* [Values and Life Styles in Urban Asia: A Cross-Cultural Analysis and Sourcebook Based on the AsiaBarometer Survey of 2003]. Tokyo: Akashi Shoten.

Ito, S. 1983. "Urban Growth in Meiji and Taisho Japan." [Meiji Taishōki Nihon no toshi seichō.] In *Sūryōkeizaishi ronshū 3 Puroto kōgyōkaki no keizai to shakai: kokusai hikaku no kokoromi* [Paper Collection on Quantitative Economic History 6 Economy and Society in the Era of Proto-industrialisation: An attempt for International Comparison], edited by Y. Yasuba and O. Saito, 305-336. Tokyo: Nihon Keizai Shimbunsha.

Kamimura, Y. 2004. "Welfare States in East Asia: For Their Comparative Research." [Higashi Ajia no fukushikokka: sono hikakukenkyū ni mukete.] In *Ajia shokoku no fukushi senryaku* [Welfare Strategies of Asian Countries], edited by M. Osawa, 23–65. Kyoto: Minerva Shobo.

Kase, K. 1997. *Shūdan shūshoku no jidai: kōdo seichō no ninaite tachi* [The Era of the Employment En Masse: The Supporters of the Rapid Growth]. Tokyo: Aoki Shoten.

Kimoto, K. 2004. "Family and Company-oriented Society: Historical Changing Process." [Kazoku to kigyō shakai: rekishiteki hendō katei.] In *Henbōsuru 'kigyō shakai' Nippon* [Transforming 'Company-Oriented Society,' Japan], edited by O. Watanabe, 299–340. Tokyo: Junposha.

Machimura, T. 2009. "Multiscalar Structure of Inequality in Contemporary Japan." [Gendai Nihon ni okeru kakusa no jūsōteki kōzō.] *Hitotsubashi Shakai Kagaku* 6: 103–123. doi:10.15057/17384

Minagawa, M. 2020. *Shuto kaizō: Tokyo no saikaihatsu to toshi seiji* [Reconstruction of the Capital: Redevelopment and Urban Politics of Tokyo]. Tokyo: Yoshikawa Kobunkan.

Miyamoto, T. 2008. *Fukushi seiji: Nihon no seikatsu hoshō to demokurashī* [The Politics of Welfare: Democracy, Employment and Welfare in Japan]. Tokyo: Yuhikaku.

NHK Broadcasting Culture Research Institute, ed. 2020. *Gendai Nihonjin no ishikikōzō* [The Structure of Consciousness of Modern Japanese People], 9th ed. Tokyo: NHK Shuppan.

Ochiai, E. 2004. *21 seiki kazoku e: kazoku no sengo taisei no mikata/koekata* [The Japanese Family System in Transition: How to View and Overcome the Post-war Regime of Family], 3rd ed. Tokyo: Yuhikaku.

Osawa, M. 2011. *Social Security in Contemporary Japan: A Comparative Analysis.* Translation edited by Michael Burtscher. Abingdon: Routledge.

Osawa, M., and S. Namba. 2011. "Explanatory Notes." [Kaidai.] In *Byōdō to kōritsu no fukushi kakumei: atarashii josei no yakuwari* [The Incomplete Revolution: Adapting to Women's New Roles], written by G. Esping-Andersen and translation supervised by M. Osawa, 179–204. Tokyo: Iwanami Shoten.

Sassen, S. 2001. *The Global City: New York, London, Tokyo.* Princeton, NJ: Princeton University Press.

Tachibanaki, T. 2011. *Muen shakai no shōtai: ketsuen, chien, shaen wa ikani hōkai shitaka* [The Truth of the No-Connection Society: How Blood Relation, Regional Ties, and Colleague Relations Have Disintegrated]. Tokyo: PHP Kenkyujo.

Takeda, H. 2012. "Company-oriented Society: The Installation to Support 'Richness.'" [Kigyō shakai: 'yutakasa' o sasaeru sōchi.] In *Kawaru shakai, kawaru hitobito: 20 seiki no nakano sengo Nihon* [Changing Society, Changing Individuals: Post-war Japan in the 20th Century], edited by T. Yasuda, J. Ōgushi, H. Takaoka, H. Nishino, and K. Harayama, 128–155. Tokyo: Iwanami Shoten.

Tamano, K. 1993. *Kindai Nihon no toshika to chōnaikai no seiritsu* [Modernisation and the Formation of Neighbourhood Associations in Modern Japan]. Tokyo: Kojinsha.

Tamano, K. 2005. *Tokyo no rōkaru komyunitī: aru machi no monogatari 1900–80* [Local Community in Tokyo: A Story of a Town 1900–80]. Tokyo: University of Tokyo Press.

Tamano, K. 2009. "Urbanisation of Tokyo Area and Formation of Suburban Districts." [Tokyo ken no toshika to kōgaichiku no keisei.] In *Tokyo daitoshiken no kūkan keisei to komyunitī* [Spatial Formation and Comunities in Tokyo Metropolitan Area], edited by K. Tamano and T. Asakawa, 225–233 Tokyo: Kokon Shoin.

Tanaka, T. 2017. *Fukushi seijishi: kakusa ni kōsuru demokurashī* [History of Welfare Politics: Democracy Against Inequality]. Tokyo: Keiso Shobo.

Tanaka, T. 2020. *Riberaru towa nanika: 17 seiki no jiyūshugi kara gendai Nihon made* [What is Liberal?: From Liberalism in the 17th Century to Modern Japan]. Tokyo: Chuokoron Shinsha.

Tanaka, Y., Y. Higashi, and K. Yugami. 2020. "The Characteristics of 'Tokyo' as a Labor Market." [Rōdō shijō 'Tokyo' no tokuchō.] *Nihon Rodo Kenkyu Zasshi* 62(5): 4–17. https://www.jil.go.jp/institute/zassi/backnumber/2020/05/pdf/004-017.pdf

Tanimoto, M. 2002. "Urban 'Small Businesses' in Modern Japan: Based on 'Tokyo Municipal Census.'" [Kindai Nihon no toshi 'shōkeiei': 'Tokyo-shi shisei chōsa' o sozai toshite.] In *Toshika to zairai sangyō* [Urbanization and Indigenous Industry], edited by T. Nakamura and N. Fujii, 3–49. Tokyo: Nihon Keizai Hyoronsha.

Tanimoto, M. 2005. "Urban Small Manufactures in the Inter-War Period Japan: The Case of Tokyo Prefecture." [Senkanki Nihon no toshi shōkōgyō: Tokyo-fu no baai.] In *Higashi Ajia kindai keizai no keisei to hatten: Higashi Ajia shihonshugi keiseishi I* [The Formation and Development of Modern Economy in East Asia: History of the Formation of Capitalism in East Asia I], edited by S. Nakamura, 201–224. Tokyo: Nihon Hyoronsha.

Tomie, N. 2007. *Kyūhin no nakano Nihon kindai: seizon no gimu* [Modern Japan in Poor Relief: The Obligation of Living]. Kyoto: Minerva Shobo.

Watanabe, O. 1990. *"Yutakana shakai" Nippon no kōzō* [The Structure of "Affluent Society," Japan]. Tokyo: Rodo Jumposha.

Watanabe, O. 2004. "The Structure and Restructuring of Japan's Developmentalism and Company-Oriented Society." [Kaihatsushugi / kigyō shakai no kōzō to sono saihensei.] In *Henbōsuru 'kigyō shakai' Nippon* [Transforming 'Company-Oriented Society,' Japan], edited by O. Watanabe, 23–114. Tokyo: Jumposha.

Yamada, A. 2012. "Income Inequality and Poverty among Elderly People: Fragile Safety Nets and Dependence on Earned Income." [Kōreiki niokeru shotoku kakusa to hinkon: zeijakuna sēfutī netto to kinrō shotoku eno izon]. In *Kakusa shakai* [Unequal Society], edited by T. Tachibanaki, 147–164. Kyoto: Minerva Shobo.

Yasui, D., M. Debnar, and H. Tarohmaru. 2013. "Global Cities and Wage Inequality: Industry, Occupation, and District." [Gurōbaru shitī to chingin no fubyōdō: sangyō, shokugyō, chiiki.] *Shakaigaku Hyoron* 64 (2): 152–168. https://doi.org/10.4057/jsr.64.152

Statistics and Data Sets

(Agencies and organisations are identified by their most current name even when changing over the course of publication.)

Cabinet Office, ed. 1964–2021. *Kokumin seikatsu ni kansuru yoron chōsa* [Survey of Public Opinion on People's Lives]. Tokyo: Cabinet Office, Government of Japan.

*for 2005–2021, accessed on August 31, 2022, <https://survey.gov-online.go.jp/index-ko.html>.

Ministry of Internal Affairs and Communications, Japan (MIC), ed. 1957–2018. *Shūgyō kōzō kihon chōsa hōkoku* [Report on Employment Status Survey], various volumes. Tokyo: Nihon Tōkei Kyōkai.

MIC. 2022. Consumer Price Index [Shōhisha bukka shisū] accessed 30 August, 2022, <https://www.e-stat.go.jp/stat-search/files?page=1&toukei=00200573&tstat=000001150147>

Tokyo Metropolitan Government (TMG), ed. 1970–2022. *Toshi seikatsu ni kansuru yoron chōsa (Tomin seikatsu ni kansuru yoron chōsa)* [Survey on Public Opinion on Urban Life (Survey on Public Opinion on Citizens' Lives)]. Tokyo: Tokyo Metropolitan Government.
*for 2016–2022, accessed on August 31, 2022,
<https://www.metro.tokyo.lg.jp/tosei/hodohappyo/press/2016/11/30/01.html>
<https://www.metro.tokyo.lg.jp/tosei/hodohappyo/press/2017/11/09/25.html>
<https://www.metro.tokyo.lg.jp/tosei/hodohappyo/press/2018/11/27/01.html>
<https://www.metro.tokyo.lg.jp/tosei/hodohappyo/press/2019/11/28/01.html>
<https://www.metro.tokyo.lg.jp/tosei/hodohappyo/press/2021/01/27/01.html>
<https://www.metro.tokyo.lg.jp/tosei/hodohappyo/press/2022/01/27/01.html>.

TMG. 1986, 1990, 1995, 2000, 2005, 2010, 2015, 2020. *Tokyo Statistical Yearbook* [Tokyo-to tōkei nenkan] accessed 30 August, 2022, <https://www.toukei.metro.tokyo.lg.jp/tnenkan/tn-index.htm>.

5 Perceived and Experienced Urban Risks and Life Difficulties

Past, Present, and Future

Tamaki Endo

Introduction

As discussed in Chapter 1, megacities are not only a space of opportunity but also a space of risk. Mega and 'global' cities are, by their nature, a risk habitat (Buscher and Mascareno 2012) where the risk production mechanism is embedded in the urban setting itself. Therefore, urban residents face various types of urban risks in the course of their daily lives, which means that urban life is inevitably a continuous process of risk responses.

The level of well-being of individuals and households going through their urban lives is defined not only by their current socioeconomic conditions but also by their vulnerability[1] and their capability to deal with urban risks and the actual shocks that they face/faced (Moser 1998, 3). These vulnerabilities and the constraints in dealing with risks and shocks differ among different social classes. In general, when daily survival is an issue, priorities will be focused on basic needs.

At the same time, in the era of uncertainty, the middle class is also not free from urban risks and shocks. Actual shocks may not only be attributed to the misfortune of individuals but also to systematic or 'covariant' risks such as macroeconomic crises, natural disasters, and pandemics which will inevitably also impact wider groups of people in a society. In particular, the new 'emerging' middle classes, who recently enjoyed upward mobility, might not stand on as firm foundations in their urban lives. Adding to that, people's concerns in urban life might not be limited to basic needs but might have multiple dimensions and priorities which change from time to time, depending on their life stage and the macro circumstances.

It is also important to note that the impact of risk and shock responses accumulate in one's life from cumulated experiences. Past events and shocks might define one's future choices and opportunities. For example, someone who had to drop out of school as the result of a financial crisis is likely constrained in their future occupational choices. Thus, how much people worry or are satisfied with their present urban life is affected by past experiences and their future prospects. In other words, both their risk perceptions and subjective well-being (life satisfaction) are defined by not only by the conditions of the individual and household

DOI: 10.4324/9781003328155-5

but also by external factors, i.e., social setting and environment which might help/ constrain their survival strategies. The historical changes in the life satisfaction level of Tokyo's lower classes provide an example which implies that not only individuals' preferences but also their social settings do matter. The lower classes in both the 1980s and 2010s faced economic difficulties, but the poor in the 1980s evaluated their lives more positively (see Chapter 4, Figure 4.3b).

In this chapter, we will look at perceived urban risks, current life difficulties, and past experienced shocks of the lower and middle classes of three cities: Tokyo, Shanghai, and Bangkok. We will compare people's priorities and the aspects that actually concern them the most. To understand the complexities mentioned above, this chapter also uses six groups for distinction (two classes in three cities) in the analysis. Both quantitative data and a qualitative survey, primarily focus group interviews, were used for the analysis. Our questionnaire survey is a one-time snapshot survey and therefore has limitations for understanding the changes in respondents' socioeconomic and subjective well-being over time. To make a more 'dynamic' understanding possible, we included questions regarding each respondent's past and present experiences as well as future perception of urban risks, difficulties, and concerns. The qualitative research provides complementary information for understanding the urban lives of the six groups in depth. Another aim of this chapter is to look at how past experiences and ongoing problems influence one's life satisfaction level (subjective well-being).

This chapter will provide some insights into people's struggles and challenges in urban life before we move on to the analysis of survival strategies connected to social networks and social settings in the following chapters. We do not go into detail on the degree of vulnerabilities and capabilities themselves, but instead this chapter aims to understand people's priorities in urban life as well as their current perceptions of these as formed from past experiences of large or small risks and shocks as well as the future prospects facing them based on their individual, household, and societal conditions.

5.1 Perceived Urban Risks and Life Difficulties of the Lower and Middle-Class Residents in Three Cities

In this section, we first explain the methodology and dataset for our questionnaire survey. Then, we briefly look at the priority 'present' perceived urban risks in people's daily and past experiences.

5.1.1 Past, Present, and Future Risks and Risk Categories

As explained in Chapter 1, urban risk is the possibility of loss connected to living in urban areas covering a variety of multi-dimensional causes. Urban risk can be both systematic and idiosyncratic (World Bank 2001). Nevertheless, local context matters a great deal, as place-specific risk accumulation processes as well as individual people's perceptions and responses mean that the impact of the same events can still be very different.

The questionnaire was organised with a focus on three temporal stages of urban risks and events: past problems, present risks and (ongoing) life difficulties, and future risks. In addition, we asked people about the social networks on which they relied when facing past problems and/or those they would rely on for present perceived urban risks. Actual questions were asked about: (Q1) actual experienced life problems (their biggest problems over the past 10 years), (Q2) whether and how they solved or did not solve them, (Q3) social networks used in coping with these, (Q4) present life problems and difficulties they face, (Q5) present perceived urban risks (up to three in order) and potential social networks in survival strategies, (Q6) perceived urban risks for the future, and (Q7) life satisfaction (scale of 1–10, where 10 is 'extremely satisfied'). Among these questions, this chapter will look at the contents of risks and actual shocks, with respondents' survival strategies (Q3 and survival strategies for Q5) discussed in the following chapters.

Questions about ongoing life difficulties and past problems were answered freely and then coded afterwards. The options were provided for perceived urban risks for both the present and future. By modifying the World Bank's classification mentioned in Chapter 1 (Table 1.1, p. 4), 19 choices which covered different types of risks were presented in the questionnaire (Table 5.1). These options were grouped into five broader categories, with economic and social risks further divided into the middle level categories, in order to acquire a better understanding of the structure of priority concerns in urban life (for our analysis 'health risk' was merged with 'social risk'). This chapter will primarily present the results at two levels as follows (middle level categories in brackets): 1. Economic (I. Financial, II. Work-related), 2. Social (III. Health issues, IV. Family issues, V. Future anxiety and isolation, VI. Community), 3. Political, 4. Environmental, and 5. Natural. Social risks are divided into personal/family sphere risks (III to V) and wider level of community risks (VI) (for details, see footnote 2 in Table 5.1). The original categories will be used when detailed investigation is needed.

5.1.2 Present Perceived Urban Risks and Difficulties

Table 5.2 shows perceived urban risks and difficulties in the present (top five most common answers for respondents' first choice to question Q5 using the middle level categories), which are the potential urban risks that concern people the most, or the actual difficulties that they are already facing. The respondents were asked to choose up to three options representing the issues which they worried about the most or which are the crucial risks to consider in their current urban life.

Regardless of city and social class, people were concerned about financial and work-related issues the most (about 70%–90%), followed by health issues in most groups. Only Bangkok's lower class and Shanghai's middle class showed a slightly different ordering of their top concerns. For Bangkok's lower class, 'Environment' (living environment) was another priority area and came second followed by work and health. This might be due to the characteristics

Table 5.1 Type of risks and dimension

Type of risks	*Idiosyncratic*	*Covariant*	
	Individual/household (micro)	*Households and communities (meso)*	*Regions and nations (macro)*
Natural			16. Natural disaster
Health	8. Illness/injury		
Social	9. Difficulty of childcare/elderly care 15. Loneliness	10. Lack or destruction of community 14. Crime/safety 17. Terrorism	
Economic	1. Unemployment/cannot find job 2. Problems or stress related occupation 3. High living cost 5. Housing cost 18. Education		4. Inflation/rise of commodity price
Political		6. Intervention by government 7. Corruption	
Environmental		11. Sanitation (basic infrastructure) 12. Environment (cf. noise, pollution) 13. Density of living area	

Source: Made by author by referring World Bank (2001) and Asia Barometer (2007).

Note: 1. Choice 19 is 'other' with free column. 2. Under large category of 'Economic risk', we set two middle categories. One is 'Financial risk and difficulties' which include risks of Nos. 3, 4, 5, and 18. Another is 'Work-related' which include Nos. 1 and 2. For 'Social risk', there are three middle categories which is 'Health issue (No. 8)', 'Family issues' (No. 9), and 'Future anxiety and isolation' (No. 15). 'Community risk' include, Nos. 10, 14, and 17 and 'Political risk' include Nos. 6 and 7. 'Environmental risk' is Nos. 11, 12, and 13 and, 'Natural risks' is No. 16.

Table 5.2 Priority in perceived urban risks and difficulties (% of first choice)

Group	*most chosen five risks and difficulties (%)*				
Tokyo-middle	Financial (50.1)	Work (23.8)	Health (9.0)	Community (4.6)	Environment (3.0)
Tokyo-lower	Financial (49.8)	Work (27.5)	Health (10.3)	Environment (3.2)	Community (2.7)
Shanghai-middle	Financial (70.7)	Work (15.3)	Environment (5.7)	Family (3.7)	Health (2.7)
Shanghai-lower	Financial (67.3)	Work (23.5)	Health (3.8)	Family (2.0)	Environment (1.8)
Bangkok-middle	Financial (49.5)	Work (26.3)	Health (6.4)	Environment (5.4)	Community (4.9)
Bangkok-lower	Financial (56.6)	Environment (10.1)	Work (8.2)	Health (7.9)	Community (4.2)
Total	Financial (55.6)	Work (22.0)	Health (7.3)	Environment (4.4)	Community (3.0)

Source: Made by author.
Note: 'Other' was excluded in ranking. For Tokyo middle class and Bangkok lower class, 'other' were 3.5% and 5.1% respectively, which were 5th if not excluded.

of the respondents in that they were all residents of informal settlements (see Chapter 3). For Shanghai's middle class, the first two answers were the same as for the other groups, but 'environment' and 'family' issues received slightly higher priority than 'health'. Despite these small differences, this indicates that the economic dimension is fundamental for all, and the social dimension on the individual level, such as health issues, also matter.

Figure 5.1 offers a plot of the categories for respondents' top three perceived urban risks and difficulties (economic and social dimensions). Two common tendencies were that among the top-ranked concerns, these broadened (1) from economic to including more social risks and (2) from personal to societal risks within the social risks. Economic risks were the biggest concern for the majority of all six groups. The lower classes in Shanghai and Tokyo showed the highest concern about economic issues, though more middle-class respondents than lower-class respondents put economic risks in the top position in Bangkok. The tendency common to all groups was that for the second and third rank risk concerns, social risks formed an increasing share of these. Priority for social risks was found in the personal sphere, such as health, family issues, and caregiving, then extended to a broader sphere, such as community related issues. Furthermore, there was interconnectivity between certain risks, a point we will return to in Section 5.2.

Regarding previous studies, there are few that have considered these issues specific to cities. Some previous studies on a national level, however, included similar questions. Asia Barometer's 2006–2007 survey included questions such as 'which, if any, of the following issues cause you great worry? Please choose all issues that cause you serious worry'.[2] There were 29 choices of social issues and the weighted answers were ranked as follows:

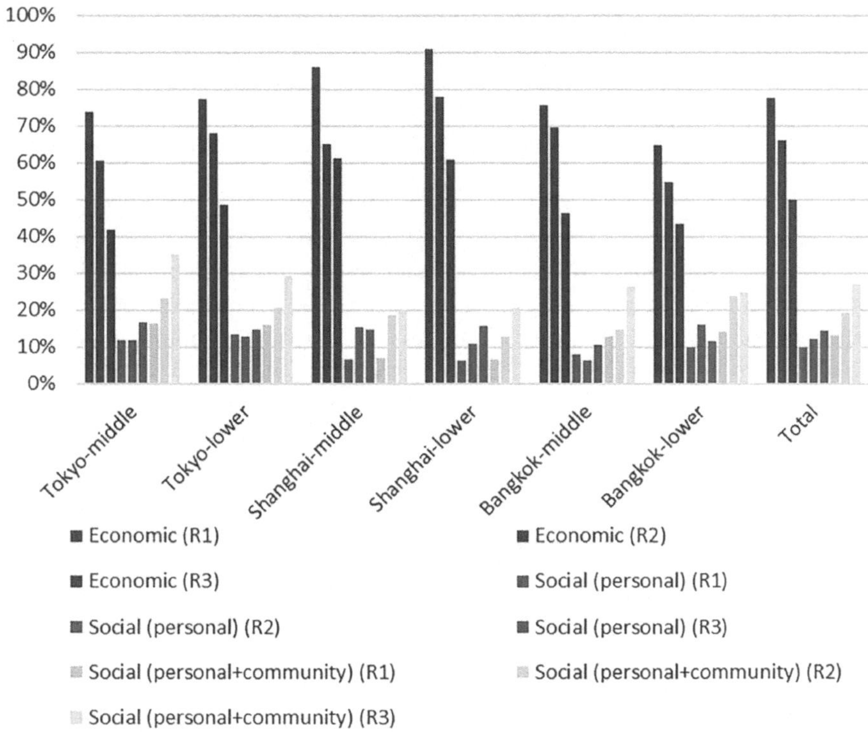

Figure 5.1 Perceived urban risks and difficulties in three cities.
Source: Made by author.
Note: Unit: %; R1=1st response, R2=2nd response, R3=3rd response.

For Japan: 1. Natural disaster, 2. Crime, 3. Environment and pollution, 4. War and disputes, 5. Deterioration of morality. For China: 1. Poverty, 2. Health, 3. Natural disaster, 4. Unemployment, 5. Corruption. For Thailand: 1. Poverty, 2. Illegal drugs, 3. Crime, 4. Unemployment, 5. Terrorism (Sonoda 2013, 29; Suehiro 2014, 4. Also see Inoguchi 2008). These results cannot be directly compared with our survey because, first, our survey's focus was concerns over risks in daily life while the Asia Barometer survey focused more on issues at a societal level, and therefore the options provided tended to be broader social issues. Second, the question did not limit the scope to 'urban' life and the respondents differed in they were not only from urban areas and also that the Asia Barometer survey included all social classes. Nonetheless, it is interesting to note that in China and Thailand, economic issues—poverty and unemployment—were the top-rated concerns.

Regarding Japan, priority for 'natural disaster' was observed in another study as well. The exploratory study by Arita on crisis thinking of the youth and middle aged in 2016 asked 'what is a crisis for you?'. The survey received 104 different answers (multiple answers) and the top five were as follows: 1. Natural disaster (not specified as to disaster type, 39.4%), 2. Earthquake (27.1%), 3. Deterioration of own household/living standard (14.9%), 4. Unemployment/lay-off (9.5%), and 5. Own health (8.5%). Arita created 20 middle and nine larger levels from 104 answers. The top five crises in the larger category were as follows: 1. Natural disaster (55.5%), 2. Individual's living standards, household account, economic-related problems (29.3%), 3. Health and life related issues (26.1%), 4. Societal issues (14.9%), 5. International relations (13.2%)[3] (Arita 2017, 4). The survey concluded that 'fear about natural disaster' is the primary worry of the Japanese.

The term used in this survey was 'crisis' which respondents might imagine as extraordinary events. Still, excluding natural disasters, we can see that the tendency, in common with our survey results, was that economic issues came first and were followed by health issues (social risks) and societal concerns. Our survey also found that the Japanese tend to be more worried about natural disasters when asked about future risks in urban life, compared with other cities (see Section 5.3.2).

5.1.3 Ongoing Problems and Past Experiences in Urban Life

As mentioned earlier, people's primary concern is the economic foundation of urban life which then gradually expands to include social risks. If we consider ongoing life difficulties and the biggest problems over the past 10 years, these actual problems show slightly different patterns among the different groups. The ratio of who has ongoing life difficulties by city and class (middle and lower classes) is as follows: Tokyo (42.5% and 59.0%, respectively), Shanghai (27.0% and 60.8%, respectively), and Bangkok (53.6% and 37.5%, respectively). As explained in Section 5.1.1, the respondents answered free response questions and we coded their answers afterwards. For those with many problems, we asked them to write them all down but to identify which one they felt was the most important.

Although the perceived fear of economic risks in urban life was high (cf., Section 5.1.2) and 'actual' ongoing difficulties also included economic issues for most people (Figure 5.2a), the data on the biggest problem in the past 10 years (Figure 5.2b) suggests that the actual degree to which people encounter economic risks and difficulties might be lower for some groups. In other words, the severity and sensibility of economic difficulties was not equal among the different groups. We will now consider the type of problems experienced by those who have/had problems in urban life.

Regarding ongoing problems (Figure 5.2a), financial problems (Economic) scored highest again for all groups among those with problems even though Tokyo and Shanghai's middle classes showed a relatively lower score. These two groups also showed relatively lower score for work-related issues as well, and Shanghai's lower classes showed a relatively higher score compared to middle class. Regarding the social sphere, both Tokyo and Bangkok's lower classes were dealing with health issues relatively more than family issues but vice versa for other four groups. In particular, Shanghai middle class, followed by Tokyo middle class, are facing challenges of family issue.

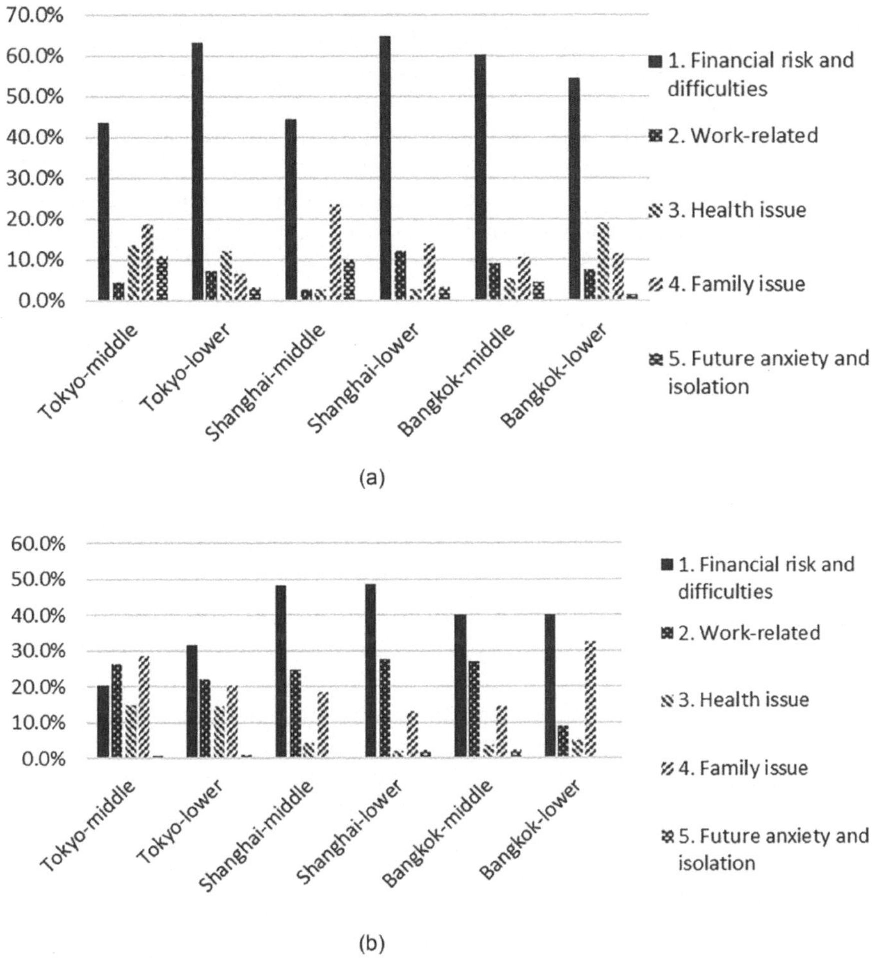

Figure 5.2 (a) Ongoing life problems, and (b) The biggest life problem in the past.
Source: Made by author.
Note: For Bangkok lower class, data is adjusted (two communities experienced fire, and 61.9% has chosen 'fire' as the biggest problem (for Figure 5.2b).

Regarding the biggest life problems in the past 10 years (Figure 5.2b), the three main past problems were 'financial', 'work', and 'family' issues for all six groups. We likewise found that 'financial' issues (Economic) came first, save for among Tokyo's middle class. For Tokyo's lower class, both classes in Shanghai, and Bangkok's middle class, finance came first followed by work-related issues and then family issues. For Bangkok's lower class, second and third place were reversed, and family issues received a higher score followed by work-related issues. However, for Tokyo's middle class, 'family' issues got the highest scores, followed by 'work-related' issues compared to financial problems. Compared to the risk perception and ongoing problems we have seen, 'family' issues (mainly caregiving) and 'work-related' problems were the biggest which meant that more people faced these problems as their biggest challenges in the past rather than 'financial' issues which were their primary concerns in the perception. It was also worth noting that both Tokyo groups scored 'health' issues relatively higher than their counterparts in the other cities.

We also asked whether this problem was solved or not and how it had been solved, and whether people dealt with it by themselves or asked for/received help from others. The ratio for those who could solve their biggest problem of the past 10 years was as follows: Tokyo (middle class: 63.8%; lower class: 52.2%), Shanghai (middle class: 63.4%; lower class: 42.4%), and Bangkok (middle class: 89.1%; lower class: 94.6%). The middle classes showed higher scores except for Bangkok. However, the high self-reported solving of the top problem by Bangkok's lower class was likely a special circumstance as two communities had faced a major fire and since then finished rebuilding permanent housing. Hence, once those who selected 'fire' as the biggest problem answered it as 'solved' had been dropped, then the ratio of those who could solve these problems decreased to 53.2%, showing a lower ratio than their middle-class counterparts.

These ratios indicate that some difficulties are persistent and continuously affect the lives of some people. Our dataset is to unable address 'why' some people can solve problems better than others, because we do not have detailed data regarding when the reported problems started (the 'timing' of problems that occur differentiate damage differently) and how severe the problems are/were (we cannot simply compare various issues because the degree of impact and severity will differ). Despite this limitation, our data still tells us that the lower classes tended to struggle with solving problems, indicating their disadvantage in socioeconomic condition and capability, thus being more sensitive to shocks (the supporting social networks will be discussed in Chapter 6).

However, an interesting feature arises when looking at a combination of perception and actual experiences in urban risks and shocks. Bangkok and Shanghai's middle classes also tended to be exposed to economic risks and problems (both financial and work-related) in their actual urban lives while in Tokyo just the middle class seemed more secure. This might be due to the fact that Tokyo's middle class has had more stable life foundations and do not face as severe financial problems as the other studied cities. They can be said to be the most stable group among the six groups while Shanghai and Bangkok's middle class included the newly emerged middle class in rapidly developing societies and therefore many are not yet free from dealing with economic concerns. We will examine what is actually happening across urban lives in these in more detail in the following section.

5.2 What Actually Matters in Urban Life?: Economic and Social Risks and Urban Well-Being

Section 5.1 showed that both perceived urban risks and actual experiences were primarily centred around the economic and social dimensions. There was a common tendency for 'financial' issues to be the primary worry for all groups, followed by 'work' related issues for the most of the groups. However, 'financial' issues were not the biggest challenge Tokyo middle class faced in the past, and 'work' related issues, which were another economic risk, were not necessarily the first concern for the respondents in ongoing difficulties they are facing; rather, 'health' and 'family' issues mattered more for some groups. In this section, we will focus particularly on the economic and social risks and difficulties that people face in urban life, by using the outcomes of both questionnaires and the focus group interviews. The latter will help us to gain an understanding of the actual contexts of daily events, people's social conditions, and their perceptions.

5.2.1 Understanding Economic and Social Risks and Difficulties

Figure 5.3 shows the original answers to the question of present 'perceived' urban risks (aggregating the first to third choices with weights) of the six groups. Regarding economic risks, first, fundamental economic issues such as 'high living cost' received high points in all groups. 'Housing' also seemed to be an issue for Shanghai's middle class as well as for both classes in Tokyo. Considering work-related issues, 'lack of job' is the fear of losing one's job or not being able to find a job and is therefore necessary for providing fundamental basic needs to sustain urban life while 'stressful job' has a more qualitative dimension. Tokyo's lower and Bangkok's middle classes showed not only stress on work but also relatively high concern for 'lack of job'.

Unsurprisingly, the concern about economic risks, especially financial issues, tended to be correlated with one another across respondents. A large number of people who chose one of the financial risks for their first choice, then chose another financial risk for their second choice as well.[4] For those with economic constraints, the risks were linked because of, for example, inflation inducing high

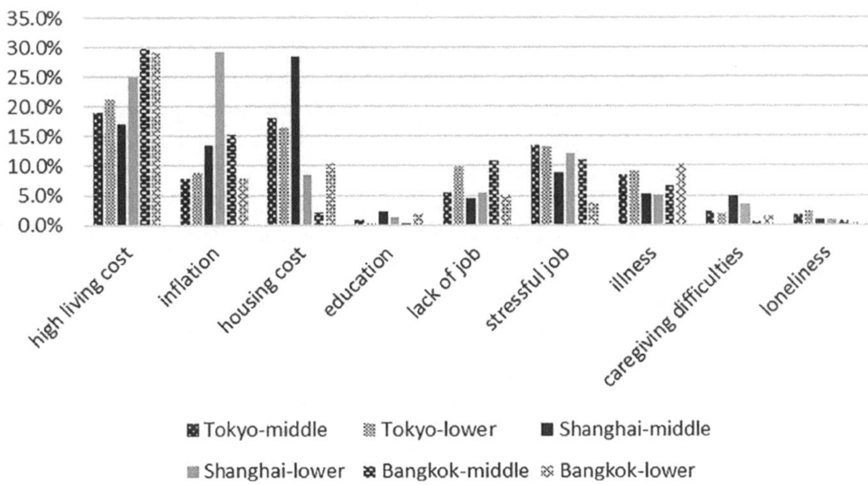

Figure 5.3 Perceived urban risks: economic and social risks.
Source: Made by author.

living costs and their economic difficulties, and the lack of their own sufficient economic resources and the provision of affordable housing in the housing market meaning that housing cost would be a burden as well.

Undoubtedly, job opportunities and conditions do matter for earning level. The average income of those who chose 'lack of job' as their first choice was lower than average. The average monthly income in US dollars for those who answered 'lack of job' as their most concerning urban risk was as follows (shown in comparison to the average income of all respondents in that group): Tokyo middle (3,656 versus 4,027 USD) and lower class (1,919 versus 1,945 USD), Shanghai middle (904 versus 1,156 USD) and lower class (331 versus 345 USD), and Bangkok middle (760 versus 837 USD) and lower class (344 versus 472 USD).

Returning to Figure 5.3, among social risks, unsurprisingly 'illness' (health issue) was the biggest concern for all groups. For other aspects, it is interesting to see that Shanghai's classes showed relatively higher concern for 'caregiving difficulties' (family issues) and both of Tokyo's classes gave higher points for 'loneliness' (future anxiety and isolation). The question arises as to why people feel loneliness in a developed city such as Tokyo, where socioeconomic well-being is believed to be better. It is unclear whether this was because family and social networks are weakened along with development and modernization, or that economic prosperity does not correlate as much with happiness as generally expected. For reference, about 10% of Tokyo and Shanghai's middle classes also chose 'future anxiety and isolation' as ongoing problems in recent life (10.8% and 9.9%, respectively) while for Bangkok's middle class, this was just 4.5%. For the lower classes, the percentages who saw this as a problem were lower: Shanghai (3.3%), Tokyo (3.2%), and Bangkok (1.5%) (see Figure 5.2a and Appendix Table 1b).

5.2.2 Different Contexts between Middle and Lower Classes: Case of Shanghai

Despite common tendencies and differences among the six groups in their priorities and actual experiences explained in previous sections, the quantitative data has limitations for understanding different contexts. For example, the lower and middle classes might have different socioeconomic conditions, needs, and aspirations for urban life. By analysing focus group interviews, Shibuya (2016) identified differences between the middle and lower classes from their testimonies and pointed out that the lower classes are seeking to satisfy their material needs while the middle classes tended to give positive evaluations of their moderate lives. Still, the middle classes are also concerned about several socioeconomic aspects preventing them from fully enjoying their urban lifestyles. Here, we would like to use qualitative research, namely the same focus group interviews that Shibuya (2016) used, for a further understanding of different contexts by social class. The interviews took place in January 2014 for samples from the lower and middle classes.[5]

A total of six people joined the lower-class group interview, who were all migrants with rural household registration and mainly service workers (e.g., cleaners, cashiers, and deliverymen/women). Their monthly income was lower than 3,000 Chinese Yuan. The moderator asked 'what is a happy life in Shanghai?' and many mentioned material needs. For example, responses included housing and income.

A: By working hard, I can move to a bigger house.
B: I want to earn a little more. I cannot buy anything in Shanghai. I need clothes, I also want to buy a house but it is impossible.
MODERATOR: What would make your life in Shanghai better?
C: We need to earn more.
D: If we earn more, our quality of life will be better.
B: Yes, if we earn more, at least our physical conditions will be better.

Many explained that things were expensive in Shanghai and that they required 'money' to improve their lives. For example, C said 'We don't need to "work" in our hometown. We have our own house and land, and we can grow vegetables there. We don't need to spend much money. But in Shanghai, we need money to rent a room'. D continued 'Yes, if we don't work a day, we don't have enough money to survive'. He said that everything is expensive in Shanghai including vegetables and most of his income disappears on daily food. F agrees too, 'I sometimes work 10 to 16 hours if I find a secondary part-time job. In my local province, I don't use money if I don't go out. I work and eat at home. In Shanghai, I feel pressure because if I don't work, I cannot do anything. Fuel and light expenses are expensive too'.

'Housing' access for migrants in the lower classes was limited as well. E bought a house in a local province where his parents and daughter live together. However, he lives in a small room of 7 m^2 (*qunzu*, divided sharing rooms) for 500 yuan a month. C explained that 'rent goes up every year. Every time I move, rent goes up. Landlords do not give long-term contracts' and then F described how it works: 'My contract is one year. I asked for a longer contract, but the landlord rejected it because he cannot increase the rent. If the landlord gives a two-year contract to us, it means he loses the chance to increase the rent'. C complained that his contract is monthly, and the rent goes up often. E says not only rent, but also electricity and water bills go up often. His wife who is also in Shanghai and living separately in a factory dormitory where she works as a cleaner, has to pay these bills and complains about increases.

In contrast, all six people in the middle-class group owned a house. Some worked in companies and others were teachers, earning between 5,000 and 15,000 yuan a month, and two of them had children who were university students abroad (Germany and Japan). They all have urban household registration of Shanghai. Some said that they were happy with their current lives in Shanghai, but others said they were not satisfied yet. Some even enjoyed traveling abroad regularly.

Discussion of 'high living cost' and 'housing' also appeared in the middle-class testimonies but in different contexts. When the moderator asked 'what is the biggest worry in life in Shanghai? What are the risks in Shanghai life?', some answered as follows: 'pollution and health' (G), 'balance between prices of goods and income' (H), and 'real estate is extremely expensive', if compared it with developed countries (I). Another said that major issues are 'housing, education, and medical services' (J). The moderator asked why 'housing' matters because everyone has their own housing. He answered, 'for the typical middle class in Shanghai, we need two houses, one in the centre and another in the suburbs. Without enough economic capacity, we cannot even get married in Shanghai. Real estate in Hong Kong and other countries is much cheaper and that is why some people start buying real estate abroad'. G and H also agreed that they needed to get another house for their children.

Regarding living costs, the middle class shared their observations of inflation and increases in the prices of goods. He explained that prices tripled in the last 15 years, comparing when she started her first job and recently. The cause of these difficulties was not survival needs but rather that her expenses increased over time after she get married and had a child. 'It is not the same as in our childhood. Children now get attention from not only their parents but from both sets of grandparents. We need to pay for schools and also for extra tuition fees for private lessons and so on'. K and I also felt that prices went up and that they needed to adjust their expenses, mainly by reducing paying for their luxury needs.

These interviews with the middle and lower classes clearly showed that there were differences in meaning and context even if they chose common economic aspects of urban risks. The middle class was concerned about quality of life, whereas the lower class's concerns were more related to basic needs. The concerns regarding 'health' clearly show these differences as well. The middle class considered the quality of health services and wider aspects of health such as the impact of air pollution and food quality for their healthier and better lives, whereas the lower class's concerns were more related to basic health services, which stemmed from their poor health insurance condition (Shibuya 2016). D (lower-class group) said 'the biggest concern in Shanghai is that we need money when we get ill. If we just get a fever, we need to pay 300 yuan and then if there are any medical tests, we have to pay an additional 1,000 yuan or more'. Most of them had limited access to medical insurance because their household registration was not in Shanghai and because paying hospitals was unaffordable, and so they bought medicine at drug stores if their illness was not severe. However, J (middle-class group) complained about the quality of medical services. PM2.5 and other pollution are damaging to personal health, and he described how medical services were insufficient, with long waiting hours at hospitals and that social security coverage was not satisfying his needs. Others also complained that social security systems in China are not well developed enough which caused anxiety about the future.

The qualitative analysis gives us actual features of class disparities in the regional context. Even priority in the risk sphere is commonly shared among classes, their expectations and needs might not be the same. Because of socioeconomic disparities, the lower classes are potentially facing more fundamental risks while the middle classes are more concerned about quality of life and services. However, both the lower and middle classes are not homogenous and it is important to pay attention to both contexts and their socioeconomic conditions for further analysis on actual risk responses and survival strategies in detail.

5.2.3 Vicious Cycle and Interconnected Difficulties

As uncertainty increases, one is also continuously required to deal with various risks and difficulties in urban life. As mentioned earlier, for those concerned with economic risks and difficulties, the financial dimension was also connected as a source of worry. In actual problems and difficulties, problems in one sphere caused other difficulties in another sphere, especially between economic and social risks/difficulties, and sometimes, this leads to a vicious cycle. We can obtain some insight by carefully looking at ongoing problems and the most severe past problems in the detailed original answers.

For many in the lower class, their difficulties were attached to basic needs. For example, the main answers of Bangkok's lower class regarding ongoing problems were 'insufficient income', 'debt', and 'health' problems. Some mentioned 'lack of social security' as well. Often, the lower classes gave clear reasons for their needs. For example, respondents said they have 'insufficient income to take care of all family members', their 'income is not enough to pay all expenses', their 'income is not enough to pay education fees for children, so I had to borrow money', and they have 'no money to pay for medical treatment for ill family'.

These difficulties are not necessarily limited to 'urban' life but apply to life in general. However, some say it is tough to be 'poor' in the city as we have seen in the testimonies from Shanghai. Tokyo's respondents also gave informative explanations in their free columns, which help us to understand their situation and background. The characteristics of Tokyo's lower class which we can read from their original testimonies are as follows: first, for 'work-related' difficulties, the majority actually have experienced serious problems such as 'bankruptcy of their own company' and being 'laid off', some due to the financial crisis in 2008 and others due to the economic downturn. To avoid being laid off, several respondents also accepted salary cuts or decreased their working hours. Second, for those with difficulties in 'financial' issues, some were struggling for survival. Some said 'I don't have enough to pay my daily expenses', 'I'm already on the edge. If consumption tax goes up, I cannot afford my daily needs', 'I used up all my saving and there is no one to rely on. I am struggling to survive', 'After I lost my work, I cannot pay health security and other tax. There is no money to pay anything'. These answers are similar to those of Shanghai's lower class given in the focus group interview. Third, with all of this distress, for those who have 'health' problems, these are not only caused by general illness and accidents but some referred to having mental illness. Of those who answered that they have a health problem or illness, 13 people gave detailed information, specifying that they actually have depression or a panic syndrome.

Regarding Tokyo's middle class, first, some people also had experienced layoffs in the middle class but were less in number than lower class group. However, all of them managed to find new jobs and when our questionnaire survey took place, they were earning enough income to be in the middle class. They tended to shift jobs quicker but there were a few cases in the lower class who took a few years to find new jobs. In the case of Bangkok's lower class, those who were laid off from their employment, either temporarily or permanently, shifted to self-employment in order to earn sufficiently to survive. This type of flexibility was not found among the Tokyo respondents. Second, there were no cases of having difficulties in 'financial' issues for survival in Tokyo's middle class, but some felt that their income was not sufficient for education fees and securing life after retirement. Third, 'health' issues were mainly related to either their own or a family member's illness, including severe cases where they had to be hospitalized for a while, but either they had recovered or have been receiving enough medical treatment to continue daily life. We found a few cases in Tokyo's middle class who were struggling with mental health but they were much fewer in number compared to among the lower class. We did not find any answers in the free response columns for Shanghai and Bangkok who specified depression or mental health problems as among their biggest ongoing difficulties.

The striking answers given by Tokyo's lower class suggest that it is important to think about why 'being poor' in Tokyo causes such high mental pressure. Partly, respondents gave some reasons for this pressure. As already introduced, one said 'I used up all my saving and there is no one to rely on. I am struggling to survive'. Tenuous social relationships can also be one reason (for details, see Chapter 6). Others grievously write, 'There is no job. my life is distressed, and I am on the edge. Thinking about how to survive, I cannot sleep well because of anxiety and sometimes, I think about suicide'. 'I had health problems and found it difficult to continue to work in Tokyo. But when I decided to go back to my hometown in Fukushima, there was the Great East Japan Earthquake, and I lost my chance to go back'.

Original answers before coding of Tokyo's lower class in the free response column provide two important implications for when we think about urban risks, shocks, and resilience. First, various spheres are interconnected and when your resources and capability are limited; in other words, in those with vulnerable socioeconomic conditions, one difficulty easily triggers a chain reaction. Illness can easily threaten employment and cause economic hardship. There is pressure in that the situation also does not allow them to be seriously ill because they cannot afford it. In theory, all Japanese people are covered by social security systems, but there are also several cases where people do not have access to benefits and support (see Chapter 7).

Second, many people do not have means and channels available to get themselves out of such vicious cycle. One said that 'I have to take care of my old mother by myself, and it was difficult to continue my own work. I cannot find a better job as well as I cannot pay back my loan for my condominium. I sold my condo but still debt was left. I was trying to work harder to pay back the debt but damaged my back and now it makes it difficult for me to look after my mother while continuing to work with my health situation'. We cannot say that this is a rare case only for an unlucky person. Other people also say that 'Just at the same time that I was laid off, I found out about my serious illness too', 'when I lost my job, my mother had a cancer operation and also a stroke. She was hospitalised for five months. I needed to take care of her, but I didn't have an income source'.

The vicious cycle cases suggest that it is important to think about not only which risks are potentially crucial in one's urban life, but also how different risks and shocks can be interconnected and can strengthen each other. For those who have limited resources and social networks to rely on, including public support and support from informal institutions, difficulties might persist. It is not only a matter of a chain reaction. Often a macro crisis induces another crisis. For example, the pandemic is not only a health crisis but it has triggered an economic crisis as well. It is partly an urban crisis because it affects cities more severely. When multiple crises happen at once, or repeatedly, vulnerable groups are more sensitive to damage and their resilience is disturbed (see footnote 1). Their weak socioeconomic condition is often an outcome of a continuous process of dealing with past difficulties and the loss they have experienced with damage accumulating for individuals and households. Thus, their perception of urban risks and life difficulties might have a path dependency, differentiating between perception and subjective well-being for present and potential future urban risks.

5.3 Risk Perception and Life Satisfaction

5.3.1 Past Experiences, Perception, and Life Satisfaction

As we have seen in Chapter 3 (Figure 3.1, p. 48), a striking characteristic is that almost 30% of Tokyo's lower class rated their life satisfaction as very low (1–3). Tokyo middle class had the second highest ratio as 13% and Shanghai lower was third but it was only 8%. For the other three groups, only a few chose the low level, 1–3 (Shanghai's lower class and both classes in Bangkok). In this section, we will consider whether experienced/perceived urban risks and shocks influence life satisfaction or not.

Chapter 3 (Table 3.6, p. 50) explained that both Tokyo and Shanghai's middle and lower classes showed correlations between life or work problems and life satisfaction, but for Bangkok, the middle class's satisfaction was correlated with ongoing life problems (but not work problems) and there were no correlations for the lower class. Table 5.3 shows life satisfaction level (high and low groups) and the ratio of unsolved/solved and have/have-not of related questions. Less satisfied groups also tended to have ongoing life problems and job-related problems. For example, regardless of city and class, when considering those who report the highest life satisfaction (scoring between 8 and 10), the share with job problems ranged from 19.1% (Tokyo lower class) to 48.4% (Bangkok lower class), indicating that most of these high satisfaction respondents did not have job problems. The same trend was observed for ongoing life problems. Among the highest life satisfaction respondents, those who answered that they had ongoing problems ranged from 16.4% (Shanghai middle class) to 38.9% (Bangkok middle class), which were actually lower rates than for the lower life satisfaction respondents in same city class groupings.

However, if we look at the lowest life satisfied respondents (scoring 1–3), the expected opposite trend is observed. Of these, 69.2% (Shanghai middle class) to 80.0% (Shanghai lower class) reported job problems, and those with ongoing life problems occupied 69.2% (Shanghai middle class) to 93.8% (Shanghai lower class) (Bangkok's case for the low score group was actually too small for analysis).[6]

Looking in a little more detail, we see that lowest life satisfaction respondents (1–3) tend to have more economic difficulties than the highest life satisfaction respondents (8–10) across all six groups. Based on our data, the nature of ongoing life problems shows clear patterns. A total of 67.6% of the middle class in Tokyo with low life satisfaction face 'economic' difficulties, whereas only 18.8% answered as such among those reporting high life satisfaction. Shanghai demonstrates a similar trend across highest and lowest satisfaction respondents, with 55.6% and 45.0% for the middle class and 83.3% and 56.0% for the lower class, respectively. However, we should be careful before concluding that this indicates a simple connection that economic condition defines the level of subjective well-being. Past experiences and their channels for solving problems also have an impact on this.

Regarding past experiences, more people among the respondents that scored highest life satisfaction, 8–10, succeeded in solving the biggest problems they faced in the past 10 years. For example, 73.7% of the middle class and 80.8% of the lower class in Tokyo could solve their past problems for the most satisfied group, but for those reporting the lowest satisfaction (score 1–3) only 36.9% and 39.2%, middle class and lower class, respectively, reported solving the biggest past problem. Shanghai had the same trend with 86.7% and 57.7%, middle

Table 5.3 Life satisfaction and past/recent well-being (unit: %)

	Job problem (ongoing)		*Life problem (ongoing)*		*Past problem (solved)*		*Dream (Have)*	
	Life S 8–10	*Life S 1–3*	*Life S 8–10*	*Life S 1–3*	*Life S 8–10*	*Life S 1–3*	*Life S 8–10*	*Life S 1–3*
Tokyo-middle	20.2	71.4	23.2	76.3	73.7	36.9	66.7	68.8
Tokyo-lower	19.1	72.2	24.0	87.4	80.8	39.2	62.7	70.9
Shanghai-middle	17.2	69.2	16.4	69.2	86.7	12.5	35.2	61.5
Shanghai-lower	25.9	80.0	29.1	93.8	57.7	12.5	53.5	71.9
Bangkok-middle	41.8	(80.0)	38.9	(100.0)	87.8	(100.0)	44.9	(80.0)
Bangkok-lower	48.4	(71.4)	31.0	(87.5)	96.2	(33.3)	69.6	(37.5)
Total	32.5	72.7	28.5	84.4	82.7	35.7	55.1	69.4

Source: Made by author.

Note: For 'Past problem (Solved)' is the ratio of those who could solve problem, among who had problem before. For 'Bangkok lower' class, sample of low score group (life satisfaction 1–3) is too small for analysis. There are only five persons for middle class and nine persons for lower class. Life S=Life satisfaction class and lower class respectively, for the highest satisfaction respondents and 12.5% for both classes of the lowest satisfaction respondents. It is interesting to note that most of Tokyo's satisfied groups showed a different trend from ongoing problems. Their past problems were more related to difficulties in the social sphere (54.5% for the middle class and 57.7% for the lower class) rather than difficulties in the economic sphere (35.4% and 34.6%, respectively). However, for Shanghai's groups, ongoing problems and past difficulties showed the same pattern, with economic difficulties showed a higher ratio in past problems (70.0% for the middle class and 75.6% for the lower class), while social difficulties were 23.3% and 19.2%, respectively (again, Bangkok's sample was too small to analyse).

5.3.2 Perception of Future Urban Risks

Table 5.4 shows perceived 'future' urban risks. We separated present and future questions because whatever difficulties they might face in their current lives, people often have both short-term and long-term life plans based on their expectations, needs, dreams, fears, and more. Sometimes their long-term target defines what they feel to be obstacles and constraints in the short-term. In their longer vision of urban life, their priority is therefore not necessarily the same as their short-term goals. Some people, indeed, have chosen different issues between present and future risks that become their priority concerns.

Tokyo's middle class was the most stable in terms of economic well-being in their current real-life situation. The top five perceived urban risks for the future (Table 5.4, also see Appendix Table 1d) also support this understanding, as there was a relatively lower rate of concern for 'financial' for the future. It is not surprising that the lower classes in Shanghai and Bangkok were concerned about

Table 5.4 Perceived future urban risks (% of first choice)

Group	*Most chosen five future urban risks (%)*				
Tokyo-middle	Work (26.8)	Financial (24.7)	Health (18.5)	Nature (14.3)	Community (4.3)
Tokyo-lower	Work (34.6)	Financial (24.4)	Health (17.9)	Nature (11.6)	Family (3.0)
Shanghai-middle	Financial (48.3)	Work (23.3)	Health (9.0)	Environment (7.0)	Family (5.0)
Shanghai-lower	Financial (56.0)	Work (25.5)	Health (6.3)	Family (5.8)	Environment (3.0)
Bangkok-middle	Financial (47.4)	Work (22.6)	Health (13.1)	Community (7.1)	Environment (4.4)
Bangkok-lower	Financial (57.1)	Health (9.4)	Nature (8.0)	Work (6.3)	Community (5.7)
Total	Financial (39.5)	Work (24.8)	Health (13.6)	Nature (7.2)	Community (3.9)

Source: Made by author.

'financial' and economic issues. Adding to that, for these two cities, middle classes also concern more on 'financial' issues for future as well. Then, after economic issues including 'work-related' issues, personal social issues were their priority as 'health' came in second and third. Considering that the most common dream of both classes in Tokyo was related to 'work' and for Shanghai, 'buying houses' (see Chapter 3, Section 3.2.5), their future risk perceptions seemed to be a reflection of their future dreams. The most common answer given by Bangkok's middle class was 'starting a business' and for the lower class, 'buying a house'. The dreams of both classes in Shanghai and Bangkok were related to 'financial' issues (economic sphere) in our risk categorisation.

Another interesting trend is that the third or fourth priorities, after economic and social issues, were unique to each city, and are attributed to urban conditions and local contexts: the fear of natural disasters (e.g., earthquakes) increased concerns about natural risks in Tokyo, which is consistent with the results of Arita's research. Concern for air pollution raised interests in environmental risks in Shanghai and a certain of Bangkok's residents; and changes in 'community' was a concern for Bangkok's residents (also see Appendix Table 1d). Regarding the case of Bangkok, especially for the lower class, urban communities function as a source of a safety net (Endo 2014) but at the same time, relocation is activated in the city nowadays. It will be interesting to analyse whether this choice is a response to current societal changes or not, but further research is needed.

Conclusion

With rapid and compressed urban change, residents face complex situations of potential urban risks and difficulties. High concern regarding economic risks, whether it be financial issues or work-related issues, indicates that economic conditions of urban life are part of fundamental basic needs and are seen as a crucial measure to fulfil people's desire for better well-being. As Moser (1998) defined the characteristics of a city from a risk perspective (also see Chapter 1), people cannot survive without an income source in the city. The testimonies of Shanghai's lower class confirmed that people have to use their own physical 'capital', otherwise they cannot satisfy their basic need to survive. To secure their economic needs, their own 'health' accordingly becomes a priority as well which is different to social classes who face disparities in access to basic medical services.

However, potential risks and experienced difficulties in actual life differ across the different groups. Although Tokyo's middle class tended to show lower life satisfaction compared to their counterparts in Bangkok and Shanghai (see Chapter 3, Section 3.2.5), they still enjoyed the most stable lives, suggested by the fact that their prominent concerns related to better quality of life. Their daily concerns were relatively more focused on social issues, like health and caregiving for their family. It is interesting to see that not only the lower classes but also the middle classes in Shanghai and Bangkok were concerned about financial issues. Whether this is due to the differences in life stability for the newly emerged middle classes in emerging cities and a developed city like Tokyo or for other reasons, such as differences in future ambition and goals to enjoy a better quality of life, we need to look beyond just aggregated quantitative data to also examine the qualitative side of people's perceptions. Another important finding to note is that, despite its economic prosperity as a city, the Tokyo's lower class showed the lowest life satisfaction and serious tensions regarding economic risks and difficulties. In an era of uncertainty and increasing risks, we must carefully look at different groups in the cities and their conditions, rather than taking a hierarchal approach according to the development stage of cities and countries.

The impacts of and sensitivity to actual shocks people encounter, and whether they can respond to risks and shocks well and to the required degree, depends on their socioeconomic condition and societal setting. In the process of responding to risks and shocks, which contribute to forming one's risk perception, individual and household condition, and societal setting interact. This is a complex mechanism because for the individual, the timing of shocks and crises over the course of one's urban life leads to different implications and damage. At the societal level as well, some event can be limited to a small group or a person, but some events amount to a crisis at the societal level. When such a macro crisis happens, wider society is affected and, the more severe it is, the more it might limit the societal responses depending on resources in the society, or in other words, the capability and resilience of the society.

As we have seen in this chapter, the lower classes in all cities were facing more fundamental economic and social difficulties. Even though the lower and middle classes shared overlapping priorities in their risks and concerns, their qualitative expectations were not the same. Adding to that, there were also differences among cities for secondary priorities depending on urban contexts. If damage of risks and shocks accumulate in one's life, vulnerable groups are the ones who suffer more. Whether shocks and crises happen at an individual or societal level, those who might have various measures to tackle them and those who have limited measures, do not share the same outcomes. Tokyo's lower class, who should enjoy a much better social security system compared with the other two cities, actually struggle to survive and express negative evaluations of their own lives. Therefore, conditions to recover from shocks and future risk perceptions are embedded in social contexts in the wider urban context. This suggests that not only formal institutions but also informal institutions matter for the resilience of both individuals and societies.

Appendix 1

Table 1a Present perceived urban risk (first to third choices, weighted)

	1. Financial risk and difficulties	*2. Work-related*	*3. Health issue*	*4. Family issue*	*5. Future anxiety and isolation*	*6. Community risk*	*7. Political risk*	*8. Environmental risk*	*9.Nature risk*	*10. Other*	*Total*
Tokyo-middle	46.0%	18.9%	8.5%	2.3%	1.7%	8.8%	0.5%	6.5%	3.6%	3.3%	100.0%
Tokyo-lower	47.0%	23.0%	9.1%	1.9%	2.3%	6.2%	0.4%	5.2%	2.3%	2.6%	100.0%
Shanghai-middle	61.5%	13.4%	5.3%	4.9%	0.8%	2.0%	1.9%	9.6%	0.2%	0.4%	100.0%
Shanghai-lower	64.0%	17.5%	5.2%	3.5%	0.9%	1.5%	2.5%	4.8%	0.1%	0.1%	100.0%
Bangkok-middle	47.6%	21.9%	6.6%	0.5%	0.6%	7.6%	4.1%	8.4%	2.0%	0.6%	100.0%
Bangkok-lower	49.6%	8.8%	10.2%	1.5%	0.4%	6.7%	1.7%	14.2%	3.4%	3.5%	100.0%
Total	51.5%	18.1%	7.7%	2.3%	1.3%	5.8%	1.6%	7.6%	2.1%	2.0%	100.0%

Source: Made by author.

Table 1b Life problem (ongoing)

	1. Financial risk and difficulties	*2. Work-related*	*3. Health issue*	*4. Family issue*	*5. Future anxiety and isolation*	*6. Community risk*	*7. Political risk*	*8. Environmental risk*	*9.Nature risk*	*10. Other*	*Total*
Tokyo-middle	43.7%	4.5%	13.4%	18.7%	10.8%	1.1%	0.0%	2.2%	0.0%	5.6%	100.0%
Tokyo-lower	63.3%	7.3%	11.9%	6.5%	3.2%	1.1%	0.0%	1.6%	0.0%	5.1%	100.0%
Shanghai-middle	44.4%	2.5%	2.5%	23.5%	9.9%	3.7%	0.0%	7.4%	0.0%	6.2%	100.0%
Shanghai-lower	64.7%	12.0%	2.5%	13.7%	3.3%	0.0%	0.0%	0.4%	0.0%	3.3%	100.0%
Bangkok-middle	60.2%	9.0%	5.4%	10.4%	4.5%	2.3%	0.0%	0.0%	6.8%	1.4%	100.0%
Bangkok-lower	54.5%	7.6%	18.9%	11.4%	1.5%	0.0%	0.0%	1.5%	0.0%	4.5%	100.0%
Total	57.0%	7.6%	10.4%	13.4%	5.3%	1.1%	0.0%	1.6%	1.1%	4.3%	100.0%

Source: Made by author.

Table 1c The biggest problem in the past ten years

	1. Financial risk and difficulties	*2. Work-related*	*3. Health issue*	*4. Family issue*	*5. Future anxiety and isolation*	*6. Community risk*	*7. Political risk*	*8. Environmental risk*	*9.Nature risk*	*10. Fire*	*11. Other*
Tokyo-middle	20.4%	26.2%	14.9%	28.6%	0.8%	2.5%		0.8%	1.4%	0.4%	3.9%
Tokyo-lower	31.4%	21.9%	14.4%	20.4%	1.0%	1.4%		1.0%	0.0%	0.0%	8.5%
Shanghai-middle	48.4%	24.7%	4.3%	18.3%	0.0%	0.0%		1.1%	0.0%	0.0%	3.2%
Shanghai-lower	48.7%	27.6%	2.1%	13.2%	2.4%	0.0%		0.0%	0.0%	0.0%	6.1%
Bangkok-middle	40.2%	26.9%	3.7%	14.4%	2.2%	0.0%		0.0%	12.0%	0.3%	0.3%
Bangkok-lower	15.3%	3.4%	1.9%	12.3%	0.0%	1.1%		0.0%	0.0%	61.9%	4.1%
Bangkok-lower*	40.2%	8.8%	4.9%	32.4%	0.0%	2.9%		0.0%	0.0%	-	10.8%
Total	32.0%	22.5%	9.0%	19.5%	1.2%	1.1%		0.5%	2.2%	8.3%	4.9%

Source: Made by author.
Note: The figure of 'Bangkok-lower' is adjusted by excluding bias of fire case.

Table 1d Perceived future urban risks (first to third choices, weighted)

	1. Financial risk and difficulties	*2. Work-related*	*3. Health issue*	*4. Family issue*	*5. Future anxiety and isolation*	*6. Community risk*	*7. Political risk*	*8. Environmental risk*	*9.Nature risk*	*10. Other*	*Total*
Tokyo-middle	27.3%	21.1%	16.6%	5.6%	4.3%	7.6%	1.0%	2.6%	12.0%	2.1%	100.0%
Tokyo-lower	29.5%	25.3%	17.0%	3.8%	3.9%	6.2%	0.4%	2.2%	10.0%	1.6%	100.0%
Shanghai-middle	50.6%	18.4%	8.8%	4.8%	1.2%	4.7%	2.5%	8.4%	0.3%	0.2%	100.0%
Shanghai-lower	55.2%	18.6%	7.8%	7.0%	1.6%	1.3%	2.6%	5.4%	0.1%	0.3%	100.0%
Bangkok-middle	41.9%	19.4%	9.9%	0.4%	0.9%	11.3%	4.0%	8.7%	2.8%	0.6%	100.0%
Bangkok-lower	48.9%	5.8%	9.6%	2.0%	0.9%	9.1%	1.6%	10.2%	8.6%	3.5%	100.0%
Total	40.0%	19.0%	12.4%	4.0%	2.4%	6.7%	1.9%	5.6%	6.5%	1.4%	100.0%

Source: Made by author.

Box 2a Security or independence: risk preference and occupational choices in three cities

Tamaki Endo

If the income were the same, which of these occupations would you choose?

A. Being an employee, which is secured/stable but do not have independence.
B. Being self-employed which you have to take risk by yourself but more independent.

What is your answer to this question? What kind of factors would you consider while making your decision?

We asked this question in three cities to find that the responses largely differed across these cities (Table BOX2-1). Across social classes, nearly 70% of Tokyo residents preferred A, to be secure, and result was opposite among Bangkok residents where more than 70% preferred B, to be independent. Shanghai residents showed similar responses to those of the Tokyo residents; in particular, its lower-class respondents preferred employment security (nearly 10 points higher than the middle class). Based on fieldwork conducted with Bangkok slum residents by author in the early 2000s, the difference between the Bangkok and Tokyo response to this question was not surprising. The Bangkok residents gave positive evaluation to be self-employed. The Shanghai results were somewhat surprising given vigorous entrepreneurial activity in China and the generally positive view of it; we were expecting to see results more similar to those of Bangkok. The Global Entrepreneurship Monitor of 2018/2019 (Bosma and Kelley 2018), which surveyed 48 economies, showed that Japan had very low entrepreneurial intention (ranked 46th), while Thailand was ranked 12th, and China was ranked 28th.

In terms of the form of employment and, from a risk response perspective, the existence/non-existence of social security support systems, employees and self-employed workers displayed fundamentally different characteristics (Endo 2014, 113). First, self-employed workers' work and income tend to be, by its very nature, less stable compared to those of employed workers such that the workers must themselves take responsibility for any investments and challenges. Employed workers, on the other hand, have a fixed income as long their employment continues. Second, the fundamental source of the risks they face is different. Employed workers face the possibility of layoffs or closure of workplace, while self-employed workers face business instability. Employed workers are usually covered by social

Table BOX2-1 Risk value in occupational choice. Unit: %

	Risk value	
	Security	*Independent*
Tokyo-middle	69.7	30.3
Tokyo-lower	68.1	31.9
Shanghai-middle	66.7	33.3
Shanghai-lower	78.8	21.3
Bangkok-middle	21.8	78.2
Bangkok-lower	26.7	73.3
Total	57.6	42.4

Source: Made by author.

security for as long as their contract lasts; however, in many middle-income countries, there is no mandated social security system for self-employed workers. Japan has a formal and designed social security scheme for covering self-employed workers, whereas Thailand and China are still limited in what provision can be offered by such systems. In these two countries, the extension of social security and safety net schemes to self-employed workers, who are usually regarded as 'informal economy workers', has been a policy priority for the past 10 years. In contrast, in all three countries, employed workers can access a social security system that is more established and legally covers most employees (although part-time workers have some disadvantages in this regard). Third, the values and occupational aspirations that people identify in these two employment forms are different. For example, self-employed workers in Bangkok valued their independence highly. A comparison of the occupational values of employed and self-employed workers would be paired as 'stable' and 'unstable', respectively. However, my previous study showed that the self-employed workers in Bangkok did not necessary consider being 'self-employed' as a negative choice. Instead, they valued 'independence' more greatly in occupations involving self-employment (Endo 2014). They also felt that the flexibility provided allowed them to find different income sources more easily (the work entry barrier was lower even if a worker had not attended university).

The interviews I have conducted in slum communities in early 2000s revealed a variety of diverse individual perceptions of 'independence'. For example, within my research site, one bike taxi driver explained independence as follows: 'being able to rest when tired, eat when hungry, and not to be given orders'. In short, they emphasised the possession of a large amount of autonomy, the right to self-discretion regarding one's time and actions, and (considering the lack of any superior whom one must answer to) the right to self-determination (Endo 2014, 259). Many workers I interviewed (including hairdressers, car repair mechanics, and carpenters, among others) valued having an occupation that did not have a supervisor and provided a strong right to self-determination.

Usually, economists examine attitudes toward risk aversion when trying to understand different levels of entrepreneurship intention and occupational choice (Tachibanaki 2001). Self-employed workers tend to have a higher dispersion of income level despite their occupational instability. Economists understand a positive intention toward entrepreneurship as a characteristics of risk takers who prefer to take risks and challenges that have 'high risk high return' results.

However, it should be noted that occupational preferences and prioritisation of stability and independence (or instability/flexibility) are not necessarily fixed priorities and that they may sometimes change. For example, self-employed workers in Bangkok and Shanghai, who were satisfied with the potential of their own work, sometimes still expected their children to take up other different types of work (e.g., banking and other types of employed work); thus, such priorities may shift even for one person. Furthermore, when labour market structures change, choices and evaluations related to employment forms could also change. People's occupational preferences reflect the labour market barriers and constraints they face and potential paths for success. Labour market structural conditions can thus be reflected in their priorities and influence what factors they consider in their occupational choices. We could not enquire about the detailed reasons underlying their occupational preferences in our questionnaire survey. Follow-up research could explore whether high stability-oriented intentions among Shanghai lower-class workers are a reflection of their constraints with regard to occupational choices and access to social security systems in urban areas; this is because some respondents had rural household registrations.

These examples show that the surrounding external environment (and its changes) can significantly influence one's occupational preference formation. In current Japan, the lack of a safety net for cushioning business investment loss or failure could be another factor for this occupational preference. In Bangkok's case, self-employed workers can build a path to upward mobility—even if this is only limited to those who have successfully overcome all risks and challenges (Endo 2014). For those who want to become well-paid white-collar employees, the education barrier is high. Self-employment, therefore, is a realistic option for many, and it provides greater business and income expansion possibilities, depending on their resources (e.g., skills, investment funding, information, networks, and so on). As self-employment jobs are diverse, the productivity levels of some self-employment jobs may be low; this is why some self-employed workers tend to consider these jobs as subsistence types. However, some self-employed businesses may encourage 'entrepreneurship' and be characterised by high productivity. Understanding these differences in occupational characteristics and people's preferences, value tendencies, and labour market conditions is crucial in the designing labour market and social security policies. Emerging countries may witness a slower growth of occupational opportunities for full-time regular employment as they accommodate new youth entries into the labour market; therefore, in such countries, large informal economies may remain in the urban areas.

Compared to the labour market situation in the first half of the 2010s (when we conducted our questionnaire surveys), digitalisation rapidly restructured this market in the later 2010s and 2020s. The gig economy's appearance and rapid expansion is one of the significant changes in this regard; also known as 'digital informality' (Endo 2021), it involves the employment of workers under short-term contracts or freelance contracts and usually involves work assigned with digital platformers. In China, it is estimated that two hundred million workers are now working in the gig economy. In Thailand, a 2017 survey of 9,300 persons conducted by Siam Commercial Bank showed that workers from the middle class also showed a strong interest in working in the gig economy, although it is not a traditional self-employment avenue (e.g., like that of bike taxi drivers) but rather a high-end freelance avenue (from interview on 18 August 2018 at Siam Commercial Bank).

One other consideration with regard to this issue is the introduction of automation in many industries and businesses. The International Labour Organization (ILO) estimates that automation could reduce job opportunities in Southeast Asia—especially manual and clerical positions—in the future (Chang and Huynh 2016). Some people in emerging countries may view the gig economy as a positive choice despite the problems in employment arrangements which must be tackled. The gig economy in developed country is often understood as the outcome of a strategy to cut employee and social security costs (see Box 2b); however, workers in emerging countries do not necessarily see gig economy as deterioration of working conditions. The traditional informal economy in emerging countries is not covered by social security scheme yet and therefore, if income level is high, people will see both options, traditional type and gig economy, as comparative choices.

While macro labour market features continue to change further in a compressed way in Asia, how will this situation change and reorganise people's occupational preferences and the actual features of social mobility? We hope to explore this question further in the future.

References

Bosma, N., and D. Kelley. 2018. *Global Entrepreneurship Monitor 2018/2019 Global Report*, accessed 18 August, 2022, <https://www.gemconsortium.org/report>.

Chang, H., and P. Huynh. 2016. "ASEAN in Transformation: Future of Jobs at Risk of Automation", Working Paper No.9, International Labour Organization (ILO).

Endo, T. 2014. *Living with Risks: Precarity and Bangkok's Urban Poor*, Singapore: NUS Press association with Kyoto University Press.

Endo, T. 2021. 'Tension and Interaction between "Digital Informality" and "Analogue Informality" in Bangkok', LSE Southeast Asia Blog, posted 17 June, 2021, <https://blogs.lse.ac.uk/seac/2021/06/17/tension-and-interaction-between-digital-informality-and-analogue-informality-in-bangkok/>

Tachibanaki, T. 2001. "Self-Employed Workers and Their Risk [Jieigousya to risuku]". In *Raifu saikuru and risuku* [Life Cycle and Risk], edited by T. Tachibanaki. Tokyo: Toyo Keizai shimposha.

Box 2b Security or independence: Historical change in risk preference and occupational choices in Tokyo

Asuka Imaizumi

Historically, in Japan, self-employed workers and their unpaid family workers have formed a high share of the total worker population compared to those in Western countries; it has been argued that this situation is one of the characteristics of Japanese economic development (Tanimoto 1998). In the era of industrialisation (from the late 19th century to the beginning of the 20th century), people primarily preferred and tried to maintain their family unit business, thus, 'being employed by others' was a socially unpreferable status. In a partial reflection of this norm, the occupations in which one was a general employee (e.g., factory work) were considered instable and lacking in security; thus, these workers were often encouraged to quit in favour of returning to the (or starting a new) family unit business (Tanimoto 2002, 2016; Tojo 2005). Daily workers and other workers under precarious conditions (e.g., rickshaw puller) were also distinguished from self-employed workers in family business (Nakagawa 1985). Thus, we must consider social norms as well when analysing preferences with regard to employment form or occupational status. 'Being self-employed', instead of 'being employed' was considered a standard form of employment in modern Japan (Matsuzawa 2022, 151–162). Of course, social norm has receded since the interwar years of the First and Second World Wars, with more stable employment options; however, the socioeconomic status of self-employed workers, regarding both income levels and political power in the local community, maintained its significance. Because of lack of access to higher education and/or the limited number of stable jobs available in large firms, people still sought opportunities to start their own businesses and run them successfully with their own family members (Tamano 1993, 2005; Tanimoto 2005, 2011). In the post-war period, small and medium enterprises (SMEs) and self-employed workers were integrated as supporters of the ruling party in national politics, and they therefore received various subsidies until the 1980s (Miyamoto 2008; Arata 2012). However, since that period, the economic balance between self-employment and employment has been reversed.

Ishii (1996) argues that the succession process in small family-owned shops started to become explicitly difficult in the 1980s; he introduces the words of workers from such businesses in the 1990s: 'I would like to live like a *salary-man* (employed office worker)' (18–19) and 'I would not like to make my daughter marry a shopkeeper' because 'a *salary-man* is more easy-going' (12–13). This change in attitude occurred because of the emergence of a new image of the ideal family (that is, the modern family) and of individual freedoms. People also started to think about the long hours without explicit leisure time of self-employment differently as they compared these working conditions with the *salary-man* or office workers (Ishii 1996, 3–48). In the 1950s, Dore ([1958]2013) asked 42 male employees in Tokyo about their preference for employment status. Among the three options, namely, being 'a wage or salary earner', 'an independent trader', and 'an independent craftsman or service worker', the latter two garnered a total of 71% (30 people) of respondences (202). The Survey of Public Opinion on Urban Life in Tokyo asked a similar question, comparing work in an organisation to that in an independent private business, in 1984, 1996, and 1997; the share who preferred the latter still exceeds that for the former up until the 1990s. The admiration for independence seemed to have survived (Tokyo Metropolitan Government 1985, 68–70, 134; 1997, 126–127; 1998, 108–114). However, when Tokyo Metropolitan Government's another survey on public opinion on labour asked a question, 'Have you ever thought that you would like to start your own business or establish your own company?' in 2001, almost 80% of the respondents answered 'no' (Tokyo Metropolitan Government 2001, 81–83). Thus, Japanese workers' preferences seem to have changed over the past decade, as part of a long run trend.

As Box 2a described, gig economy workers are now increasing in Japan as well. In Japan, where self-employed family businesses once dominated the socioeconomic landscape, the expansion of gig work may not return this landscape to its previous state but rather lead a transformation of Japanese society toward an expansion of individualised and atomised job opportunities. Self-employment in Japan primarily denoted family unit businesses, and self-employed workers showed a higher marital rate mainly because of the necessity of recruiting new family workers to run or continue the businesses (Tanimoto 2002, 2011). However, platform businesses do not usually require their family member co-workers to work alongside gig workers. Employment Status Survey (Statistics Bureau, Ministry of Internal Affairs and Communications 2018, 228–239) indicate that the number of self-employed workers has remained relatively stable over these several decades, whereas the number of unpaid family workers has drastically declined (see also Chapter 2). Self-employment can both invite and avoid family formation based on the form of the relevant self-employment, which may also affect worker's perception of risks in different employment forms.

References

Arata, M. 2012. *Shōtengai wa naze horobirunoka: shakai, seiji, keizaishi kara saguru saisei no michi* [Why a Shopping Street Becomes Extinct: A Way to Reformation Considering from Social, Political, and Economic History]. Tokyo: Kobunsha.

Dore, R.P. (1958) 2013. *City Life in Japan*. Paperback edition. Abingdon: Routledge.

Ishii, J. 1996. *Shōnin kazoku to shijōshakai: mōhitotsu no shōhishakairon* [Shopkeeper Families and Market Society: Another Argument on Consumer Society]. Tokyo: Yuhikaku.

Matsuzawa, Y. 2022. *Nihon kindai shakaishi: shakai shūdan to shijō kara yomitoku* [A Social History of Modern Japan: Social Groups and a Market Economy 1868–1914]. Tokyo: Yuhikaku.

Miyamoto, T. 2008. *Fukushi seiji: Nihon no seikatsu hoshō to demokurashī* [The Politics of Welfare: Democracy, Employment and Welfare in Japan]. Tokyo: Yuhikaku.

Nakagawa K. 1985. *Nihon no toshi kasō* [The Urban Lower Classes in Japan]. Tokyo: Keisoshobo.

Statistics Bureau, Ministry of Internal Affairs and Communications. 2018. *Heisei 29nen shūgyō kōzō kihon chōsa hōkoku todōfuken hen* [2017 Employment Status Survey Results for Prefectures]. Tokyo: Sōmushō Tōkeikyoku.

Tamano, K. 1993. *Kindai Nihon no toshika to chōnaikai no seiritsu* [Modernisation and the Formation of Neighbourhood Associations in Modern Japan]. Tokyo: Kojinsha.

Tamano, K. 2005. *Tokyo no rōkaru komyunitī: aru machi no monogatari 1900–80* [Local Community in Tokyo: A Story of a Town 1900–80]. Tokyo: University of Tokyo Press.

Tanimoto, M. 1998. "Another Industrialization: The Range of the Argument of Indigenous Economic Development [Mōhitotsuno kōgyōka: zairaiteki keizai-hattenron no shatei]." In *Sekai rekishi 22 sangyō to kakushin: shihonshugi no hatten to henyō* [World History 22 Industry and Innovation: The Development and Transformation of Capitalism], edited by K. Kabayama et al., 151–177. Tokyo: Iwanami Shoten.

Tanimoto, M. 2002. 'Urban "Small Businesses" in Modern Japan: Based on "Tokyo Municipal Census" [Kindai Nihon no toshi 'shōkeiei': 'Tokyo-shi shisei chōsa' o sozai toshite]'. In *Toshika to zairai sangyō* [Urbanization and Indigenous Industry], edited by T. Nakamura and N. Fujii, 3–49. Tokyo: Nihon Keizai Hyoronsha.

Tanimoto, M. 2005. 'Urban Small Manufactures in the Inter-War Period Japan: The Case of Tokyo Prefecture [Senkanki Nihon no toshi shōkōgyō: Tokyo-fu no baai]', In *Higashi ajia kindai keizai no keisei to hatten: higashi ajia shihonshugi keiseishi I* [The Formation and Development of Modern Economy in East Asia: History of the Formation of Capitalism in East Asia I], edited by S. Nakamura., 201–224. Tokyo: Nihon Hyoronsha.

Tanimoto, M. 2011. 'Women's Work and Household Economy in Modern Japan [Kindai Nihon no setai keizai to josei rōdō: "shōkeiei ni okeru "jūgyō" to "kaji"]'. *Ohara Shakaimondai Kenkyūjo zasshi* 635/636, 7–25 doi: 10.15002/00008784

Tanimoto, M. 2016. '"Industrial Revolution" and the "Indigenous Economic Development": 1885–1914 ['Sangyō kakumei' to 'zairaiteki keizaihatten' 1885-1914nen]'. In *Nihon keizaishi: Kinsei kara gendai made* [The Economic History of Japan: From the Early Modern Era to the Present], edited by M. Tanimoto, and M. Sawai, 143–245. Tokyo: Yuhikaku.

Tojo, Y. 2005. *Kindai, rōdō, shiminshakai: kindai Nihon no rekishi ninshiki 1* [Modernity, Labour, and Civil Society: The Recognition of History in Modern Japan 1]. Kyoto: Minerva Shobo.

Tokyo Metropolitan Government, ed. 2001. *Rōdō ni kansuru yoron chōsa* [Survey of Public Opinion on Labour]. Tokyo: Tokyo Metropolitan Government.

Tokyo Metropolitan Government, ed. 1985, 1997, and 1998. *Toshi seikatsu ni kansuru yoron chōsa* [Survey of Public Opinion on Urban Life]. Tokyo: Tokyo Metropolitan Government

Notes

1 According to Moser's (1998) theoretical survey, the meaning of 'vulnerability' has expanded to include a range of elements and situations of 'livelihood security', including exposure to risks, hazards, shocks, and stress, difficulty in coping with contingencies, and is linked to net assets. There are two dimensions of vulnerability: its sensitivity and resilience. The former is the magnitude of a system's response to an external event and the latter is related to the ease and rapidity of a system's recovery from stress. Therefore, urban studies define vulnerability as insecurity and sensitivity in the well-being of individuals, households, and communities in the face of a changing environment, and implicitly in this, their responsiveness and resilience to risks that they face during such negative changes (1998, 3).

2 The respondents were between 29 and 49 years old (3,400 people). The respondent rate for the question on crisis was 69.7% (2,370 people).

3 The 6th to 9th were as follows: 6. Other (9.7%), 7. Family relation, family issue (6.6%), 8. Care giving (5.2%), 9. Food, environment (nature), and resource related issues (2.7%). In our survey, 7th and 8th were categorized as 'family issue' in the middle category. By using our category, family issue would be 11.8% in Arita's survey.

4 The ratio was as follows (middle and lower classes): Tokyo (53.8% and 51.7%, respectively), Shanghai (55.5% and 65.1%, respectively), and Bangkok (58.1% and 49.7%, respectively). This equates to around one-third of all respondents for each group: Tokyo (27.2% and 25.9%, respectively), Shanghai (39.1% and 43.8%, respectively), and

Bangkok (29.1% and 29.0%, respectively). The ratios of those who chose financial risks for all of their three choices were as follows: Tokyo (middle class: 13.3%, lower class: 13.6%), Shanghai (middle class: 24.9%, lower class: 18.3%), and Bangkok (middle class: 11.0%, lower class: 12.5%).

5 The focus group technique is a data collection method that uses semi-structured interactive interviews with a small group of individuals that have some common characteristics but are unfamiliar to each other. The group discussion in a close-to natural setting helps to gather the real voices of the group on a particular topic and to understand why they have certain opinions. The participants were recruited through a local firm for the session. After screening for potential participants based on pre-set criteria such as annual income, age, and gender, 12 participants were selected and then divided into two groups based on their income level (middle and lower classes) prior to the focus group session (for detail, see Shibuya 2016).

6 Only five people in the lower class and nine people in the middle class had chosen life satisfaction levels 1–3.

References

Arita, S. 2017. '*What is "Crisis" for People?: Analysis on Free Answers for Panel Survey by Institute of Social Science* [hitobitono kangaeru "kiki" tohananika?: Shaken paneru tyousa jiyuukijyutukaitou no bunseki]', Social Sciences of Crisis Thinking Discussion Paper Series No. 2. Institute of Social Science, University of Tokyo.

Buscher, C., and A. Mascareno. 2012. 'Mechanisms of Systematic Risk Production.' In *Risk Habitat Megacity*, edited by D. Heinrich, et al., 39–63. Berlin: Springer.

Endo, T. 2014. *Living with Risk: Precarity & Bangkok's Urban Poor*. Singapore: NUS Press in association with Kyoto University Press.

Inoguchi, T, ed. 2008. *Human Beliefs and Values in Incredible Asia: South and Central Asia in Focus Country Profiles and Thematic Analyses Based on the AsiaBarometer Survey of 2005*. Tokyo: Akashi Shoten.

Moser, C. 1998. 'The Asset Vulnerability Framework: Reassessing Urban Poverty Reduction Strategies.' *World Development* 26 (1), 1–19. DOI: 10.1016/S0305-750X(97)10015-8

Shibuya, M.K. 2016. 'Definition of Happiness in Shanghai: A Focus Group Study.' *The International Journal of Interdisciplinary Global Studies* 11 (4): 1–11. DOI: 10.18848/2324-755X/CGP/v11i04/1-11

Sonoda, S, ed. 2013. *Risuku no nakano higashi ajia* [Risk in East Asia]. Tokyo: Keiso shobo.

Suehiro, A, ed. 2014. 'Employment and Social Security and New Risk Responses in East Asia [Higashi ajia no koyou-seikatsuhosyo to aratana syakairisukuheno taiou]', ISS Research Series No. 56, Institute of Social Science, University of Tokyo.

World Bank. 2001. *World Development Report 2000/2001: Attacking Poverty*. Washington: World Bank.

6 The Networks of Received and Anticipated Supports as a Risk Response to Urban Life in Asia

Momoyo Shibuya

Introduction

Urban life requires individuals to equip themselves with some measures, often described as some form of 'capital', to survive in an environment full of risks. It has been argued that in an increasingly urbanised and globalised society, individuals are more likely to suffer from diverse risks while remaining 'disembedded' from local communities and workplaces (Beck and Beck-Gernsheim 2002). It is now widely recognised that community formation and revitalisation within cities are by no means exceptional, but it has also become clear that not everyone is equally connected to their local communities. We can all recall, for instance, that in during the most recent coronavirus pandemic, vast number of us self-isolated, lost community activities, and often confronted the situation as individuals. Some survived in isolation, while others found new ways of connecting to the community. It is, therefore, essential to understand an Asian urban space by clarifying whether people living in contemporary Asian cities are in a state where they must deal with risks individually or, in case of the alternative, examine the kinds of relationships they rely on in times of need. It is also vital to understand what kind of people, if any, are experiencing individualisation, becoming disembedded from communities, in the context of urbanisation.

This chapter considers urban residents coping with risks and difficulties by looking at two types of personal support networks: anticipated and received/enacted. Anticipated support networks are those which people believe and expect that they can rely on when in need, and which have been reported as a major influential resource of risk response for individual well-being (e.g., Cohen and Wills 1985; Krause, Liang, and Gu 1998). In contrast, received support networks are those that people really could ask or already have asked for help and utilised when the need arose. For this type of support network, studies have shown mixed results in relation to actual stress reduction, though they are said to play an auxiliary role when individuals face acute difficulties (Barrera 1986). Incidentally, many relationships today exist in virtual spaces and play a major role in the life of some people, but examining these were outside of the scope of this study. This is an area for future research and will be left for another occasion in the future paper.

DOI: 10.4324/9781003328155-6

6.1 Personal Support Networks: Anticipated and Received

To obtain a quantitative understanding of the kinds of relationships developed in Asian cities and how they were formed, a questionnaire survey method was employed. Participants across three cities were asked to list and rank up to three people whom they could most rely on when facing difficulties in urban life.

In all cities, the respondents were more likely to name 'family members' (parents, children, siblings, and other relatives) as the support they would depend on in times of need; among the three people they could list, family members appeared most often for respondents from Shanghai at 1.6 people per respondent, and lower in both Tokyo and Bangkok at 0.9 family members listed. Family members were dominant at almost double the rate of other personal and social relationships, such as colleagues, friends from school, or social clubs (0.6 in Shanghai, 0.5 in Tokyo, 0.4 in Bangkok, respectively). As for public services listed, such as government and non-governmental organisations available for risk response, the data showed that despite the varied social conditions, the degree of perceived availability and reliability of such public services were similar across the three cities (0.6 in Shanghai and 0.5 in each of Tokyo and Bangkok).

Considering the data for Tokyo and Bangkok, the average number of people that the respondents listed as 'counted on in times of need' in the categories of 'family members', 'social relationships', and 'public services' showed a similar trend, although minor differences were observed. For instance, within the 'family members' category, Tokyo and Bangkok showed opposing trends, with respondents in Tokyo relying more on their parents and siblings, and those in Bangkok, on their spouses, children, and relatives. This is at least partly attributable to the proportion of unmarried persons being higher among respondents from Tokyo than Bangkok. In fact, the data for married people in Tokyo showed a high level of dependence on their spouses. Yet, the same distancing tendency towards children and relatives was also observed among married respondents in Tokyo. Differences were also found in perceptions of neighbours, alumni friends, or other friends within the 'social relationship/community' category. Respondents in Bangkok anticipated that they could rely on their neighbours, whereas those in Tokyo considered their alumni and other friends as available to provide support. These data suggest that the definition of family members and the development of social relationships could differ between the two cities.

Shanghai had a significantly higher proportion of respondents who cited someone in the 'family' category as 'dependable', about twice as many as in Tokyo and Bangkok. Over half of the responses comprised close (immediate) family members, including spouses, parents, siblings, and in-laws. Conversely, the average number cited in the social relationship category was only slightly higher than in the other two cities, and yet the difference was marginal. The inclination to rely on family members was notable and evident.

The relationships between respondents and sources of anticipated personal support are plotted by frequency of contact and the ease of requesting help in

Figure 6.1 and detailed by city in Figure 6.2. Respondents rated the extent of the two indicators with scores ranging from 1 ('not at all') to 4 ('very much') for each person. In the figures, the X-axis represents the frequency of contact and the Y-axis the ease of making requests, while the size of the bubble represents the frequency of response, with larger bubble and higher positions on the right indicating a closer relationship for many. Figure 6.1 illustrates the positive correlation in each city between the number of people who are identified as 'dependable' and their closeness. This resulted in families being plotted with a larger bubble in the upper right-hand corner and public support services with a smaller bubble in the lower left-hand corner. Friends and other social relationships come in between. However, compared to the closeness of family members in Shanghai, it can be inferred (from the size of the bubbles and the position of the X- and Y-axes) that the familial relationships of the participants from Tokyo and Bangkok are a little weaker, both quantitatively and qualitatively. This further confirms the existence of a support network structure that is heavily biased in favour of family/relatives in Shanghai. Each category of family, social relations, and public services broken down into more detail specifying the various relationships can be seen in Figure 6.2. From these figures, it appears that Bangkok has some very strong personal relationships, not limited in scope to the family, that relationships in Shanghai are heavily centred on the family, and that Tokyo has relationships that are generally distant including a certain amount of non-family relationships.

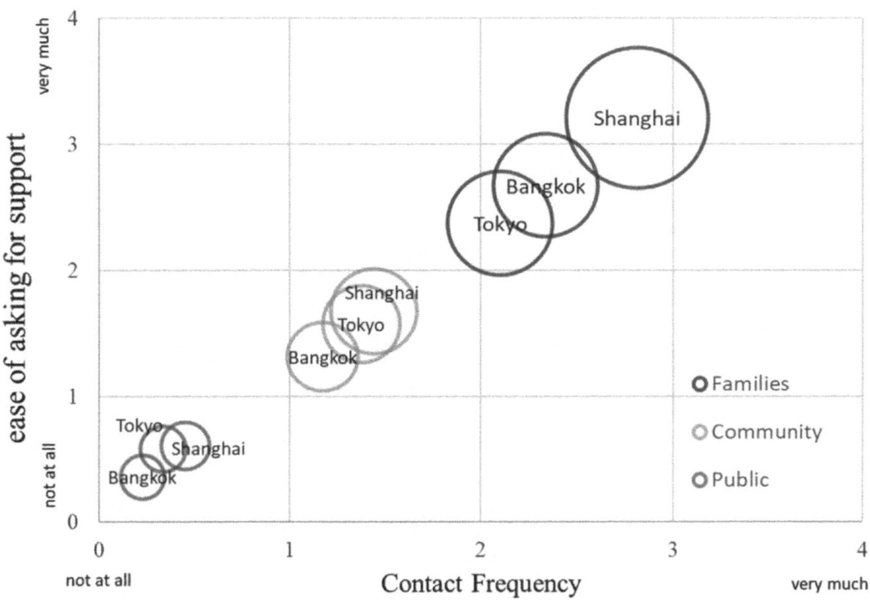

Figure 6.1 Relationships with perceived personal supporters by category.
Source: Graph by author.

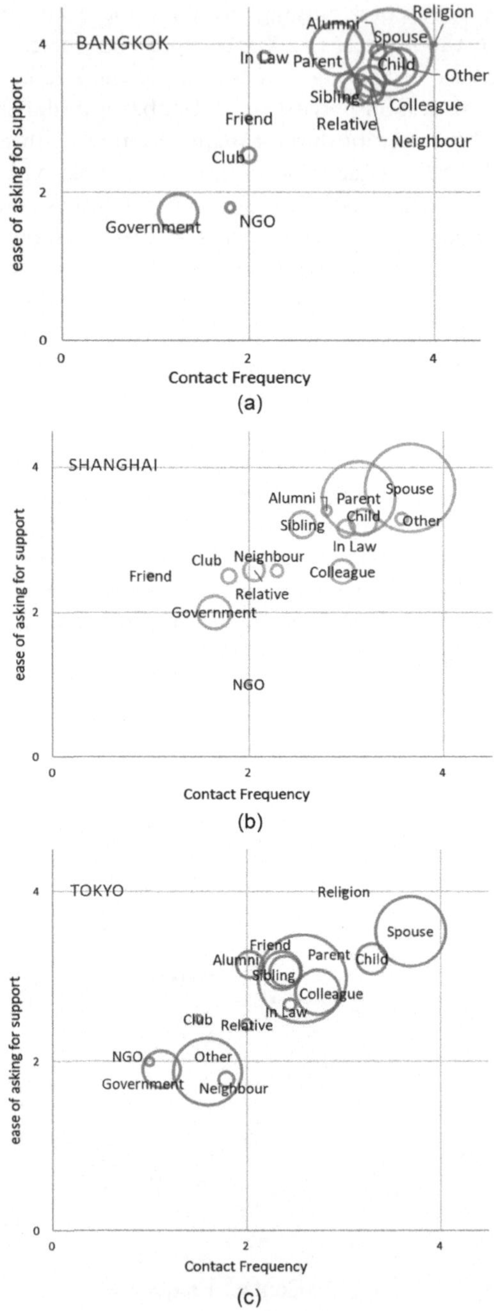

Figure 6.2 Relationships with perceived personal supporters by city, (a) Bangkok, (b) Shanghai, and (c) Tokyo.

Source: Graph by author.

The network structure of received support in the face of adversity shows a similar trend to the anticipated support network. Practically utilised support networks were extrapolated from the data collected when respondents were asked who they had depended on when solving the biggest problems they had encountered over the last decade. Among those who answered, support was primarily received from family members, followed by social relationships, and finally, from public services. In Bangkok, for example, the average number of times help was received was 1.0 for family members, but only 0.4 for social relations and 0.1 for public resources. In Tokyo, social relations were slightly more common, with 0.5 (against 0.9 by family members and 0.1 by the public service). Shanghai has extremely few respondents who reported receiving public assistance, close to zero (in contrast to 0.8 from family, similar to Tokyo, and 0.3 for social relationships, similar to Bangkok). Moreover, the findings also revealed individuals who did not seek any help from others in all three cities. Shanghai and Bangkok followed a similar pattern, except that more Bangkok participants used public and family support than in Shanghai. In Tokyo, fewer respondents tackled problems alone (0.3) than in Shanghai and Bangkok (0.7 each) and were in turn more likely to seek help from colleagues and friends. (See also Box 3, for further discussion on surviving in the city by solving problems alone.)

When classifying the types of problems faced by the respondents as either economic or social issues, it was observed that different supporters were sought for different types of problems across the three cities. Commonly, many respondents tried to solve economic problems on their own, while more relied on their family members for social problems. Further, different supporters were relied on for different types of problems. In Tokyo, respondents were often assisted by relatives and neighbours for family care issues, but seldom for financial problems. Interestingly, people in Tokyo even turned to their colleagues for help with family issues – apparently colleagues may even be considered friends outside of work in Tokyo. Shanghai residents also sought help from their colleagues in caregiving; however, unlike in Tokyo, they did not seek help for other family issues. In Bangkok, people did not anticipate their colleagues would be part of the support network for any family related issues. Nor are friends from religious organisations considered supporters in economic matters, although Bangkok is perceived to have a more religious environment than Tokyo or Shanghai.

Taken together, these factors reveal the scope for community formation across the three cities. Tokyo, with its long history of urbanisation and industrialisation, has certain social conditions underpinning its increasing individualisation. Indeed, it appears to reflect a form of progress with disembedding and distancing from traditional institutions such as family and work communities. Compared to other cities, traditional ties of kinship and neighbourhood tend to be tenuous, though reliable and supportive communities seem to be established based on their bonds of personal association. In this sense, Tokyo seems in line with the argument of 'community liberated' (Wellman 1979) that the community has been transformed in urbanisation.

Meanwhile, Bangkok is a core city in rapidly developing Southeast Asia; and yet, urbanisation seemingly exerts a low impact on social relationships. The residents are still embedded in families and local communities. In fact, association networks, such as those formed by alumni or hobby gatherings, are few and far between, whereas kinship and neighbourhood bonds appear more significant. The anticipated availability of such primary connections outside the so-called nuclear family (regardless of whether they are actually used or not) may function as an informal form of risk response. However, it should also be noted that the sense of religious community is weak and seems to be transforming into a somewhat individualistic practice of religion, as Yano (2006) has pointed out, rather than a persistence of traditional ways of engagement.

Finally, Shanghai has achieved rapid economic development due to changes in socio-economic policies; however, the city still maintains a gemeinschaft mode of social relationships in which strong family support networks sustain individual lives. Nevertheless, it should also be pointed out that a certain degree of individualisation may have evolved, as many respondents tried to solve their adversities alone, with or without success. Furthermore, they showed little sense of belonging with respect to local communities, such as neighbourhoods, despite some being embedded in association networks such as workplaces and hobby groups. In this sense, too, their personal relationships do not seem to be reflecting a simple traditional communal space.

These results indicate that urban life in East Asia does not follow a simple linear argument assuming that urbanisation leads to individualisation, but rather that it has developed in its own way. In Shanghai, people appear to live a life embedded in consanguine family and relatives, the blood gemeinschaft, even in the context of urban social development. In Bangkok, they seem to live and function deeply embedded in a more open local community, gemeinschaft by place, not only within their families, whereas in Tokyo, their lives seem to be embedded in association networks of colleagues (*sha-en*), alumni (*gaku-en*), and hobby gathering (*shu-en*), reflecting gemeinschaft of mind. Certainly, the ties between individuals and communities are reasonably strong in all cities, yet it is not a simple gemeinschaft world – more of a bi-layered structure. Gemeinschaft-like human relationships are built within a social environment premised upon a gesellschaft-like communication space facilitating individualisation. It will be interesting to see if and how the urban communication space will transform gemeinschaft-like relations in the future.

6.2 Personal Networks and Context: Cultural and Social Capitals

We now discuss other individual characteristics that may have an effect on the structure of support networks. In our survey, respondents reported demographics including education, income, occupation and turnover experience, gender, family size, neighbouring relatives, type of house and length of residency, and experience of migration. The data were analysed vis-à-vis the number and types of support networks with which the respondents were connected. A comparative analysis by variables such as income (middle/lower), work (full-time/part-time), gender (male/female), marital status (married/unmarried), children (have/do not have), and place of origin (city/other region) revealed some interesting findings.

In Tokyo, many residents had a similar structure of support networks, regardless of whether they belonged to the middle- or lower-income bracket, indicating that the pattern of personal relationships is unaffected by wealth. Lifestyles and values may not yet be so divided by income level that the differences reflect these social support relationships, perhaps a holdover from the 'all-Japanese-are-middle-class' mentality that dragged on from the 1970s until the economic bubble burst. For other variables, however, differences were found. Comparing full-time and part-time workers, the former tended to have closer relationships with their families and relatives than the latter. In a comparison of the genders, it was found that men had closer relationships with their families and relatives than women did, who instead had closer and richer social relationships outside of their families. Those who were married or had children maintained larger and more closely related family support networks than their unmarried or childless counterparts. Similarly to women, singles had richer social relationships outside the family. Furthermore, those who had migrated from other regions were less likely to have close relationships with their families and relatives. This means that having an established family life, rather than income bracket, determines what support networks people in Tokyo rely on. Among them, those in non-regular employment and those from other regions tend to live in more isolated (or 'individualised') circumstances, not expecting to receive informal support when problems arise. Public support will be essential for these people to survive in the city.

Respondents from Shanghai, as previously mentioned, had stronger family networks compared with the other cities. This trend was more evident in those who belonged to the middle class, were full-time employees, married, had children, and were born in the city. Regarding intimacy, the middle class, full-time employees, and women maintained closer relationships. In contrast, those who were single, migrants, or childless, had closer association friendships. Interestingly, the middle-class respondents had a strong dependence on their families and relatives and only a small number of dependable friendships. The lower-class respondents neither relied on others nor on public services, to get through demanding troublesome situations. In other words, the middle-class respondents in Shanghai were more dependent on primary support networks of kinfolk, while the lower class were more characterised by individualisation within urbanisation, where people face and survive risks independently. Hence, unlike in Tokyo, where income class disparities were less clear, Shanghai's income classes actually enclose the other variables; the lower-class population overlaps with more vulnerable non-mainstream groups (i.e., singles, migrants, non-regular employees), who do not have access to informal support.

The opposite was true in Bangkok, where the lower economic status respondents and part-time employees had larger and richer family and social relationships. The anticipated support network in the middle class was not large, with fewer dependable social relationships, as well as weak dependence on family and relatives. In fact, participants did not rely on other people, or public services. Moreover, those who were unmarried, childless, and migrants were found to have richer social relationships than their counterparts who were married, had children, and were born in the city, respectively. These results suggest that in Bangkok, those who are vulnerable and precariously situated are better able to access informal support, while the lifestyles of those considered more stable in middle-class and full-time employment are more individualised.

Interestingly, support network structures were manifested in a different manner in the three cities. In Bangkok, where the middle class is increasingly individualised and the lower class remains embedded deeply in a primary gemeinschaft-like network of local community, personal connections serve as informal support. In contrast, Shanghai has a middle class deeply embedded in more primary networks of kinfolks, and a seemingly disembedded lower class. Support networks have a reinforcing role in helping those with connections to lead even more stable lives, despite the challenging situation in which vulnerable groups cannot access these networks as an informal support resource in Shanghai, and possibly in Tokyo as well.

Underpinning this, the correlations between the size of the support networks and selected sociodemographic and relationship variables are examined. The respective correlation coefficients are shown in Table 6.1. In Shanghai, the size of anticipated support networks was weakly but positively correlated with education and income levels, as was the size of received support networks with job changes. A richer human capital, or a wider sphere of activities, could lead to a wider perceived set of options (or, this could be vice versa, having a wider world makes human capital richer, and increases the possibility of job change). Oppositely, levels of income and education, sizes of family/neighbouring relatives, as well as the relationship with neighbours were negatively correlated with self-help. It follows that those who have to depend on themselves are vulnerable in terms of their economic, cultural, and social capitals. In Tokyo, variables related to an individual's capitals, such as income, education, and job change, were not correlated with the support network size. However, good relationships with family and neighbours were positively correlated with network size, and those without such relationships had no choice but to help themselves. That is, good relationships were the only meaningful variable for network building. Similarly, both types of support networks in Bangkok showed negative correlations with income level and positive correlations with frequency of moving house. Furthermore, those with higher education did not have access to support and were more likely to solve their problems alone. The size of the support networks can assume the opposite relationship between moving house and jobs. Moving house expands personal networks (or one can move house because one is rich in personal networks), while changing jobs loses them (or one can change jobs because one does not have personal networks). It is often thought that education increases human capital, or that the sphere of activities expands through job

Table 6.1 Correlation coefficient of selected variables

	Bangkok			*Shanghai*			*Tokyo*		
	Self-help	*Support (past)*	*Support (future)*	*Self-help*	*Support (past)*	*Support (future)*	*Self-help*	*Support (past)*	*Support (future)*
City-born	−0.02	−0.01	−0.03	−0.18**	−0.10**	0.11**	0	0.04	0.14**
Age	−0.09*	0.17**	0.06+	0.13**	−0.03	−0.03	−0.04	0.01	0.03
Class	−0.42**	0.45**	0.41**	0.71**	0.07+	−0.25**	0.07*	0.03	−0.03
Education	0.21**	−0.21**	−0.10**	−0.54**	−0.02	0.21**	−0.04	0	0.03
Moving house	0.14**	0.28**	0.21**	0.18**	0.03	−0.09*	−0.03	0	−0.01
Length of residence	−0.25**	0.20**	0.17**	−0.07+	−0.07+	−0.07+	−0.04	0.01	0.14**
Job change	0.31**	−0.10**	−0.15**	−0.05	0.23**	0.12**	0.04	−0.02	−0.01
Length of employment	−0.10*	0.17**	0.10**	−0.04	−0.11**	0.02	−0.03	−0.01	0.03
Family size	−0.21**	0.18**	0.20**	−0.41**	−0.03	0.16**	−0.13**	0.04	0.10**
Number of children	0.01	0.01	−0.01	−0.07+	0.01	0.07+	−0.12**	0.08**	0.04
Relatives in area	−0.11*	0.26**	0.13**	−0.50**	−0.01	0.15**	0.01	0.01	0.06*
Family relationship	−0.12**	0.23**	0.24**	−0.04	0.02	0.05	−0.24**	0.19**	0.25**
Comm. relationship	−0.28**	0.19**	0.22**	−0.41**	0.05	0.18**	−0.10**	0.33**	0.33**

Source: By author.

Note: Support (future) is anticipated support networks; support (past) is received support networks. $^{**}p < 0.01$, $^{*}p < 0.05$, $^{+}p < 0.10$.

change, which in turn expands social network, and this was actually the case in Shanghai. However, in Bangkok, in terms of responding to problems, the skills and ability developed through education may lead to a sense of confidence and efficacy, in turn resulting in self-help aspirations. Changing jobs does not seem to lead to networking for support either; instead, moving their residence to a new location seems to help networking.

The above differences can be attributed to the impact of socio-economic development and globalisation on Shanghai, Tokyo, and Bangkok. In Shanghai, strong family networks provide the 'capital' for the stable livelihoods of the middle class, while in Bangkok, support networks serve as an important informal resource for the survival of the lower class. The situation is slightly different in Tokyo, where income level and education are not particularly meaningful variables for the structure of support networks. To nevertheless draw conclusions, it is necessary to consider the extent to which formal support resources in society have been developed and to what extent individuals have access to them. In fact, a weak correlation was observed between anticipated public support networks and age ($r = .218$, $p < .01$) in Tokyo. This may be due to the fact that people become more aware of the public support service which they need and are available as they get older, such as with parenting and for elder care, though no such correlation was observed in the other two cities. By examining how public support is provided and how it is anticipated, together with the enrichment of informal support networks, it may be possible to identify the characteristics of desirable living arrangements and lifestyles in different societies.

6.3 Influence on Life Satisfaction

Let us now consider how these support networks contribute to the degree of actual life satisfaction. Life satisfaction measures cognitive aspects of subjective well-being, and our questionnaire-based survey asked respondents to rate their perception of their own living conditions on a 10-point scale.

First, the correlations of self-assessment of life satisfaction with the size of respondents' anticipated support network, as well as their received support networks, were examined. None of these were statistically significant in Tokyo or Bangkok. That is, individuals' life satisfaction may not be influenced by the number of their supporters in these cities. In Shanghai, there was a slight negative correlation between self-help and life satisfaction ($r = -.250$, $p < .01$), meaning that life satisfaction was higher if there was someone to ask for help in times of need. However, no significant differences were found regarding whom and how respondents were connected. It is thus difficult to say from the data that life satisfaction depends on support networks.

Figure 6.3 plots the average scores of life satisfaction (*X*-axis) and the size of support networks (*Y*-axis) for economic and social problems/risks in the three cities. The plotted markers distinguish between family and non-family social relations, and between economic and social problems. It is evident from the figure that life satisfaction is not necessarily directly proportional to the size of the support networks. However, a close look reveals that life satisfaction is likely

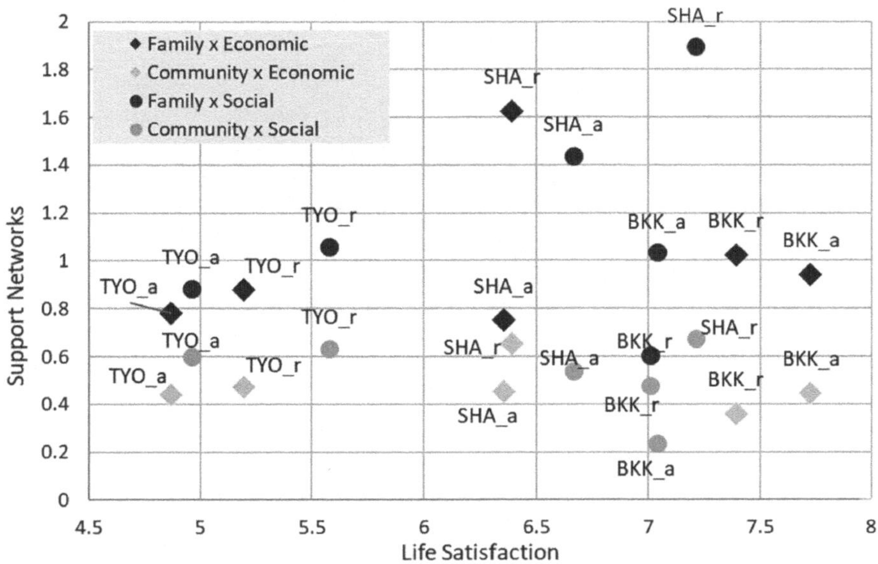

Figure 6.3 The relation of support network size and life satisfaction.

Source: Graph by author.

Note: Family x Economic=support for financial problems by family; Community x Economic=support for financial problems by social relationship/community; Family x Social=support for social issues by family; Community x Social=support for social issues by social relationship/community: TYO=Tokyo; SHA=Shanghai; BKK=Bangkok: a=anticipated support; r=received support.

to be higher for those who received support from sources they did not anticipate and those who had larger anticipated support networks.

Regarding the size of the support networks, the following points were found. First, the size of the anticipated support network and the received support network with the life satisfaction self-assessment were different from one another. For instance, the size of anticipated support network for future risks is greater in the high life satisfaction group than in the low. Although the Tokyo data did not confirm a direct proportion between life satisfaction and anticipated network size, a clear positive correlation can be observed in the Bangkok data. In the case of Shanghai, the size of support network was in general larger than other cities, and it was found to gradually increase further with increasing life satisfaction. In contrast, the size of the received support network was mixed in relation to the level of life satisfaction. A clear correlation was observed in Bangkok, where the low- and high-satisfaction groups had a small and large network, respectively. Meanwhile, Shanghai had a smaller network size to begin with and even had an inverse correlation with the high-satisfaction group. For Tokyo, the network was indeed larger for the high satisfaction group, but it was almost the same for the low and even smaller for the medium groups (Figure 6.4).

Second, the relationship between the quality of the support network and life satisfaction showed similar trends in each city. As previously noted, families and relatives were significant supporters in times of need in the surveyed cities.

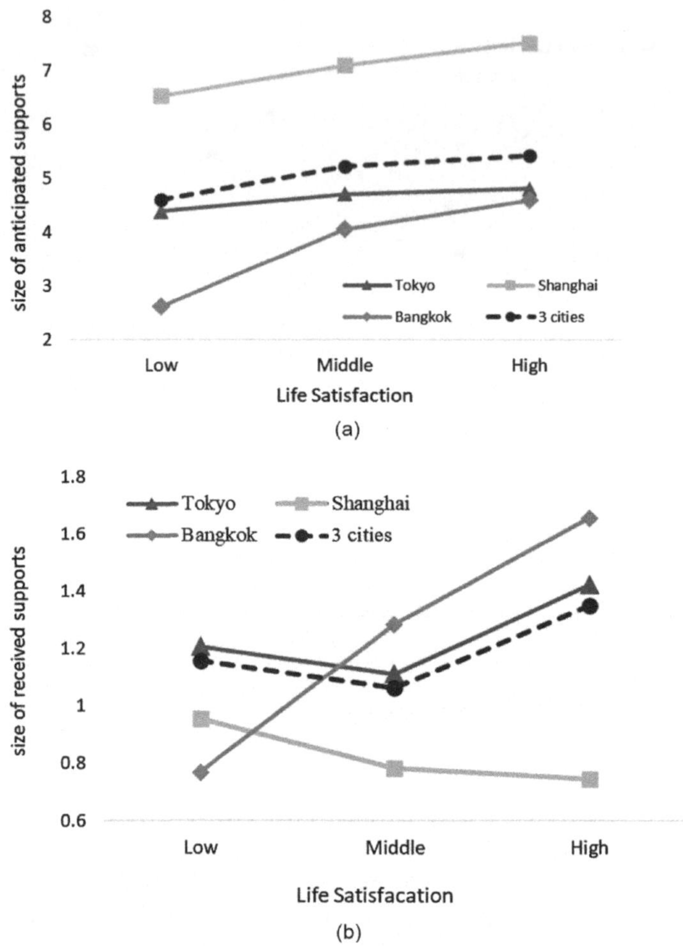

Figure 6.4 The size of (a) anticipated and (b) received support network, by category of level of life satisfaction.

Source: Graph by author.

Note: Life satisfaction is categorised: Low=score 1 to 3; Middle=score 4 to 7; High=score 8 to 10.

However, understanding life satisfaction also needs consideration of intimacy with family members, as well as the proportion of family members in their entire support networks. Intimacy with family members was found to be directly proportional to life satisfaction, despite a plateau at higher life satisfaction in Bangkok (Figure 6.5). Additionally, higher levels of satisfaction were associated with lower proportions of non-family supporters or a higher proportion of family members (Figure 6.6).

From what has been seen, it can be argued that family relationships are key in Asian cities when considering support networks in relation to life satisfaction. While the size of the support network cannot be ignored, size only makes sense in terms of anticipated support networks, and the received support networks may

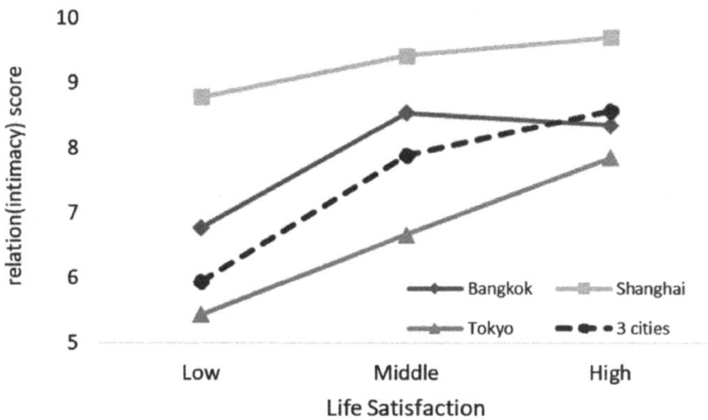

Figure 6.5 Average score of family relation, by category of level of life satisfaction.
Source: Graph by author.
Note: Life satisfaction is categorised: Low=score 1 to 3; Middle=score 4 to 7; High=score 8 to 10.

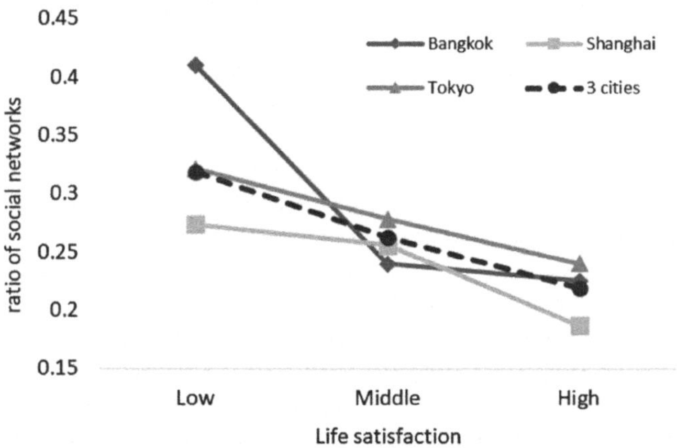

Figure 6.6 Ratios of social relationship among support networks, by category of level of life satisfaction.
Source: Graph by author.
Note: Life satisfaction is categorised: Low=score 1 to 3; Middle=score 4 to 7; High=score 8 to 10.

not always increase satisfaction. Rather, maintaining good relationships with a high percentage of dependable family members and relatives are thought to contribute more to individuals' life satisfaction and well-being.

Further comparisons between the cities looking at the support network's contribution to life satisfaction through regression analysis confirmed the differences among the three cities. In the analysis, life satisfaction was used as the dependant variable, with the 10-point scale scores re-categorised into three levels (low [1–3], medium [4–7], and high [8–10]). The independent variables were selected from those involved in support networks reflecting the respondents' social capital. The variables used here were the size and closeness of expected and actual supporters in family and social relationships, self-help experience, together with the number of family members, children, and neighbouring relatives, marital status, age, education, city-born, number of moves and years of residence, length of employment, and frequency of job changes.

Each city was analysed in an ordinal logistic regression analysis with the same variables entered. Table 6.2a shows the results of the analysis. All results confirm that support networks do not directly explain the level of life satisfaction, yet subtle differences in impact among variables became visible. In the Shanghai model, variables such as city-born, number of relatives living nearby, and job changes contribute to the model, in addition to the anticipated number of support sources from social relationships and their closeness. By contrast, variables of received support networks do not contribute meaningfully to the model as much. Separate stepwise analyses for the middle and lower classes showed that not only were there different relevant variables in the resulting models for each but they were also different from the model for Shanghai as a whole (Table 6.2b). The variables included in the resulting middle-class model were number of children and neighbouring relatives, self-help experience, and job changes. None of the variables directly related to support networks were employed in the model of this group. In the lower-class model, the only variable which remained was being city-born. Nevertheless, its classification predictions of life satisfaction levels were not low (71.1%), making it interesting to find that whether or not born in the city is related to life satisfaction for the lower class.

For the Bangkok model, the two variables which were statistically significant were closeness to the supporters from social relations and the frequency of job changes (Table 6.2a). Notably, no variables related to the support network size or family contributed prominently to the model. Exploring the variables identified by the stepwise regression (Table 6.2b) clarified that the model for the lower classes used the number of supports received, along with closeness to supporters from social relations. Alternatively, in the model for the middle class, a completely different variable – city-born or not – was the only one used. This resulted in the same basic model as that for Shanghai lower class. Despite a slightly weaker fit than the Shanghai lower-class model, the predictions of life satisfaction classification were comparable to those of the overall Bangkok model (60.6% and 59.4%, respectively).

The model for Tokyo significantly consisted of contributions from the following variables: age, education, number of family members and children, moves, and years of residence, along with intimacy with family members (Table 6.2a). This model infers that a sound family situation with a stable living environment contributes to life satisfaction compositely, but conversely there is no decisive variable. Each of the middle- and lower-class models uses slightly different variables, but again there is no decisive variable in either case (Table 6.2b). The middle-class model included variables of intimacy with family members, the size of the social relationships, the size of received support networks, years of residence, age, education, and family size. In contrast, the model for the lower class included variables of years of residence, length of employment, age, as well as intimacies with family and social/community relationships.

Table 6.2a The results of ordinal regression analysis

Variable	*Bangkok*			*Shanghai*			*Tokyo*		
	OR	*95% CI*		*OR*	*95% CI*		*OR*	*95% CI*	
Age	1.017	0.987	1.047	0.998	0.977	1.018	1.017**	1.004	1.03
City-born	1.399	0.807	2.425	1.627*	1.02	2.595	1.115	0.854	1.457
Marital status	1.301	0.75	2.257	0.987	0.586	1.664	1.147	0.81	1.624
Family size	0.947	0.801	1.12	1.052	0.926	1.196	0.761**	0.664	0.873
Number of children	0.86	0.672	1.101	1.267	0.858	1.871	1.198*	1.005	1.43
Neighbouring relative	1.113	0.94	1.318	1.244**	1.085	1.425	1.033	0.881	1.211
Years of residence	1.000	0.998	1.001	1.000	0.999	1.001	1.001*	1.000	1.002
Number of moves	0.954	0.767	1.185	0.99	0.913	1.074	0.943+	0.882	1.009
Length of employment	1.001	0.998	1.003	0.998	0.997	1.000	0.999	0.998	1.000
Job change	0.850+	0.703	1.027	0.820**	0.709	0.949	1.000	0.998	1.003
Education (year)	1.001	0.946	1.059	1.052	0.978	1.131	1.110**	1.069	1.153
Self-help	1.181	0.682	2.046	0.953	0.621	1.463	1.169	0.819	1.667
Total received support	1.446	0.864	2.419	1.225	0.399	3.759	1.118	0.738	1.693
Support – family (received)	0.817	0.449	1.485	0.834	0.267	2.612	0.954	0.632	1.441
Support – community (received)	0.623	0.304	1.28	0.777	0.222	2.723	1.048	0.679	1.618
Total anticipated support	1.041	0.795	1.363	1.115	0.946	1.314	1.069	0.948	1.205
Support – family (anticipated)	0.975	0.751	1.266	0.988	0.846	1.154	0.954	0.84	1.083
Support – community (anticipated)	1.176	0.836	1.654	0.855+	0.713	1.026	0.864*	0.752	0.994
Family relation	0.989	0.947	1.034	0.996	0.949	1.045	1.051**	1.025	1.078
Community relation	0.914*	0.847	0.986	1.044+	0.993	1.097	1.025	0.991	1.061
pseudo R^2	.113*			.139**			.111**		

Source: By author.
Note: ** $p < 0.01$, * $p < 0.05$, + $p < 0.10$.

Table 6.2b The results of ordinal regression analysis (stepwise)

Variable	*OR (95% CI)*					
	Bangkok (middle)	*Bangkok (lower)*	*Shanghai (middle)*	*Shanghai (lower)*	*Tokyo (middle)*	*Tokyo (lower)*
Age					1.016* (1.000-1.031)	1.017** (1.004-1.031)
City-Born	2.287* (1.196-4.372)			2.488** (1.427-4.340)		
family size					.789** (0.668-0.932)	
number of children			1.791* (1.14-2.82)			
neighbouring relative			1.232* (1.04-1.46)			
years of residence					1.001* (1.000-1.002)	1.001* (1.000-1.002)
length of employment						.997** (0.996-0.999)
job change			0.829* (0.695-0.989)			
Education (year)					1.105** (1.028-1.187)	
self-help			0.286* (0.093-0.877)			

total received support		1.312** (1.121-1.536)			1.194* (1.038-1.371)	
support -community (anticipated)					.852** (0.774-0.938)	
family relation					1.053** (1.016-1.091)	1.033** (1.001-1.065)
community relation		0.903** (0.849-0.961)				1.040* (1.002-1.078)
pseudo R^2	.045*	.137**	.107**	.049**	.118**	.073**

Source: by author.
Note: ** $p < 0.01$, * $p < 0.05$, + $p < 0.10$. Blank columns in the table are variables that were entered into the analysis but removed due to their small contribution. The following variables were also removed for all six groups: marital status, number of moves, support - family (received), support - local (received), total expected support, support - family (expected).

When comparing the data analysis results of support networks across the three cities from the perspective of life satisfaction (i.e., social capital for risk response), the differences between the cities became apparent. In Bangkok, having received support networks, rather than an anticipated support network of family, relatives, and community in which they were embedded, proved more meaningful in relation to life satisfaction. However, the results of ordinal logistics regression showed that the middle-class model only included the variables of city-born or migrant, suggesting a need for reconsideration on what meaning this may have. Moreover, the result that having support networks is not necessarily a key to life satisfaction foreshadows a possibility that subjective well-being may not be captured by existing approaches, including variables such as economic conditions. In Shanghai, being connected to families and relatives, and perceiving that they would receive help when in need, was more likely to enhance life satisfaction. At the same time, ordinal regression analysis revealed that such contributions were limited to the Shanghai-wide model. Rather, the lower classes in Shanghai shared with the Bangkok middle class a model, in which variable of being city-born was an explanatory one. Although its meaning itself needs to be considered, further discussion would be called for on whether this has the same meaning as for both Bangkok and Shanghai residents. In contrast, in Tokyo, maintaining a positive and close relationship with family and relatives was more meaningful than social relationships with regard to life satisfaction, albeit more modest than in Shanghai and Bangkok. This is the case for the middle class and was also shown markedly in the ordinal regression analysis, though even for the lower class it is still of significance whether they have someone among their social relationships with whom they have a good enough rapport to be able to ask help.

Personal networks as a risk response or crisis countermeasure are relevant for life satisfaction but can be only effective in an indirect way as a safety net. Still, the meaning of those support networks differs depending on the city and social class in which people live. Having anticipated supporters may be crucial to their survival for a group, while having received support may be for another group. Being embedded in a community may work as a resource for satisfactory problem-solving for a group, whereas community networks are not valued in the first place for another. Being connected is certainly important and meaningful even in urban life, if not directly linked to life satisfaction; still, there is no 'right answer' as to who to be connected to and how.

Conclusion

This chapter has attempted to understand the informal risk-response resources in the form of support networks for people living in three Asian cities. Against the backdrop of rapid economic growth, Bangkok and Shanghai experienced a phenomenon that cannot be expressed as the simple notion of 'individualisation', reflecting the manifestation of complex structures within the cities. Their personal relationships as a risk-response resource have become polarised, with a notable number of people responding to risk as individuals, while others are deeply embedded in the safety net of their personal relationships. The reasons for these different orientations seem to differ between Shanghai and Bangkok. In Bangkok, the middle class has acquired an individualised lifestyle in the course of urbanisation, while in Shanghai, the lower class seems to face the potentially risky individualisation outlined by Beck and Beck-Gernsheim (2002), Giddens (1991), or others. In Tokyo, the marketisation of human relationships has quietly progressed during the long urbanisation process, and they seem only to have fragile networks in return for people's freedom from existing relationships. With good public services available, there may be no need for personal relationships to serve as a safety net; conversely, life can be very tough and challenging for those who are unable to have personal relationships in such a context.

While many differences exist within and between these cities, the impression that there are underlying commonalities also persists. A common thread that runs through the three Asian megacities is the importance of family networks. Families are the people who are most dependable and reliable in risk response, and they indeed provide help in times of crisis. Nevertheless, when considering who family members are and what kind of relationships they have with each other, it may be a risk to proceed with the discussion by assuming that people in the three cities share the meaning of 'family' and 'relatives'. Similarly, variations probably exist in what kind of relationship is considered desirable.

Given so many variations and differences, it is difficult to grasp Asian cities all in one unified form. However, reviewing the findings of our survey based on an understanding of the context in which each city is situated provides some insights for further study of the challenges Asian cities pose.

Box 3 Surviving alone

Naoki Oishi

One section of our questionnaire survey asked respondents to select from multiple choices "Who helped you to solve the problem you faced?" to identify the networks they employed when confronted by a serious problem of urban life. The responses were unexpected and intriguing. As discussed in Chapter 6, it goes without saying that the existence of social networks possessed by individuals was important. On the other hand, particularly notable was the high percentage of respondents who selected "solved by myself" among the multiple choices given for the response to all the people involved in solving the problem.

What this signifies is that many people either choose or are compelled to grapple on their own with the most serious problems and concerns they have faced in their urban life. Here, we have labelled this phenomenon of dealing alone with the risks of life in a large city as "Surviving Alone", in an analogy of Robert D. Putnam's *Bowling Alone*.

The 'surviving alone' phenomenon that characterises urban life is also thought to be an outcome of the changing trends in household composition. Of course, there are people 'living and surviving alone' in all three cities, but most notably Tokyo owes much to this change in the composition of households. According to the national census, between 1995 and 2015, the total number of households in Tokyo increased from 4.95 million to 6.67 million, but the average household size dropped from 2.34 to 1.99 persons. The average number of persons per household is now below 2. This means an increase in the single-person household rate (from 38% to 47%) due to an increase in single-person households (from 1.88 million to 3.16 million). As long as this continues as a structural change, the trend of surviving alone in large cities can be expected to continue in the future.

Therefore, we looked at the reality of surviving alone, focusing on the results of a survey of Tokyo's lower-income group, who has a particularly large number of single-person households. In this survey, several respondents indicated that the biggest problem they faced in the past decade was changing jobs. While some sought to change their work environment or shift to a new career, others were compelled to change jobs due to their employer's restructuring or bankruptcy.

Typical responses included the following: "My company went bankrupt. I was only able to find a new job after I accepted a lower salary" (39-year-old woman, accounting/HR); "I was forced to change jobs due to my company's circumstances" (47-year-old man, call centre supervisor); "They didn't clearly say it was a restructuring, but it was" (48-year-old woman, financial institution sales); "I changed jobs through a headhunting, but my duties were different than what I had been originally told they would be. The stress made me sick" (51-year-old woman, management). What we see here is the lack of fluidity in Japan's labour market which is premised on long-term employment within the same company, typified in its tradition description as a lifetime employment system.

In fact, there were only a few cases in which a respondent said they chose to change jobs to advance their career. More typical was the response of a 37-year-old woman who worked as a clerk in a credit card company, who said, "I discarded all my hopes and looked for work that would sustain my livelihood". There were not just a few cases like this in which people opted for jobs they did not really want simply to sustain their urban livelihood. Likewise, many of these people were compelled to search long and hard for a new job: "After my company restructured and I was let go, it took me over a year to find another job" (42-year-old man, pharmaceutical R&D); "Twice, it took me two years to find a new job" (61-year-old man, accounting). For some, the process of seeking another job often led to new problems: "I ran out of money while looking for a new job and had to take out a consumer loan to get through" (38-year-old man, relaxation

Table BOX3-1 Life satisfaction of people who have solved problem

		By myself			*By cooperating with others*		
		Life satisfaction	*No.*	*%*	*Life satisfaction*	*No.*	*%*
Tokyo	Middle	5.92	85	27.2%	6.21	227	72.8%
	Lower	4.87	61	23.6%	5.35	197	76.4%
Shanghai	Middle	6.18	11	18.6%	7.27	48	81.4%
	Lower	6.70	125	77.6%	6.75	36	22.4%
Bangkok	Middle	7.12	227	79.6%	7.19	58	20.4%
	Lower	7.81	142	53.8%	7.89	122	46.2%

Source: By author.

therapist); "My debt was around 4 million yen while I was searching for a job" (61-year-old man quoted above).

What these cases tell us is that, even when confronted with a problem that threatened their ability to sustain their urban life, these people had to attempt to solve the problem on their own. The fluidity of the labour market has been increasing with the slowing of economic growth since the 1990s, but it is not functioning smoothly to match people to jobs which they want or for which they are best suited. In fact, under conditions of labour shortages, risk of changing jobs generating new problems, such as workplace maladjustment or over-pressure from employers.

Of course, it is not appropriate to dismiss surviving alone as a negative phenomenon. It should not be forgotten that it can, after all, also be viewed positively as an indication of a high degree of autonomy in surviving urban life. Additionally, it should be noted that in comparing the degree of life satisfaction among those who solved their past problems on their own and those who did so with the help of others, life satisfaction was lower for the former than for the latter in all three of the cities surveyed (see also Chapters 3 and 5).

Still, when it comes to coping with the difficult problems of one's health, need for nursing care, and death, then help from others is essential. In fact, several respondents said they were able to change careers and find new jobs thanks to the help of their family, co-workers, and friends. The survey results clearly indicate that these people were able to overcome the various risks and difficulties of urban life by making use of diverse networks.

Our survey results suggest that in addition to fostering the skills needed for surviving urban living on one's own and securing the conditions to do so, fostering a network which can be relied upon in times of shocks and crisis are another important factor, not only in increasing the probability of being able to cope with urban risks but also in improving life satisfaction.

References

Barrera, M. Jr. 1986. "Distinctions between social support concepts, measures, and models". *American Journal of Community Psychology* 14 (4): 413–445.

Beck, U. and E. Beck-Gernsheim. 2002. *Individualization: Institutionalized individualism and its social and political consequences.* London: Sage.

Cohen, S., and T. A. Wills. 1985. "Stress, social support, and the buffering hypothesis". *Psychological Bulletin* 98(2): 310–357.

Giddens, A. 1991. *Modernity and self-identity.* Cambridge: Polity Press.

Krause, N., J. Liang, and S. Gu. 1998. "Financial strain, received support, anticipated support, and depressive symptoms in the People's Republic of China". *Psychology and Aging*, 13(1): 58–68.

Wellman, B. 1979. "The community question: the intimate networks of East Yorkers". *American Journal of Sociology*, 84(5): 1201–1231.

Yano, H. 2006. *Gendai tai ni okeru bukkyo undo* [Buddhist movements in contemporary Thailand: Thammakai meditation and Thai society in transition]. Tokyo: Toshindo.

7 Life Satisfaction and Social Security in Three Megacities

Masato Miyazaki

Introduction

Well-being is related to government activities to some extent. We use public services and sometimes receive benefits. Social security related to health care, long-term care, unemployment, pensions, etc. are essential to our lives, and we pay taxes or insurance premiums to finance them. The relationship between government activities such as spending and burdens and well-being is one of the important themes of economics.

This chapter examines the relationship between well-being and social security systems in Tokyo, Shanghai, and Bangkok. Specifically, the life satisfaction survey employed in this book is treated as an indicator of subjective well-being. As has already been discussed, the average level of life satisfaction varies from city to city, and there is an apparent link to the fiscal activities and support available from the respective governments. For example, benefits through schemes such as pensions and health insurance may increase people's life satisfaction and security, while having to pay the taxes and insurance premiums that finance such benefits may decrease this, with the balance between these depending on how the specific systems function. That is, even if each country nominally offers coverage through medical insurance system, the mere existence of the system might well not raise the life satisfaction of the people if the vital service delivery and access does not function adequately and people cannot receive health services when needed.

This suggests that it is important not just to examine the relationships between burdens such as taxes and insurance premiums and benefits such as medical services with life satisfaction independently, but rather to examine how much the burdens are offset and compensated for by the benefits. Therefore, this chapter examines the relationship between life satisfaction and social security systems, by considering the relationship between burden and benefit.

The chapter is organised as follows: After reviewing previous studies in Section 7.1, Section 7.2 examines the impact of social security systems using residents' self-reported life satisfaction as measured with our questionnaire surveys in Tokyo, Shanghai, and Bangkok; Section 7.3 further analyses the three city samples by dividing them into middle- and low-income groups; and in Section 7.4,

DOI: 10.4324/9781003328155-7

we argue that the health care supply system has an impact on life satisfaction and that institutions are important.

7.1 Reviewing the Relationship between Life Satisfaction and Social Security Systems

According to International Labour Organization (ILO n.d.), social security guarantee income security and health protection, thereby contributing to the prevention and reduction of poverty and inequality, and the promotion of social inclusion and human dignity, through the provision of benefits, in cash or in kind. It intended to ensure access to medical care and health services, as well as income security throughout the life cycle, including retirement and old age, but particularly in the event of illness, unemployment, employment injury, maternity, family responsibilities, invalidity, loss of the family breadwinner. The nine principal branches of social security are medical care, sickness, unemployment, old age, employment injury, family, maternity, invalidity, and survivors' benefits.

Regarding the effects of social security system or fiscal expenditures on well-being or happiness, they are mostly based on data from Western countries. The conclusions drawn by previous researchers are mixed. For example, Veenhoven (2000) finds that increases or reductions in social security expenditure are not related to a rise or fall in the level of health and happiness. Ouweneel (2002) concludes that the level of social security has hardly any beneficial (or detrimental) effect on the well-being of the unemployed, which is perhaps due to state-provided benefits being a poor consolation for the impact of unemployment. Another explanation could be that in not so generous nations, social security can be substituted by an equally effective private care system of either traditional welfare institutions like family, community, and church or by modern institutions like commercial insurance companies and pension funds. Bjørnskov et al. (2008) analyse the impact of fiscal and political decentralisation on subjective well-being in a cross-section of 60,000 individuals from 66 countries, finding that general government consumption significantly reduces well-being. Furthermore, Hutchinson et al. (2017) measure happiness by the probability of committing suicide and find that higher state income taxes reduce happiness in the USA.

In contrast, Ram (2009) argues that evidence is lacking a significant negative association between government expenditure and population happiness in broad, cross-country contexts. Considerable caution is therefore urged in interpreting the policy implications of earlier studies which find negative association between government spending and life satisfaction in a given population. Hessami (2010) suggests that the effect of government size on well-being follows an inverse U-shape and that it depends positively on the extent of decentralisation and negatively on the level of corruption based on data for 12 EU countries over the period 1990–2000. Kotakorpi and Laamanen (2010) examine the impact of publicly provided health care services on individuals' subjective well-being in Finnish data, showing that higher relative expenditure on local service provision has a positive influence on the life satisfaction of the average citizen. Further, they examine how this effect varies among different groups. Their results show that devoting more resources to the provision of public services has a positive effect on well-being, although this effect may vary across groups.

Kiya (2012) provides the following empirical evidence from US data: First, the size of general expenditure is positively related to life satisfaction. Second, tax revenue size is negatively related to life satisfaction, while non-tax forms of revenue, such as intergovernmental transfers, are positively related. Third, considering the government expenditure and tax structures together, the positive impact of government expenditure and the negative impact of overall tax revenue are both smaller for higher income groups.

As we have seen, the conclusions based on data from Western countries are mixed. Therefore, it is important to also examine data from other regions, and it is necessary to take the institutional background of the quantitative analysis into consideration when examining the results. In addition, Albanese et al. (2015) analyse this issue in 10 European countries by examining whether happiness is impacted by the percentage of taxes returned to the population in the form of social provision, using the proxy of taxes paid for the 'value for money', or share of welfare, offered to taxpayers in return. Additionally, they analyse whether the sensitivity of happiness to the social expenditure–tax ratio was strengthened by the 2008 financial crisis, finding strong evidence of a relationship between social–tax ratio and happiness. Moreover, the Happiness Index showed high responsivity to the social–tax ratio during the crisis. While the previous study simply analysed the relationship between well-being and the benefits of government spending, this study also considers the burdens.

The importance of clarifying the relationship between life satisfaction and social security systems is considered to have increased further under COVID-19. Around the world, there were many reports of the workload on health services from COVID-19 patients and the pandemic's impact on staffing and supplies. The resulting varying degrees of 'health care system collapse' leaving patients unable to access medical care despite the existence of a health insurance system demonstrates the importance of not only the existence of a health insurance system but also the ability to delivery health services. Although the data discussed in this chapter were collected before the pandemic, they are very suggestive of the knock-on effects from such stresses on health care systems. This is because, as will be discussed below, it will be clear how lack of access to health services affects life satisfaction, even when health insurance exists.

7.2 Empirical Analysis of Life Satisfaction Indicators

This chapter uses the previously introduced questionnaire survey of residents in Tokyo, Shanghai, and Bangkok to analyse life satisfaction, scored on a 10-point scale ranging from 1 (the most *dissatisfied with*) to 10 (the most *satisfied with*) (see Chapter 3). The empirical analysis was carried out using this self-reported life satisfaction score as the explained variable. In this analysis with multiple explained variables, an ordered probit regression is adopted for the analysis. The explanatory variables covered demographic factors, living arrangements, employment, and financial related variables. These were gender, age, householder status (i.e., being head of household), marital status, city of origin, academic background, length of residence in the city to date (months), number of times of moving in the city, number of people living together, number of children (including separation), number of families and relatives living nearby, length of service in the current job, average monthly income (USD), average working hours per day, whether or not they were engaged in secondary job, number of job changes while living in the city, whether or not they owned their own house, status as employees, and whether or not the social security system is applicable. The regression modelling examines whether these factors affect the life satisfaction score of respondents.

For clarity, the variables as used on the modelling are: Gender is a dummy variable with 1 for men and 0 for women (male dummy). 'Marital status' is a dummy variable with 1 married and 0 for unmarried, divorced, or widowed (marriage dummy). 'Whether or not someone is from the city' is a dummy variable that takes the value 1 for people from the study city (Tokyo, Shanghai, and Bangkok) and 0 for people from other cities (birthplace dummy). The "academic background" is a dummy variable that takes 1 for a university degree and 0 otherwise (university graduate dummy). 'Whether or not they are doing a secondary job' is a dummy variable in which when the respondent has secondary employment is set to 1 and in the case of no secondary employment is set to 0 (secondary job dummy). 'Whether or not you own a house' is a dummy variable where owner-occupied status is set to 1, and rental housing, rental room, illegal occupation, and lodgings are set to 0 (homeowner dummy).

For 'position as an employee', the following four dummy variables are used. First is a dummy variable which is set to 1 in the case of a regular employee (private sector) (regular employee (private sector) dummy). Second is a dummy variable which is set to 1 in the case of a regular employee (public organisation) (regular employee (public organisation) dummy). Third is a dummy variable which is set to 1 in the case of non-regular employee (private sector) (non-regular employee (private sector) dummy). Fourth is a dummy variable which is set to 1 in the others (manager, non-regular worker (public organisation), day and seasonal worker, side job, and unpaid family worker). The reference category is the case of self-employment. Finally, for 'application of the social security system', the following three dummy variables are used. First is a dummy variable which takes the value of 1 when health insurance is applied. Second is a dummy variable which takes the value of 1 when unemployment insurance is applied. The third is a dummy variable which takes the value of 1 when a pension is applied. The descriptive statistics for these variables in the overall sample in each city are provided in Tables 7.1–7.3. Given the focus of this chapter, the participation in the social security and support systems for each city's sample is worth noting. For the Tokyo sample, the share with health insurance is 0.76, unemployment insurance is 0.71, and a pension is 0.70, while the statutory social security systems clearly cover nearly all people. The sample from Shanghai is in a similar situation, with 0.68 and 0.78 health insurance and pension coverage, respectively. However, the unemployment insurance coverage is a little lower at 0.40. In Bangkok, though the health insurance coverage is 0.62, the unemployment insurance rate is just 0.10 of the sample and the pension is 0.04, which are all very low. The unemployment insurance and pension are applicable to very few people.

For the model estimation, the endogeneity of health insurance is addressed. The problem of endogeneity has been found relevant as it gains more attention in econometric methods. Endogeneity, the correlation between the error term and the explanatory variables, arises due to the characteristics of observed data in all fields of social science, and it is the subject of a large body of research in the field of econometrics.

For example, Tran et al. (2017) point out that some of the same factors that determine life satisfaction may endogenously determine a person's health insurance status and they seek to account for this endogeneity through the identification of instrumental variables. The resulting analysis finds that not having health care coverage decreases life satisfaction. Knowing that one would not be able to afford needed health care can lead to other psychological and financial worries, as individuals can quickly exhaust their savings and incur debt in the event of required major medical procedures, given such high out-of-pocket costs for those without health insurance.

It is known that models estimated without considering the endogeneity problem in econometrics have biased parameters. In Japan and Thailand, employees are automatically covered by health insurance (in the latter for formal employees). On the other hand, in China, while employees with urban registration are automatically covered by health insurance, the health insurance does not automatically apply to farmers or those with rural registration working in urban areas. In Shanghai, which is discussed in this chapter, individuals, including those with rural registration, must choose whether or not to join a comprehensive insurance system in which medical care, pension, and insurance for industrial accidents are included. Hence, the problem of endogeneity arises in whether life satisfaction affects the decision to enrol in the insurance.[1] Therefore, we calculated estimates for Shanghai using an instrumental variable. The answers to the questions on risk were made into a dummy variable and an instrumental variable.[2]

Table 7.4 shows the estimated results for the three cities. The impact of the social security system on life satisfaction is as follows. First, people who have health insurance in Shanghai have lower well-being and in Bangkok higher well-being. Although the social security system should bring benefits to the population, health insurance enrolment has a negative impact on life satisfaction among the Shanghai sample. The results are contrary to our intuition and will be discussed in detail later by considering burden and benefit trade-off mentioned earlier. Second, in Shanghai, those who are enrolled in the pension system have higher well-being. Third, in Bangkok, life satisfaction rises with unemployment insurance, one of the key social security supports.

Table 7.1 Descriptive statistics (Tokyo)

	Sample	*Mean*	*SD*	*Minimum*	*Maximum*
Life satisfaction	1,261	5.34	2.19	1	10
Gender dummy	1,261	0.52	0.50	0	1
Age	1,261	44.83	14.08	21.00	85.00
Householder dummy	1,261	0.86	0.34	0	1
Marital status dummy	1,261	0.32	0.47	0	1
Birthplace dummy	1,261	0.47	0.50	0	1
University graduate dummy	1,261	0.30	0.46	0	1
Length of residence	1,261	336.64	239.63	2	974
Number of times of moving	1,261	3.03	2.15	1	16
Number of people living together	1,261	1.98	1.17	1	7
Number of children	1,261	0.61	0.97	0	6
Number of families and relatives living nearby	1,261	0.59	1.29	0	24
Length of service	1,261	105.91	122.78	0	690
Income per month	1,225	2,800.87	1,542.34	0	6,803.24
Average working hours per day	1,127	8.52	2.24	1	24
Secondary job dummy	1,127	0.15	0.36	0	1
Number of job changes	1,261	3.12	17.02	0	600
Homeowner dummy	1,261	0.41	0.49	0	1
Regular employee (private) dummy	1,261	0.53	0.50	0	1
Regular employee (public) dummy	1,261	0.05	0.22	0	1
Non-regular employees (private) dummy	1,261	0.20	0.40	0	1
Other employee positions dummy	1,261	0.06	0.24	0	1
Health insurance dummy	1,044	0.76	0.43	0	1
Unemployment insurance dummy	1,044	0.71	0.45	0	1
Pension dummy	1,044	0.70	0.46	0	1

Source: Made by author.

Table 7.2 Descriptive statistics (Shanghai)

	Sample	*Mean*	*SD*	*Minimum*	*Maximum*
Life satisfaction	700	6.48	1.74	1	10
Gender dummy	700	0.50	0.50	0	1
Age	700	37.82	11.17	20	65
Householder dummy	579	0.52	0.50	0	1
Marital status dummy	700	0.70	0.46	0	1
Birthplace dummy	700	0.75	0.43	0	1
University graduate dummy	700	0.34	0.47	0	1
Length of residence	700	363.77	208.33	6	781
Number of times of moving	700	2.73	2.55	1	12
Number of people living together	700	3.00	1.33	1	10
Number of children	700	0.64	0.56	0	3
Number of families and relatives living nearby	700	1.14	1.44	0	8
Length of service	700	83.36	91.85	0	453
Income per month	614	739.51	519.75	123.02	2,368.82
Average working hours per day	614	8.57	1.38	2	14
Secondary job dummy	614	0.04	0.19	0	1
Number of job changes	700	2.20	1.28	0	9
Homeowner dummy	700	0.75	0.44	0	1
Regular employee (private) dummy	700	0.49	0.50	0	1
Regular employee (public) dummy	700	0.33	0.47	0	1
Non-regular employees (private) dummy	700	0.08	0.27	0	1
Other employee positions dummy	700	0.06	0.24	0	1
Health insurance dummy	614	0.68	0.47	0	1
Unemployment insurance dummy	614	0.40	0.49	0	1
Pension dummy	614	0.78	0.41	0	1

Source: Made by author.

Table 7.3 Descriptive statistics (Bangkok)

	Sample	*Mean*	*SD*	*Minimum*	*Maximum*
Life satisfaction	769	7.32	1.77	1	10
Gender dummy	769	0.48	0.50	0	1
Age	766	42.80	11.30	17	78
Householder dummy	769	0.49	0.50	0	1
Marital status dummy	765	0.61	0.49	0	1
Birthplace dummy	769	0.35	0.48	0	1
University graduate dummy	768	0.26	0.44	0	1
Length of residence	769	331.51	179.67	12	840
Number of times of moving	766	2.72	1.52	1	12
Number of people living together	769	2.89	1.60	1	14
Number of children	573	1.63	1.13	0	9
Number of families and relatives living nearby	577	1.21	1.42	0	10
Length of service	768	120.57	98.50	0	552
Income per month	754	669.37	572.92	0	8,159.97
Average working hours per day	732	8.99	2.64	1	24
Secondary job dummy	765	0.09	0.29	0	1
Number of job changes	764	2.09	1.29	1	11
Homeowner dummy	768	0.57	0.50	0	1
Regular employee (private) dummy	755	0.25	0.43	0	1
Regular employee (public) dummy	755	0.06	0.23	0	1
Non-regular employees (private) dummy	755	0.11	0.32	0	1
Other employee positions dummy	769	0.07	0.25	0	1
Health insurance dummy	766	0.62	0.49	0	1
Unemployment insurance dummy	701	0.10	0.31	0	1
Pension dummy	701	0.04	0.19	0	1

Source: Made by author.

Table 7.4 Estimation result (three mega cities)

	Tokyo		*Shanghai*		*Bangkok*	
Gender dummy	−0.275	***	−0.00229		−0.0256	
Age	−0.0102	**	−0.0148		−0.00352	
Householder dummy	−0.222	**	0.133		0.416	***
Marital status dummy	0.167	*	0.257	*	0.276	*
Birthplace dummy	−0.0898		−0.245		−0.348	*
University graduate dummy	0.0711		0.0349		−0.0325	
Length of residence	0.000621	**	0.000180		0.00158	**
Number of times of moving	−0.0108		−0.0396	**	−0.0140	
Number of people living together	−0.158	***	0.0768		0.00981	
Number of children	0.109	**	−0.0499		−0.0876	
Number of families and relatives living nearby	−0.0235		0.115	***	0.0516	
Length of service	−0.0000363		0.0000945		−0.000366	
Income per month	0.000225	***	0.000588	***	0.000317	***
Average working hours per day	−0.0407	**	−0.0924	**	0.00751	
Secondary job dummy	−0.0171		−0.0643		−0.172	
Number of job changes	0.000970		−0.0865	**	−0.0641	
Homeowner dummy	0.272	***	0.229		0.0187	
Regular employee (private) dummy	−0.0756		0.160		−0.359	*
Regular employee (public) dummy	0.243		0.201		0.0195	
Non-regular employees (private) dummy	−0.177		−0.0742		0.168	
Other employee positions dummy	−0.205		−0.191		−0.111	
Health insurance dummy	0.0442		−1.690	***	0.209	*
Unemployment insurance dummy	0.00983		−0.00367		0.411	*
Pension dummy	0.0796		0.722	***	0.171	
Number of obs.	1,008		508		324	

Source: Made by author.
Note: ***, **, and * denote significance at the 1%, 5%, and 10% level.

Next, apart from the social security system, a common tendency among the three cities is that the higher the monthly income, and if married, the higher the degree of life satisfaction. Other common trends are as follows. In Tokyo and Shanghai, life satisfaction is lower when working hours become long. This result is consistent with our intuitions. The duration of residence was significantly positive in Tokyo and Bangkok. Contrasting results were observed for the head of household dummy in Tokyo and Bangkok. In Tokyo, being the head of household lowers life satisfaction, while in Bangkok it raises it. This is a good juncture to describe the other characteristics of each city. In Tokyo, the life satisfaction of a person who has many children and lives in an own house is high, but that of men who are older and live with many others is low. (The number of children includes children who live separately and household size includes non-children living with the respondents, so there is no contradiction with the sign of the coefficient for the number of people living together.)

In Shanghai, those who can expect help from family and relatives are more satisfied with their lives, while those who move residents or change jobs more frequently have a low degree of life satisfaction. In Bangkok, life satisfaction is lower for people born in Bangkok.

Thus far, we have considered the model results using the whole sample of each of the three cities. In this chapter, we are mainly interested in the effect of the social security system on life satisfaction. Summarising the estimation results overall, life satisfaction is lower for those who are covered by health insurance and higher for those who are covered by pension in Shanghai. Life satisfaction is higher the more unemployment insurance applies in Bangkok. However, the impact of social security systems on life satisfaction may differ among income groups. To examine this issue, the samples of the three cities are thus divided into middle-income groups and low-income groups and ordered probit estimation is carried out for each sub-sample. The definitions of the middle- and low-income groups used in this book are applied in this analysis.

7.3 Analysis by Income Group

Table 7.5 shows the estimated results of dividing the sample of three cities into middle- and low-income groups. In the estimation using the Shanghai sample and the instrumental variable, the method was continued to be used; the answer to the question on the future dream was made into a dummy variable.[3]

The impact of the social security system on life satisfaction is as follows. First, the health insurance dummy shows a significantly negative association for the middle- and low-income groups in Shanghai and a significantly positive one for the middle-income group in Bangkok. In Shanghai, it was found that health insurance coverage had a negative impact on life satisfaction for both groups. Second, the coefficient of the pension dummy was significantly positive in Shanghai for both income groups. Unlike health insurance, however, pension insurance coverage has a positive impact on life satisfaction. Third, the unemployment insurance dummy showed a significantly positive association for the low-income group in Bangkok.

Table 7.5 Estimation result (three mega cities/income group)

	Tokyo				*Shanghai*				*Bangkok*			
	Low-income		*Middle-income*		*Low-income*		*Middle-income*		*Low-income*		*Middle-income*	
Gender dummy	−0.326	***	−0.305	***	0.270		−0.0798		0.0864		−0.106	
Age	−0.00816		−0.0103	*	0.0172		−0.0157		−0.0117		0.00285	
Householder dummy	−0.217		−0.189		0.562	***	0.00378		0.729	***	0.106	
Marital status dummy	0.153		0.217	*	0.807	***	0.143		0.235		0.451	*
Birthplace dummy	−0.0607		−0.124		0.117		−0.302		−0.502	*	−0.190	
University graduate dummy	0.112		0.0532		0.726	***	−0.139		−0.208		0.0876	
Length of residence	0.000945	**	0.000659	**	−0.00165		0.000424		0.00158		0.00159	
Number of times of moving	−0.0585	*	0.0239		−0.0131		−0.104	**	0.116		−0.153	**
Number of people living together	−0.0743		−0.214	***	0.158		0.0272		0.0842		−0.140	*
Number of children	0.0483		0.147	**	−0.493	**	0.207		−0.117		0.0492	
Number of families and relatives living nearby	−0.0705		−0.0000598		0.307	**	0.0683		−0.0153		0.0510	
Length of service	−0.00137	*	0.0000232		0.000896		−0.000685		−0.000624		0.000869	
Income per month	0.000107		0.000216	***	0.00424	***	0.000507	***	0.000294		0.000376	**
Average working hours per day	−0.0218		−0.0457	*	−0.108	**	−0.0220		0.0268		0.0237	

(*Continued*)

	Tokyo		*Shanghai*		*Bangkok*	
	Low-income	*Middle-income*	*Low-income*	*Middle-income*	*Low-income*	*Middle-income*
Secondary job dummy	−0.161	0.173	−0.383	0.0701	−0.239	0.127
Number of job changes	0.00116	−0.0520 **	0.0136	−0.106 **	−0.0429	−0.0564
Homeowner dummy	0.0926	0.356 ***	0.0147	0.362	−0.390	0.120
Regular employee (private) dummy	0.231	−0.0237	0.655	0.370	−0.629 **	−0.148
Regular employee (public) dummy	0.929	0.144	0.840 *	0.409	0.665	−0.713
Non-regular employees (private) dummy	0.0775	−0.0140	0.272	0.827	0.235	−0.777
Other employee positions dummy	−0.0123	−0.0482	−0.515	0.153	−0.152	−0.0888
Health insurance dummy	0.260	−0.188	−2.069 ***	−2.062 ***	0.0848	0.337 *
Unemployment insurance dummy	−0.046	0.0988	0.162	0.117	0.832 **	−0.449
Pension dummy	−0.050	0.231	0.492 **	1.270 ***	−1.116	0.827
Number of obs.	413	595	208	300	167	157

Source: Made by author.
Note: ***, **, and * denote significance at the 1%, 5%, and 10% level.

In Table 7.4, we may note that common characteristics of the three cities are that higher monthly income and being married both positively improve self-reported life satisfaction scores. These characteristics are observed for the middle-income in Tokyo, the middle-income and low-income groups in Shanghai, and middle-income in Bangkok for monthly income, and in the middle-income in Tokyo, low-income group in Shanghai, and middle-income in Bangkok for marriage. Compared with the results in Table 7.4, the class separated results in Table 7.5 offer additional detail. Life satisfaction decreases in the middle-income in Tokyo and the low-income group in Shanghai when the working hours increase. In addition, length of residence was significant for the middle- and low-income groups in Tokyo, but not in Bangkok when the sample was divided into economic classes.

For the head of household dummy, the impact is not consistent. While it is insignificant in Tokyo, it has a significantly positive impact on life satisfaction scores for the low-income groups of Shanghai and Bangkok. Other results from each city are as follows. In Tokyo, the number of children and homeownership dummy showed significantly positive association with life satisfaction. Being male, age, number of persons living together, and number of changing jobs were significantly negatively associated with life satisfaction for the middle-income. In the low-income group, being male, moving frequency, and length of service in the current job had significantly negative association with self-reported life satisfaction.

In Shanghai, for the associations of the number of moves and job changes had a significantly negative impact on life satisfaction. For the low-income group, being a university graduate, having family members or relatives living nearby, and being a regular employee (in the public sector), and having fewer children improved self-reported life satisfaction. In Bangkok, life satisfaction is low in Bangkok for the middle-income when the number of moves and the number of people living together are large, and in the low-income group for people from Bangkok.

7.4 Considering the Social Security System

The effects of the various social security systems on life satisfaction, the focus of this chapter, may be summarised as follows. First, life satisfaction of those enrolled in health insurance is low for both middle-income and low-income groups in Shanghai, while it is high in the middle-income of Bangkok. Second, life satisfaction is high in the low-income group when they are covered by unemployment insurance in Bangkok, and it is high for both the middle-income and the low-income group when they receive a pension in Shanghai. Third, none of the social-security-system dummies showed a significant association in Tokyo. Considering these results, it can be said that the effect of the social security system on the life satisfaction differs not only by city but also by income group, and the variance seem to reflect the differences in the systems which make the effect of the system in each city different.

Regarding the dummy variables for the various social security systems, as with the other explanatory variables, these varied in their significance across the groups. When significant, pension and unemployment insurance showed positive associations with life satisfaction, and health insurance was less clear having both positive and negative results. The reason for these results is that the effect of the system of pension and unemployment insurance results when the cash is given, while the effects of the system of health insurance are exerted when the individual actually visits the medical institution. Therefore, the benefits of the system of health insurance cannot be fully realised when problems in supply chains and capacity prevent medical treatment. On the other hand, in the case of 'insurance', the insured person is required to pay insurance premiums, and a situation where the insured person must pay the insurance premium even though they cannot receive medical care is simply the burden of the insurance premium.

In Thailand, as there are many private medical institutions in urban areas, the coefficient of Bangkok is positive because the middle-income group does not perceive a problem in the medical supply, while in Shanghai, the coefficient is negative because both income groups perceive problems in the medical supply (also see Chapter 5).

In China, it is said, '[i]t is difficult to receive medical care, and the medical expenses are high even if you receive it', so there is a problem of access to medical treatment.[4] Therefore, it can be said that enrolment in health insurance is not directly associated with improved access to medical treatment. Therefore, the insurance premium burden of the health insurance is a mere burden which might lower people's life satisfaction.

Though the GDP (gross domestic product) per capita in Thailand was about US$2,100 (IMF database) in 2002, Thailand implemented publicly financed national health insurance (Universal coverage for health care: USC) in 2002, which covered 76% of population, including informal economy workers, who were not covered by scheme for public officers and private employees (ILO 2008). In addition, prior to 2002, employees covered by health insurance can visit both public and private hospitals contracted with the insurer. It was considered a model case of medical policy in developing countries (Matsuda and Fujimoto 2019). Therefore, access to medical treatment in Bangkok seems to be easier than in China, and the estimation results that life satisfaction rises with coverage by health insurance seems to verify this service value for the middle-income group.

In examining the relationship between the social security system and life satisfaction, it is insufficient to simply measure 'value for money' quantitatively; it is necessary also to consider institutional problems of in-kind benefits such as health services.

Conclusion

The factors which affect how life satisfaction is impacted by the availability of social security systems have been examined. The factors which affected life satisfaction differed not only by city but also by income group, and it was shown that there was such a tendency for the social security system to impact life satisfaction.

It was also shown that the effect on the life satisfaction differed across health care access and supply systems, even with the same health insurance system. That is to say, in Bangkok, a rise in life satisfaction is associated with health insurance coverage, since the middle-income group does not perceive problems in the medical supply. On the other hand, in Shanghai, the feeling of the burden of the health insurance premium may be connected with the lowered life satisfaction, since both income groups perceive problems in the medical supply. Therefore, it is important in these cases to improve the health insurance system as well as the medical supply system.

The empirical analysis in this chapter was conducted to determine the micro relation of health insurance enrolment to individual and life satisfaction, and as a result, it was shown that the macro- or semi-macroscopic mechanism of the medical supply system in one country or city affected life satisfaction. This cannot be explained simply by examining the relationships of burdens and benefits with life satisfaction independently. Therefore, the institution is important contributor to life satisfaction; furthermore, both the micro aspects of individual attributes as well as the 'macro foundation' are important.

During the recent COVID-19 pandemic, the demand for health care services has drastically exceeded the medical supply, and 'health care system collapse' in which the medical supply becomes impossible to provide has become a problem. The analysis in this chapter reveals that the method of medical supply affects the degree of life satisfaction, and it can be said that COVID-19 clarifies this fact through this extreme condition of life and death. It is critically important that people have access to medical services when they become ill. It is thus useful not only in normal conditions but also in crisis to improve the medical supply system, which affects people's life satisfaction, and to reduce popular dissatisfaction. In addition, it is important to operate the system at a level ensuring little dissatisfaction in normal conditions, since it is impossible to rapidly increase the medical supply in times of crisis.

Box 4 Surviving the COVID-19 pandemic: Infection experiences in three cities

Masato Miyazaki and Tamaki Endo

COVID-19 challenged formal and informal institutions of all three cities. We also had a hands-on experience of reflecting on how our societies would be.

In Tokyo, one of the three megacities analysed in this book, COVID-19-infected residents with mild symptoms were instructed to quarantine at home. In fact, I (Masato Miyazaki) had my entire immediate family, except myself, all infected with COVID-19 in January 2022. At the time, the Omicron variant had been spreading rapidly, and infections were rising sharply in Japan. Japan was in the midst of the "sixth wave" of infections, and ambulances were constantly racing across Tokyo and Saitama (the neighbouring prefecture in which the authors work) every day. Here is my report on the experience:

I suspected that my children had COVID-19 because they came down with a sudden fever and we therefore tested the whole family using commercially available medical antigen test kits. The tests confirmed that my wife and children were infected and that I was not. As per official guidance, I called the Coronavirus Call Centre and the Tokyo Fever Consultation Centre and asked for information on medical institutions where they could receive treatment. However, since they were already confirmed 'positive' for COVID-19 infection through the antigen tests, it was therefore ironic that we were told that the number of medical institutions in which we could receive treatment were very limited to prevent the spread of COVID-19 to those who were uninfected. At the same time, with just the informal at-home antigen tests, we were not considered to be 'officially' infected yet. Thus, our family struggled to even be counted among the 'officially' confirmed infections. Furthermore, we faced an unexpected situation where we could not access any medical services even though we had health insurances.

Three days after we conducted that first test using the antigen test kits, we finally underwent PCR tests at a medical institution and became officially designated as 'infected' and thus eligible for receiving assistance. In

Photo BOX 4-1 Assistance package from Tokyo Municipality (photo by Masato Miyazaki, January 2022)

Tokyo, those eligible for assistance receive food and drinks like those in the picture (Photo BOX 4-1). The Government used a private courier service to deliver these boxes (later, this service became optional and only offered when necessary). Four cardboard boxes filled with relatively long-lasting food and drinks arrived. We also borrowed a pulse oximeter for measuring oxygen saturation in the blood to be returned after recovery. However, all these items arrived at our doorstep around the end of the quarantine period (14 days). It is likely the delivery was delayed because the number of infected people was increasing rapidly and so was the demand for the packages. Fortunately, we had a sufficient stock of food and drink in our home, and no one developed any serious symptoms; therefore, we did not face many problems. However, it is questionable whether the government support was sufficient; the situation would have become dire if we had not had a sufficient stock of food and drink, or if any of us had developed any serious symptoms. The procedures were not elderly-friendly; they faced many impediments in digital access for making hospital appointments (when online booking was recommended) or simply being on hold and dealing with overloaded telephone reception for hours while unwell with COVID-19. Furthermore, the degree and quality of the government services provided differed across prefectures; and public expectations regarding assistance therefore greatly depended on the capabilities of local governments.

Regarding COVID-19 cases in Bangkok, there were some similarities in the basic services provided there for supporting infected person, but they seemed to be greater flexibility. The long-term research sites (informal settlements for low-income groups in the inner city of Bangkok) of other author of this Box (Tamaki Endo) have experienced a cluster of infections during the third wave of COVID-19 (the Delta variant) followed by spread of the Omicron variant. This community, which consists of low-rise housing typically comprising two floors having three rooms and one bathroom, has 250 households. The residents said that once the infection took hold in the community, it was difficult to prevent the infection of other family members and neighbours. Subsequently, 200 persons became infected with the Delta variant; the cases were counted by a community leader, who also works as a health volunteer under the supervision of the Ministry of Public Health and the district office. When the Omicron variant emerged in 2022, the community leader stopped counting the cases, as most of families had been infected at least once.

However, before the Delta variant emerged, the community had managed COVID-19 infections relatively well, with health volunteers testing all the residents at the community office when case numbers rose and the volunteers also taught residents how to use self-test kits. Private company provided support to community by offering heavily discounted antigen test kits (at half of the market price). As in Tokyo, infected persons with serious symptoms were sent to hospital, including temporary field hospitals (which the government had constructed around Bangkok), sent to quarantine facilities (e.g., hotels or temporary shelters), or asked to stay at home for 10–14 days, depending on the government's regulation at the time. The official case count only included cases confirmed using the PCR tests, but the Government also announced the number of positive cases that had been confirmed using antigen self-test kits every day. In interviews (conducted during January–March and August 2022) of community leaders and other residents, the interviewees mentioned some flexibilities in the practice for confirming "official" infections. During big waves, when medical capacities were under pressure, those who confirmed themselves to be 'positive' by using antigen tests contacted the community leader, who then took a photograph of these positive results. This leader then reported the results to the local office of the Ministry of Public Health. People in home quarantine were provided with medicines and an oximeter as well as a daily delivery of three cooked meals. Nevertheless, the community leader recalled that the community faced some difficult moments from time to time. For example, during the first wave of 2020, no medicines were provided to the patient under home isolation. The residents therefore followed postings on SNS, which claimed that some natural herbs were good for aiding recovery. Ginger was noted as one of these home remedies and, regardless of its actual efficacy, the price of this spice went up. Next, the residents started to grow ginger and other herbs in the community garden. During the third wave, which consisted of the Delta variant, hospitals were unable to accommodate all the infected people, so residents helped each other find oxygen tanks and jointly procured these, as a community, for the seriously ill members. Seven residents lost their lives since the pandemic started.

As NGOs, private companies, and the Government began to provide funds and assistance from time to time, mutual support among residents became possible. Because of its vulnerability to the pandemic due to the dense arrangement of its residential setting, the community used these funds to arrange frequent testing and supports for home isolation (delivery of necessities and goods and other activities). I (Tamaki Endo) was impressed by their Facebook posts during 2020, which detailed how the community committee members and volunteers cooked 500 lunch meal boxes every day to help people who were losing their jobs and incomes during the lockdown. As the case numbers increased, vaccination drives were also organised within the community. Government officials visited the community and administered the vaccinations (especially to the elderly and vulnerable people) in the residential area. Actually, the community leader had already been given four shots (I had had only two shots at that time because the regulatory approval and relevant procedures were slow in Japan) when I was talking with her in February 2022. Although the community has been struggling to prevent the spread of the infection because of its density, some informal institutions were trying to take on various roles in order to reduce the risks of infection and provide support for the infected in the low-income groups of Bangkok. It should be noted that the national Government of Thailand fully utilised digital tools, including managing to deliver initial cash transfers (5,000 bahts) to informal economy workers (about 14 million persons from among those who registered) within two weeks after registration in May 2020. It helped low-income groups at the initial stage of the pandemic. In contrast, Japan, which conducted manual cross checking of the registrations, took several months to complete this process; the registration started in June 2020, and actual cash transfers were almost completed by August 2020 (100,000 yen for each household).

Unfortunately, we could not visit Shanghai during the pandemic; therefore, we do not have first-hand information regarding the cases in Shanghai. According to Takaguchi's work (2021), Shanghai made strong use of digital tools for tracking, infection management, and delivery of services for isolated persons. At the same time, interestingly, the community committees took on important roles as well. For digitally vulnerable people in communities who were not good at using digital tools, the delivery of assistance goods was made to the community's leaders house, and the leader delivered them to each house or community members were allowed to pick them up at the leader's house.

The COVID-19 pandemic is still ongoing (as of August 2022, when we are writing this essay). However, it is clear that countries' performance in dealing with this crisis differed and that each country's economic development level did not necessarily explain the efficiency and effectiveness of its formal institutions in dealing with the crisis. Other factors (e.g., degree of digitalisation, resource availability, social expenditure, and trust in formal/informal intuitions) may differentiate service efficiency, scale, and effectiveness in different countries. Furthermore, from residents' perspectives, formal institutions and the availability of informal institutions can significantly affect survival strategies. In Japan, the quality of medical services available to ordinary people is certainly high; however, once the citizen is disconnected from the formal services, self-help is their only option. In particular, we must consider the nature of the pandemic, which restricted human contacts and increased difficulties in asking for help from friends and neighbours. In contrast, the high residential density of Bangkok's communities increased the risk for infection but, simultaneously, allowed these spaces to deploy and exercise informal networks even during the pandemic. In Shanghai, digital solutions were fully utilised with the supplement of the community networks for serving the disadvantage groups. In Tokyo, formal institutions serviced everyone equally. However, if the elderly cannot overcome the first step of making appointments for tests, they may find it hard to access medical treatments. In Bangkok and Shanghai, at least the informal institutions offered some additional support to aid the elderly and vulnerable groups in navigating such obstacles. To understand how much this combination of formal and informal institutions helped to prevent infections, aided in recovery, and provided economic support, we must conduct further analysis. We are sure that there are many lessons we can learn from each other, at the local level, regardless of the developmental stages of our cities and countries.

Takaguchi, K. 2021. *Chugoku korona huuji no kyojitsu* [China's COVID 19 responses]. Tokyo: Chuokouronshinsha.

Notes

1 In Japan and Thailand, the health insurance in which one is enrolled is automatically decided by occupation (the regulations in Thailand require all enterprises with more than one employee to provide social security benefits and employee with social security is regarded as formal employment). Therefore, it is assumed that existing life satisfaction does not affect decisions regarding insurance subscription.

2 In the questionnaire, the respondent was asked, 'If you had the same income, which job would you choose?' with two response options, 'as an employee with job stability but whose independence is limited' and 'a self-employed person (include entrepreneur) who must take risks but who has independence'. For those who chose the latter option (risk loving), an instrumental variable for a preference for risk which could affect whether to enrol in health insurance but does not directly affect life satisfaction.

3 In the questionnaire, the respondent was asked 'Do you have any dreams or hopes that you want to realize in the future?', and the two alternatives of 'Yes' and 'No' were provided. A dummy variable taking the value 1 when the respondent chose the former was made an instrumental variable, on the assumption that future hopes seem to not directly affect present life satisfaction, though they do affect enrolment in health insurance, because individuals would like to be healthy until such a time when their hopes are realised.

4 https://www.chinanews.com.cn/m/gn/2019/09-26/8966535.shtml

References

Albanese, M., M. Bonasia, O. Napolitano, and N. Spagnolo. 2015. "Happiness, taxes and social provision: A note." *Economics Letters* 2: 100–103.

Bjørnskov, C., A. Drehe, and J. A. V. Fischer. 2007. "On decentralization and life satisfaction." *Economics Letters* 99: 147–151.

Hessami, Z. 2010. "The size and composition of government spending in Europe and its impact on well-being." *KYKLOS* 63(3): 346–382.

Hutchinson, T., I. Ahmed, and P. Buryi. 2017. "Impact of income tax on happiness: evidence from the United States." *Applied Economics* Letters 24(18): 1277–1279.

ILO (International Labour Organization) Subregional Office for East Asia. 2008. *Thailand: Universal Health Care Coverage through Pluralistic Approaches.* Bangkok: ILO.

ILO. *International Labour Standards on Social security.* https://www.ilo.org/global/standards/subjects-covered-by-international-labour-standards/social-security/lang--en/index.htm

Kiya, K. 2012. "Life satisfaction and public finance: Empirical analysis using U.S. micro data." *SSRN Working Paper* 2126357: 1–52. https://ssrn.com/abstract=2126357.

Kotakorpi, K., and J. P. Laamanen. 2010. "Welfare state and life satisfaction: Evidence from public health care." *Economica* 77: 565–583.

Matsuda, S., and K. Fujimoto. 2019. "Current status and issues of Thailand's public health insurance system [Tai no kouteki iryouhokenseido no genjou to kadai]", *Shakaihoken Shumpo* 2764: 6-20.

Ouweneel, P. 2002. "Social security and well-being of the unemployed in 42 nations." *Journal of Happiness Studies* 3: 167–192.

Ram, R. 2009. "Government spending and happiness of the population: Additional evidence from large cross-country samples." *Public Choice* 138(3/4): 483–490.

Tran, N. L. T., R. W. Wassmer, and E. L. Lascher. 2017. "The health insurance and life satisfaction connection." *Journal of Happiness Studies* 18: 409–426.

Veenhoven, R. 2000. "Well-being in the welfare state: Level not higher, distribution not more equitable." *Journal of Comparative Policy Analysis* 2: 91–125.

8 Towards Better Urban Well-Being in Asian Megacities

Momoyo Shibuya and Tamaki Endo

Introduction

Globalisation and urbanisation prevailed; megacities in various countries were connected to one another, bringing national borders out of the shadows. The world had come to be understood through networks of cities. However, the novel coronavirus disease 2019 (COVID-19) pandemic—spreading quickly worldwide since early 2020—has brought our attention back to national borders. Countries closed their borders temporarily to prevent further spread of the disease, many international flights were cancelled, and people were restricted from travelling freely across national borders.

Cities were believed to be cosmopolitan spaces where diverse people gather and live. Yet, the world is not completely flattened, and the COVID-19 crisis has reminded us that cities are inseparable from the larger society in which they are situated. Cities undertook different measures to control the pandemic, reflecting their social contexts. Combining existing formal systems and available informal support within society, while simultaneously enacting countermeasures to balance economic and social activities, societies went through a continuous process of trials and errors. Some societies saw existing problems come to the forefront, while social vulnerabilities previously invisible were revealed in others. We have also come to realise that the so-called developed countries do not always cope well with crisis situations.

8.1 Individual Well-Being in the Era of Uncertainty

We seek better opportunities and life and believe that cities offer it to us. Some may leave their hometowns and eagerly head to the cities hoping for better economic opportunities and a more convenient and comfortable life for their families or their futures. Others may have drifted into cities after losing their place to be. Yet, others may have ended up living in cities as a result of urban development swallowing up their hometowns. Whatever the circumstances, an increasing number of people are living in cities, and cities continue to grow, fuelled by our desires to live well. A dense and large population lead to more efficient infrastructural development in the area. Instead of using energy

DOI: 10.4324/9781003328155-8

and technology to ensure basic sanitation, such as clean water, and to make comfortable living possible through, for instance, constant access to air conditioning and products, cities have become environmentally hazardous spaces. Simultaneously, an urban system has been established where money serves as a common medium for diverse people to live together, and various services can be provided without personal relationships, if paid for. The urban system has allowed us to have some control over the natural and social environment (or so we have believed). However, it has led to the exploitation and destruction of nature, along with the dilution of human relationships or individualisation, thus creating new risks and challenges for us to confront.

Megacities become not only a space of opportunities but also a space of risks, with a risk-generating mechanism embedded in the urban setting itself (Buscher and Mascareno 2012). As discussed in Chapters 1 and 5, dense layouts and high-rises increase vulnerability to natural and environmental hazards. A diversified market economy ensures a convenient and comfortable urban life if we can afford it, but once income sources are lost, survival in the city suddenly becomes difficult. Individual labour and health are therefore important capital for meeting material needs and improving the quality of life in cities. While for some people tenuous relationships may mean freedom from old norms, it is also true that once faced with shocks and crisis, they limit resilience and become the very cause of vulnerability.

What is more, risks or crises occur within the mutual interactions of each of the three—people, society, and environment—that threaten our lives in a constant and multifaceted way. Some risks and crises affect only individuals (idiosyncratic), whereas others strike the society as a whole (systematic), irrespective of individual conditions and attributes. However, individuals from different social classes and other attributes might have differential sensitivity to the shocks and, thus, may appear to experience different degrees of damage. Furthermore, one crisis can trigger other crises, resulting in compound shocks, forcing a multifaceted response at once with limited resources. For example, during the COVID-19 crisis, some individuals experienced a chain reaction of limited economic activity due to behavioural restrictions, unemployment, loss of a place to live and loss of health, on top of the risk of the COVID-19 infection. It was a health crisis as well as an economic crisis. What is more, in an era of uncertainly, one might be faced with multiple crises simultaneously. Amidst the ongoing pandemic, some regions in the world also had to deal with other crises such as war, hurricane, extreme heat and fire, and flooding.

Individual and societal resources are limited. When societal shocks and crises occur as a domino effect, it is difficult to cope with them, as budgets are limited, and the capability of formal institutions is damaged and weakened. If an individual faces a single spot shock, they are more likely to succeed at solving problems using their own resources and the help of others, unless they are exposed to continuous multiple shocks and crises. The risks of urban life are inevitable; from the perspective of individuals, it is important whether and how one recovers from shocks as quickly as possible and escapes from the vicious circle, where the consequences of a previous shock increase vulnerability to the subsequent risks and shocks in urban life. Difficulties might persist because the various risks and shocks are interconnected and potentially reinforcing each other, and the resources and capabilities of social networks are limited. The damage can chronically accumulate in the life course of individuals and households, and continuous responses to past difficulties and loss might erode their socioeconomic foundation for resilience (Chapter 5). Therefore, it is important to employ a dynamic perspective when we discuss the components of an individual's urban well-being, such as how people deal with and overcome difficulties, rather than the static perspective of what resources and networks they currently have available. As previous chapters showed their life satisfaction (subjective well-being) also correlates with the process of dealing with risk or crisis and the outcome of overcoming these difficulties.

The question then arises whether and how the quality of life of such urban dwellers can be improved or made better in the era of uncertainty. The concept of people 'living well', or well-being, has both objective and subjective definitions. Objective well-being, a material, quantitative approach of well-being based on externally observable factors, often uses indicators such as health and high education, in addition to income, food, housing, and other living conditions. Development discussions have paid much attention to improving these objective conditions, and our obsessive efforts have also looked to improve social infrastructure and other aspects of the urban environment. Of course, these objective aspects cannot be ignored, but the improvement in individual well-being cannot be naturally attained only through the enhancement of these objective well-being indicators (e.g., Easterlin 2001). Subjective well-being plays an important role as well. Individual subjective well-being is presumed from self-evaluation (life satisfaction) and emotions (happiness) (Diener and Suh 1997; D'Acci 2011). Even if the material conditions, which are indicators of objective well-being, are fulfilled, the overall quality of life cannot be considered good unless subjective well-being increases accordingly and vice versa. It is possible to maintain a certain level of individual well-being as long as a subjective, self-affirming situation can be created, even if the actual material conditions are not sufficiently met. In the case of urban dwellers, their objective well-being is easily maintained at a certain level, though this cannot be guaranteed when they are exposed to multiple or combined risks and crises. The evaluation of their lives may even go down accordingly. When the promised environment collapses and risks and crises loom, we can also choose to reassess the new situation from a different perspective and adapt to the new environment in a way that increases our subjective well-being. Initiating this positive cycle involves looking at the situation from a broad and pluralistic perspective and utilising the resources at hand to move towards a solution. At this point, as described above, it is more important to understand and be able to practise how to utilise the resources you have, rather than what you have as resources. As risk and shock response processes are also embedded in social context, involving multiple stakeholders (Chapters 1, 6 and 7), the nature of formal and informal institutions woven at the societal level becomes the key to understanding dynamic process of forming urban well-being.

8.2 Formal and Informal Institutions in Surviving Urban Lives

As mentioned, the way risks manifest and are perceived differs from city to city, but when analysing Asian megacities at the city level, our research found that there are many commonalities among either lower class groups in their struggle for survival or middle class groups pursuing quality of life in these cities. Despite the assumption that Tokyo, a fully mature city, would be contrasted with Bangkok and Shanghai, which embody dynamic and compressed change, this was not the case. Rather, the discrepancies within each city were conspicuous and emphasised the need to adopt a cross-sectional view of the cities.

One of the key puzzles of our research was remarkable desperation and pressures that the Tokyo lower classes showed, among all six groups, in their daily survival in the city. At the time of our research, Tokyo seemed to have all the conditions required for the so-called urban life, with a well-developed social infrastructure and favourable financial situation. Nonetheless, access to such public resources in the urban space was not enjoyed by everyone in the population, especially the lower classes, who lived with limited resources. Their well-being was considerably low, possibly due to the marketisation of relationships preventing them from functioning well within an informal safety net. Further, because they perceive a gap between the situation surrounding them and their own situation, they are prone to a sense of relative deprivation.

In Shanghai and Bangkok too, the middle and lower classes lived different daily realities, though they seemed to lead more subjectively fulfilling lives than both classes in Tokyo. People in Bangkok evaluated their lives positively, using personal informal measures to cover the lack of social infrastructure, such as social security. For the middle class, objective well-being indicators such as education supported them and compensated for their deficiencies, whereas for the lower class, community ties and support from their relationship networks seemed to lead to positive evaluations of their lives (as the survey is community-based, there may be some sampling bias). Many people in the lower class in Shanghai were unable to lead the life they wanted, due to lack of access to familial relationships where they can expect informal support, which the middle class can utilise, and insufficient formal support. As a result, they had difficulty achieving sufficient subjective well-being to compensate for their negative objective well-being status (Chapter 6).

The lower class in each of these cities has a common vulnerability stemming from limited access to public resources or objective well-being indicators. They are exposed to multiple risks and crises, many of which cannot be easily resolved due to the limited resources available to them. Simultaneously, despite such vulnerabilities, the range and options of social networks vary among groups. By combining and utilising various networks, there are also people who have adapted to urban life. They used informal safety nets as an alternative to insufficient public resources and objective well-being indicators. Of course, informal support is often insufficiently stable and functional, and vulnerability is not eliminated. Even in Bangkok, where the lower class can rely on informal support, dependency on others is still unstable and unreliable compared to the resources of the middle class. However, when one is disconnected from formal institutions and society does not allow informal mechanisms to operate, the current quality of life and prospects are affected, which end up lowering people's life satisfaction and future expectations (Chapter 4). The case of Tokyo's lower class is implicative to think about the future of the urban well-being of the residents of Bangkok and Shanghai, locations which are now facing a turning point due to compressed urban development (Chapter 2).

Having presented the abovementioned implications, we would like to emphasise that we are not dismissing the importance of formal institutions. Extension of social security is one of the policy priorities for emerging countries where access to service and benefits largely differ among different groups. The social security system can strengthen individual and societal capability and resilience, thus extending accessible services as well as improving quality of social security services, which have been challenges for countries with relatively weak financial foundations. From the individual perspective, it is not simply a matter of the levels of contributions and benefits one can pay for/receive, but how the social security system is designed and enforced to meet different needs; these impact one's life satisfaction (Chapter 7). One of the biggest challenges of the coming decade is how different social classes can achieve social consensus and contracts for establishing and maintaining sustainable social security systems to ease rising inequalities. There is not much time left for these complex challenges to be tackled. For example, if Bangkok and Shanghai's population start ageing, as has been the case recently in Tokyo, with only one-third of residents covered by pension, which is the current scenario in Shanghai and Bangkok, how can we guarantee decent urban life for residents? This also raises questions of whether there will be more options of formal institutions to rely on, and still a variety of informal institutions available to people. Understanding the needs of different groups, actual features of social division and conflict, and characteristics of the social setting of the city will be even more crucial. Formal and informal institutions are not exclusive but can mutually supplement each other. A cross-regional and non-hierarchal approach is required to learn mutually across Asian megacities. Our study is one of the trials to explore and deal with these new academic and social challenges.

8.3 Concluding Remarks: Towards Better Urban Well-Being in Asian Megacities

The presence of resilient urban people overcoming their vulnerability to risk and actual shocks is instructive for making urban life better. Even those with high objective well-being now may lose it at some point, or the city as a whole may fall into such a situation. When that happens, we need to look beyond and learn from past experiences, but also come up with different approaches and combine the resources available to us to respond. The risks and crises in the urban age merged with uncertainty will lead to new challenges. As described in Chapter 2, emerging cities such as Bangkok and Shanghai, along with other Asian megacities, must deal with challenges that developed cities and developing cities face simultaneously. Instead of imitating and following approaches used by developed countries, the solution would lie in learning from each other and responding flexibly while identifying the social characteristics of each city.

Currently, 10 years after the survey, it is unlikely that the people in the three cities will be in the same condition. As discussed in Chapter 4, people's lifestyles change with the social environment, as do their values and sensibilities. Particularly in cities, where people from diverse cultures interact on a daily basis, changes are rapid and dramatic, as new values can easily emerge constantly from stimulation and excitement. Hence, a one spot time survey cannot tell much, and more dynamic and time series analysis is needed. Still, we should consider that the characteristics of Bangkok, Shanghai, and Tokyo that were visible at the time of the survey have important implications because the direction of change is determined by the social context and, thus, is path dependent. The context here means a combination of the cosmopolite 'city' and the historical context of each city—its place in global society, its Asian social structure, and the orientation of its people. This results in the cities showing changes that have commonalities but also unique characteristics.

As globalisation can cause further restructuring of megacities across Asia and the world simultaneously, cross-regional analysis among megacities on the driving forces of socioeconomic changes as well as urban problems will become even more meaningful than perhaps a city-specific analysis. Regardless of the developmental stage of society, given the existence of social groups with commonalities across cities, we might find new ideas and solutions from other cities. At the same time, our research confirms that the boundaries and manifestations of division vary from city to city. Thus, deepening city-specific analysis is also significant. As we have pointed out, survival strategies of residents are often embedded in each city's context. Yet, income classes or other social groups within our world are not determined and fixed only within national borders. Combining cross-regional and city-specific time series analysis is challenging but worth considering.

Existing social systems and values have been fluctuating in recent years. The concept of 'living well' for us may well change, when we are faced with the limits of efforts to improve the objective and subjective aspects of our lives, and we experience the associated risks and increasing complexity. While much has been revealed, our research has also reaffirmed the difficulty of quantifying well-being. Further studies should determine how to capture the invisible parts of well-being. We look forward to the future of Asia, where urban studies will be further developed and where we will continue to learn from each other to search for a flexible and changing environment for 'living well'.

References

Buscher, C., and A. Mascareno. 2012. "Mechanisms of systematic risk production." *Risk Habitat Megacity*, edited by D Heinrich, K Krellenberg, B Hansjürgens and F Martínez, 39–63. Berlin: Springer.

D'Acci, L. 2011. "Measuring well-being and progress." *Social Indicators Research* 104: 47–65.

Diener, E., and E. Suh 1997. "Measuring quality of life: economic, social, and subjective indicators." *Social Indicators Research* 40 (1-2): 189–216.

Easterlin, R. 2001. "Income and happiness: towards a unified theory." *Economic Journal* 111: 465–484.

Index

Note: **Bold** page numbers refer to tables, *italic* page numbers refer to figures and page numbers followed by "n" denote endnotes.